Fascists, Communists, and the National Government

FASCISTS, COMMUNISTS, AND THE NATIONAL GOVERNMENT

Civil Liberties in Great Britain, 1931–1937

Gerald D. Anderson

University of Missouri Press
Columbia & London, 1983

Library of Congress Catalog Card Number 82–10985
Printed and bound in the United States of America
University of Missouri Press, Columbia, Missouri 65211

Library of Congress Cataloging in Publication Data

Anderson, Gerald D., 1944–
Fascists, communists, and the national government: civil liberties in Great Britain, 1931–1937.

1. Civil rights—Great Britain—History. 2. Internal security—Great Britain—History. 3. Communism—Great Britain—History. 4. Fascism—Great Britain—History. 5. Great Britain—Politics and government—1910–1936. 6. Great Britain—Politics and government—1936–1945. I. Title.
JC599.C7A75 1983 323.4'0941 82–10985
ISBN 0-8262-0388-4

to my parents
Wilferd and Violet

Acknowledgments

I wish to acknowledge the helpful services of the library staffs of the British Museum, the British Public Records Office, the Trades Union Congress, the University of Iowa, the University of Minnesota, and Luther College. I am also indebted to my friend and adviser Dr. Laurence Lafore, of the University of Iowa, without whose tireless assistance and academic inspiration this book would not have been possible.

G. D. A.
July 1982
Luther College, Decorah, Iowa

Contents

Chapter 1

Introduction

Out of the upheavals of World War I, the Russian Revolution, and the Great Depression, radical movements emerged that threatened the existing order in western Europe. They were more successful in some countries than in others, but few parliamentary governments avoided a challenge from extraparliamentary groups. In places where democracy was weak or where liberal regimes were unsatisfactory or novel, conservative dictatorships were installed. By the mid-1930s, fascism challenged democracy in virtually every European country. With the success of the Fascists came a revival of the fortunes of their foremost opponents—the Communists.

Fascism and communism represented different but related threats. To some extent they were reciprocating polarities: each tended to grow in response to the other. Fascism flourished in part because it seemed a way of preserving capitalism and destroying communism. It fostered fear of communism and exploited that fear to gain power. Communism was therefore a necessary enemy of fascism, and it too exploited its role as a defender—against fascism. In places where communism was weak, such as in Great Britain, fascism was usually never more than an annoyance. In countries where communism appeared to be a genuine threat, as in Italy in 1922 and Germany in 1933, Fascists succeeded in gaining power. Later, in places where the Communists and their allies gathered influence and support, fascism also grew.

By 1937, Fascist groups operated in all European countries. In Belgium there were the Rexists under Leon Degrelle. In France, the Croix de Feu had been dissolved but had been partially reconstructed as the Parti Francais Social, and other groups, more or less explicitly Fascist, proliferated. Switzerland had several local Fascist fronts, particularly in the cantons of Zurich and Geneva. Norway had the National Socialists of Vidkun Quisling, while the

Netherlands Fascists followed Mynheer Mussert. The Blueshirts of Ireland followed General O'Duffy. Denmark and Sweden each had their local brands of fascism. In Britain, the black cloak of leadership was worn by Sir Oswald Mosley.

In the early 1930s, the position of the Communist party underwent a significant change. Following the directives of the Seventh World Congress of the Comintern, the individual national sections of the Communist party began to work for a common front of all leftist parties, which the Communists hoped to use to effectively oppose fascism. To diplomatically isolated Russia, this was a prime consideration. The revolution, then, was indefinitely postponed in the interests of the Communist fatherland. In joining with other leftist parties, the Communists worked for the preservation of the regime that offered them legal protection. Exploiting the civil war in Spain as an example of a world struggle between fascism and social democracy, they were able to command the support of a large segment of the non-Communist Left.

Most European societies were not faced with a genuine or immediate threat of Communist revolution or, save in Spain, with the prospect of drastic social reform and were therefore never induced to choose fascism as a defense of their economic order. Fascism was tolerated in some cases, perhaps, as a possible future defense, but so long as communism remained a distant threat, fascism was not likely to gain ascendancy. The governments of western Europe protected their regimes through existing legal institutions; in doing so, some traditional civil liberties were sacrificed.

Finland was one of the first democracies to take strong legislative action. In 1930, the Finnish Riksdag passed a law outlawing those parties that urged the forceful change of the political and social order. Originally directed against the Communists, the same law was applied in December 1931 to outlaw a Fascist organization. In 1933, Finland prohibited the formation of private armies within political parties and followed with an antiuniform bill the following year. The measures proved effective. In Czechoslovakia, such regulations were perhaps the most direct. In 1933, a statute was passed empowering that government to dissolve any political group that it thought was "apt to endanger the constitutional unity, integrity, the republican-democratic form of the State or the safety of the Czechoslovakian Republic." This involved the control of meetings, processions, uniforms, and indeed almost every political activity of an outlawed group.[1]

More or less identical laws prohibiting political uniforms were passed in Sweden, Norway, and Denmark in 1933 and in the Netherlands and Belgium in 1934. Belatedly, and only after extreme provocation, was Britain's antiuniform bill passed in 1936. Sweden, Denmark, Belgium, and the Irish Free State passed laws regulating private armies in 1934, while France and Holland joined Britain in passing such a law in 1936. Laws against inciting members of the armed forces to sedition or disaffection were passed in Belgium, Holland, and Great Britain in 1934, after several other countries already had such a law. Carried out by parliamentary action, often at the insistence of public sentiment, this legislation existed as a defense of moderate constitutional ideas. To some extent, all European legislation of this sort was implicitly legislation against change and involved infringements of what some regarded as inherent personal rights. In some European countries, this defense was specifically anti-Communist; in others, it was directed equally against the Fascists and the Communists.

Britain witnessed a milder brand of fascism and communism than did most other European countries. Neither the extreme Left nor the extreme Right ever assumed proportions that directly threatened the regime or even approached any major electoral displacement. But Britain eventually took its place with those countries that passed laws curtailing Fascist and Communist activities and, in the process, certain traditional civil liberties. The following chapters study Fascist and Communist groups in Britain during the 1930s and the actions taken by the National Government to prevent their growth and to preserve public order.

The British working class regarded the National Government with extreme suspicion from its birth in 1931. Part of the distrust came from the way the Government had been formed—the Labour party had been gravely weakened by the very people who held leadership in the new regime. Another part of the distrust came from the Government's attitude toward unemployment, the means test, and distressed areas. The Government's handling of foreign affairs did not inspire working-class confidence, either. Liberals and leftists suspected that instead of fighting the dictators, the National Government was prepared to join them. The heavy concentration of Conservatives in the House of Commons also caused grave apprehension among the Opposition, for that party held a virtual dictatorship under a National label.

British democracy was a blending of a rigid and antique class structure with universal suffrage and some traditional freedoms. Because of the structure of the Government, change was difficult. The task that it faced was to prevent the growth of extraparliamentary groups without destroying or infringing upon traditional civil liberties. To a certain extent, the task was impossible. Herbert Samuel considered such a situation when he wrote:

> Liberty conduces to welfare in its widest sense. Happy are the people who are fitted, and able to enjoy liberty in all its forms together. They will not deny that crises may come when one kind of liberty has to be subordinated for a time for the sake of another. But they will need clear proof of it before they will consent to so great a sacrifice.[2]

In April 1934, when the incitement to disaffection bill was introduced, there was no clear proof of a crisis in Britain, despite the noisy presence of Communists and Fascists. Mussolini had long been admired in many circles, and the staid crawl of the National Government was frequently and unfavorably compared to the staccato march of the Third Reich. Mosley was often seen as no more than a Conservative with the courage of his convictions. It is not surprising, therefore, given the conservative composition of this Government, that the first law to protect the regime would be directed against the Left. The incitement to disaffection bill was intended to suppress Communist propaganda among the armed forces, but it was so loosely worded in its original form that it could have been used against virtually any opponent of the Government. To the Left, smarting under decreased unemployment benefits and earlier trade union restrictions, it indicated that the National Government was adopting a Fascist spirit of its own, and the Communists attempted to exploit the issue by drumming up support for an unofficial common front. In the absence of clear proof of a crisis, however, seven months passed before the bill, heavily amended, became law.

The second major act against extraparliamentary political groups was the Public Order Act. This act, which was introduced shortly after the massive East End disturbances of 4 October 1936, prohibited forming political armies, wearing political uniforms, and carrying arms in processions. The British Union of Fascists (BUF) was the primary instigator of disorder, but the act was directed as much against the British Left as against the Fascists. Far more comprehensive than the Incitement to Disaffection Act, it passed through all legal stages in less than six weeks. The public order bill was readily accepted because, unlike the earlier measure, disorder had provided evidence of the need for it.

Maurice Petherick, a Conservative M.P. for Penryn and Falmouth who had served in the Foreign Office, told an anecdote while discussing a Fascist-Communist clash at Olympia Meeting Hall in June 1934 that reflected the attitude of the Government concerning extremist parties. Petherick said a friend had been asked by a foreigner why it was that Britain allowed such extreme latitude to radical groups. His friend replied, "You see, we have a different method of dealing with these people in England. What we do is to turn them into Hyde Park under police protection, and let them have their revolution in time for everybody to get back comfortably for dinner."[3] By November 1936, the dinners were getting very cold.

It would appear, on close examination of events, that the problem of extremism was viewed as a domestic one. Foreign developments heightened British awareness, but the clear proof that such legislation was needed came to Britain not from Austria, the Rhineland, Ethiopia, or Spain, but from the streets of London. The Communist Party of Great Britain (CPGB) adhered meticulously to the Comintern line after 1929, but it attracted little attention until it took to the streets to oppose the Fascists. Mosley frequently met with Hitler and Mussolini, and the lira reportedly backed B.U.F. ventures, but few noticed the British Blackshirts until blood was spilled at Olympia on 7 June 1934. In the two-and-one-half years that passed between the introduction of the incitement to disaffection bill and that of the public order bill, the attitude of Parliament changed considerably.

It is highly doubtful that the conservative National Government would have adopted such legislation without the impetus of domestic necessity. When order broke down in London's East End, though, that was a problem far more real than the loss of other nations' liberties, and one that could not be ignored. The British Union of Fascists developed in reverse ratio to fascism on the Continent. As Hitler and Mussolini grew more successful, and hence more threatening, Mosley's support faded, but when Fascists and Communists met in the Battle of Cable Street on 4 October 1936, the National Government was forced to take action.

The action taken and almost universally accepted did infringe, however, on certain traditional civil liberties. The Public Order Act was not only an anti-Fascist measure; it affected the Left and significantly increased the power of the executive. Public order had been challenged. When it became a choice between civil liberties and order, civil liberties were sacrificed.

The actions of the National Government were severely criticized by both the Right and the Left. On the Right, the Government was seen as timid and indecisive. Many decried its unwillingness to take forceful action against the Communists, who, they claimed, were endangering free speech by obstructing Mosley's meetings. Many non-Fascist conservatives sympathized with Mosley's attempt to gain a hearing and decried the Government's failure to insure order. On the Left, the same criticisms were turned upside down. Many non-Communist Liberals and Labourites denounced the inaction of the Government concerning Fascist provocations and saw in the failure to keep order a sinister plot directed at the Left. Both sides openly exploited fears that their particular civil liberties were being threatened.

An examination of the National Government's action does not, however, reveal any sinister motives. The Left might have interpreted the Government's reluctance to act against fascism as a signal that it was planning to use fascism to prop up the sagging social structure, but there is no evidence that the Government ever saw the BUF as a possible ally. Indeed, all indications point to a genuine disdain within the Government for the BUF. The National Government may not always have been candid, as in the confusing introduction of the incitement to disaffection bill, but it was not engaged in duplicity. It was, however, ponderous and slow—it only acted when it could no longer afford to procrastinate. Fascism and communism were both foreign imports, and their presence in Britain was considered by many to be a foreign threat, but only after these groups became a domestic source of disorder did the Government act. It is doubtful if either fascism or communism would ever have taken root in the complacent, self-assured social structure of Britain, but in acting to insure domestic tranquillity, the National Government also acted to insure its own political security.

Survival is, of course, one of the primary motives of any government. Compared to the upheaval and the loss of liberties in other nations of Europe, the British experience with extremist politics was of minor consequence. But this knowledge comes to us through history. At the time of the Battle of Cable Street, there was no certainty that the British democratic society could be preserved. The National Government was guilty of many failures, but as extremist politics threatened to undermine public order, it did successfully defend itself. In protecting the existing society, traditional civil liberties were threatened, defended, and, in some cases, compromised. The effectiveness of the National Government's action to preserve order and defend itself was never critically tested, yet this in itself may testify to its success.

Chapter 2

Legislation Affecting Civil Liberties from 1918 to 1928

The law in Great Britain is usually regarded as providing relatively adequate protection in ordinary terms against infringement of civil liberties by officials. The fundamental rules of the realm relating to personal freedom are rooted in common law and the public conscience, from which common law is deemed to spring. Civil rights may be extended, refined, or restricted by statute or in some degree by executive act. The effectiveness of limitations imposed by Parliament or the government depends in some measure on the willingness of the public to accept them. In times of tension, citizens are usually willing to make more concessions to the state's power and duty to maintain public order than in normal times.[1]

The interwar period in British history was such a period of tension. The guns of Europe fell silent at eleven o'clock on the morning of 11 November 1918, but the spirit and rules prevailing in wartime were not so quickly ended. During the war, His Majesty's subjects were governed under the broad terms of the Defence of the Realm Act. This act, passed in 1914 and amended several times in the next four years, gave the state the power to try citizens for any act considered detrimental to the war effort.[2] In a bill passed in late 1914 to consolidate the Defence of the Realm Act with its many amendments, Parliament gave the government the power to "issue regulations for securing the public safety and defence of the realm, and as to the powers and duties for that purpose the Government could by such regulations authorise the trial by courtsmartial."[3]

An act so broad in its language, strengthened by prosecution without trial by jury, could impinge upon the citizens in almost any activity. The subject could be prosecuted for simply whistling for a cab.[4] Traditional civil liberties were suspended; but it was wartime, and such emergency regulations were perhaps justified by the demand of public safety and were similar to those in force in other belligerent countries. The Defence of the Realm Act expired with the peace, but many of its features were included in later legislation.

The Coupon Election of December 1918 gave the coalition of Lloyd George a decisive victory but was even more decisive for the Conservatives. There were 179 company directors in the new House and 86 members associated with commerce and finance.[5] This conservative and propertied profile did not augur well for the hopes of Labour. Except for the brief interruptions of Labour rule in 1924 and from 1929 to 1931, the Conservative party would control the government throughout the interwar years.

When the incitement to disaffection and the public order bills were introduced in the thirties, several critics of the Government saw them as part of a patterned attack on civil liberties that had begun in the previous decade. There is no evidence that any of these acts constituted a consistent and planned attempt to deprive the subject of his liberties, but against the background of the earlier acts, the actions of the National Government did appear to many as a concerted attack on its opponents. In order to understand the apprehensions with which the later bills were greeted, therefore, it is necessary to examine these earlier acts.

In the decade after World War I, four major acts were passed that in one sense or another infringed on what many considered to be traditional civil liberties: the Police Act of 1919, the Emergency Powers Act of 1920, the Official Secrets Act of 1920, and the Trades Disputes Act of 1927.

The Police Act of 1919

During the summer of 1918 the conditions of pay and pension for the police forces were becoming intolerable. The cost of living had increased significantly during the war, but police wages had remained constant. In the Metropolitan Police Force of London, there were about twenty-one thousand five hundred men. Added to this number were about 58 county police forces in England and Wales and 128 city and borough forces. In all, perhaps sixty thousand policemen were receiving substandard pay.[6] The deterioration of the force finally compelled the police rank and file to take action. The National Union of Police and Prison Officers had been formed before the war, and in August 1918 over twelve thousand police struck to achieve recognition of their demands for higher pay.[7] The Government was caught off guard by the strike, and since the pressure of the war made it virtually impossible to replace the strikers, the authorities granted substantial increases in pay and pensions and even gave limited and qualified recognition to the union. According to the report of the police commissioner, the strike was handled to a large degree by the Prime Minister himself, who ordered the raise in pay pending a general inquiry. During the interim period, the members of the force were not prohibited from joining the police union as long as the union did not interfere with the discipline or regulations of the force.[8] The police, having temporarily achieved their goals, returned to their duties.

But within the velvet glove was a mailed fist; the Government set out almost immediately to crush the union. General Nevil Macready, who had commanded troops at the miner's strike at Tonypandy in 1910, was appointed commissioner of the Metropolitan Police. The major fear of the Government was that soldiers would follow the example of the police and organize their own union. Macready would later write that any concessions made to the police on union recognition would "be more than a stepping stone toward a similar state of affairs in the army."[9]

After studying the situation, the Inspectors of Constabulary submitted a report to Parliament that showed little sympathy for the police union. Recognizing that "an organised attempt to seduce the police from their duty met with a regrettable amount of success," the constabulary report came down hard on the striking policemen. Noting the oaths taken by policemen and their positions in the national community, the report went on to say, "The men who broke their promise of faithful service, whether their motive was favour and affection for their own interests or personal fear induced by the intimidation which no doubt affected many of them, showed that a promise means little to them and can be sacrificed to their own interests."[10]

The inspectors, like almost everyone in the kingdom, nevertheless agreed that the police had legitimate complaints. They recommended the establishment of a national organization to coordinate increases in pay, allowances, pensions, and rank, which would supplant the National Union of Police and Prison Officers.[11] A police bill embodying the increased wages and pensions and calling for the creation of such a national union was presented for a second reading on 18 July 1919.

In presenting the police bill, the Secretary of State for the Home Department, Mr. Edward Shortt, Liberal member for Newcastle West who had been relatively successful as chief secretary for Ireland and had been transferred to the Home Office to deal with the threatened police strike, gave the background of the situation. Noting the discontent of the previous summer, he admitted that many of the same conditions that had spawned the police strike still existed. He traced the activities of the Police Committee under Lord Desborough, which had been appointed to "consider and report whether any and what changes shall be made in the method or recruiting for and the conditions of service of, and the rates and pay, pensions and allowances to the Police Forces of England, Wales and Scotland."[12]

There were two main grounds upon which the Opposition objected to the bill. One was that for the first time since the inception of the trade union movement, the Government had set out to suppress a registered trade union—a precedent that caused Labour party members great anxiety. The second major objection concerned clause 3, which said:

> If any person causes, or attempts to cause, or does any act calculated to cause disaffection amongst the members of any police force or induces or attempts to induce, or does any act calculated to induce any member of a police force to withhold his services or to commit breaches of discipline, he shall be liable on conviction or indictment to imprisonment, with or without hard labour, for a term not exceeding two years, or on summary conviction, to imprisonment, with or without hard labour, for a term not exceeding three months, or to a fine not exceeding fifty pounds.[13]

It was not what the clause said that aroused apprehensions; it was what it did not say. M.P.s began to fear interpretations that might later be given the vague phrase "attempts to cause disaffection," and these fears were not allayed when Shortt admitted that the press could be liable to prosecution if it incited a police strike by its criticisms. Shortt also made a bad impression by blurting out, "A policeman who is charged under this Bill, is, in fact, a traitor, nothing more, nothing less." When challenged, Shortt, somewhat flustered, quickly corrected himself and said that he had, of course, meant only those policemen who were convicted, not simply charged. To those members who feared such a miscarriage of justice, the slip was suggestive.[14] Captain James O'Grady, the Bristol Labour leader and M.P. for Southeast Leeds since 1906 whose attitudes had been shaped by working in a mineral water factory at the age of ten, spoke for a large majority of Labour when he asked that the bill be divided into parts. O'Grady, who would later serve as governor of Tasmania and the Falkland Islands, said that the first part, dealing with better standards of pay and hours for policemen, was enthusiastically supported by Labour. The second, dealing with the establishment of a Police Federation to supplant and outlaw the Police Union, was, of course, inimical to trade unionism.[15]

Because Lord Desborough's committee had lumped all police concerns into one omnibus package, the Labour members of Commons were at first in an awkward position. In voting against the bill, they would be rejecting the sizable pay increases. In voting for it, they would be rejecting the principle of a trade union for police. The Home Secretary, however, relieved part of their embarrassment by announcing that the pay increases would be provided regardless of the fate of the bill.[16]

When the bill returned from committee for its third reading in the House of Commons, the Labour opposition formulated its objections into amendments. J. R. Clynes, Labour member for Manchester and previously a piecer in a cotton mill who would become the Labour leader in Commons in 1921 and would later serve in the first and second Labour Cabinets, moved that subsection 2 be deleted from the bill. This subsection read, "The Police Federation and every branch thereof shall be entirely independent of and unassociated with any body of persons outside the public service." Clynes, reflecting his association with the Union of General and Municipal Workers, noted that the subsection denied to policemen "all contact or association with their fellow wage earners in different trades and occupations."[17]

Shortt had an answer to this complaint. He pointed out that similar terms had been accepted by the police themselves at the time of the establishment of the National Union of Police and Prison Officers. They had agreed that the police union would be "entirely within the force, and [would] be entirely independent of, and unassociated with, any outside body."[18] Nevertheless, the new bill was judged a grave threat to trade union activity among government servants. For while the restrictions provided for in subsection 2 and those of the original police union were virtually identical, the organizations differed fundamentally in origin and character; the proposed union was in effect a company union, and the Labour party could not accept a governmental bill to outlaw an existing, legal union. Their amendment to delete this portion of the bill was defeated by a four-to-one margin on a division of the House. The margin approximately paralleled that of the Opposition strength in Parliament. A further amendment by J. R. Clynes to leave out all of clause 2, which specifically forbade members of the police force to become members of a trade union, was rejected without a division.[19]

It was clause 3, however, that seemed to carry the greatest threat to civil liberties. By the wording of this clause, any trade unionist who expressed an opinion that the police should have the same rights of organization as others was liable to severe penalties. Clynes said that it would deprive some men of their right to voluntary combination, and Shortt, in replying, was thought to have revealed one of the hidden purposes of the clause when he admitted, "It is the agent of disaffection and of revolution and the agent of real mischief which is aimed at in this clause."[20] In other words, the bill was intended, in part, as an anti-Communist measure. Given the temper of the times, it was an aim that seemed to many people sufficiently urgent to override concern about the rights of labor.

The Opposition was unable to make an appreciable dent in the original wording of the bill. Labour M.P.s protested that it was offered as a "remedy against conditions of discontent" yet was not directed at the base of the problem. Clynes said that clause 3 would be the source of recurring discontent in the future. The majority of the House thought otherwise, however, and the bill passed into its third reading without a division.[21]

As the discussions on the bill had progressed, the police had received the support of the London Trades Council and the *Daily Herald*. In an attempt to prevent it from becoming law, the National Union of Police and Prison Officials, hearing the opening tones of its own dirge, called for a strike on 1 August 1919.[22] But support for the union had waned since its initial success. The strike failed; the police bill became law on 15 August. Out of 60,000 policemen, only 2,365 went on strike, a response so small that the police authorities were able to dismiss practically all of the strikers from the force with corresponding loss of pensions.[23] According to the report of the police commissioner, the experience gained from the strike of 1918 and the passage of the Police Act of 1919 "indicated clearly the failure of the experiment of allowing men to belong to a union which was unable to keep within the bounds necessary for the due observance of duty by the police to the state.''[24] From this second police strike, the Government learned that its police force was more loyal than it had supposed and could be trusted in an emergency. Perhaps even more important, it learned that other workers showed little interest in striking over a constitutional issue. The strikers received a little money and a lot of verbal encouragement from the trade union movement, but no official support through sympathy strikes.[25]

The Police Act of 1919 isolated the police politically from the trade union movement and reinforced this political isolation with corresponding social isolation.[26] The act made it illegal for policemen to join any association having as its object the influencing of pay, pensions, or conditions of service in the force. Instead, all policemen below the rank of superintendent automatically were made members of a Police Federation. Meetings of this union were to take place on official time and at official expense.[27]

The Police Act was generally used judiciously during the next two decades, but there were exceptions. In 1921 a man was successfully prosecuted under its terms. He was tried at Leeds Assizes and sentenced to six months for crying out at a meeting of unemployed men, ''Policemen! You fought for us in France. Don't help the capitalists now.'' Later that same year, the editor of a bimonthly newspaper published by the National Administrative Council of Unemployed was tried, with the printer, for having published an article calculated ''to cause disaffection.'' The article, entitled ''To the Coppers,'' was accompanied by cartoons showing the police ''zooping the unemployed with batons.'' The magistrate refused to take the case seriously; he fined the editor, Lillian Thring, ten pounds, and bound the printer over for one year. Thring, stubbornly devoted to her principles, refused to pay the fine and served a short jail term instead.[28]

In the spring of 1922, many members of the National Unemployed Workers Movement (NUWM) were arrested, imprisoned, or fined for sedition, obstruction, or acting in a manner to cause a breach of the peace. The editor of *Out of Work,* a national publication associated with the NUWM, was imprisoned for three weeks under the terms of the Police Act of 1919 for appealing to the police not to use their batons against the unemployed.[29]

Because of its close cooperation with the Communist Party of Great Britain, the NUWM was carefully watched by police during the next decade. In 1932, the NUWM headquarters were raided and hundreds of letters and documents were seized. Wal Hannington, head and founder of the organization and himself a Communist, was arrested and ordered removed from the leadership of the group because he had attempted "to cause disaffection among members of the Metropolitan Police, contrary to the Police Act of 1919."[30] Although it appeared of minor importance at the time, it was out of this police raid that the specifics for the later landmark case *Elias* v. *Pasmore* would be drawn.[31]

The Official Secrets Act, 1920

In December 1920, the official secrets bill was presented to Commons for its second reading. In moving the second reading, Attorney-General Sir Gordon Hewart, who would serve as Lord Chief Justice from 1922 until 1940, said that it was simply a bill to amend the Official Secrets Act of 1911. His stated reason for strengthening the 1911 act was the "elaboration of the systems and the methods of spying." The Official Secrets Act of 1911, he pointed out, was essentially a reenacted and amended version of the Official Secrets Act of 1889, and now it was the position of the administration that this act should be amended further.[32]

The bill was the work of an interdepartmental committee that included, among others, representatives from the War Office, the Admiralty, and the Home Office. During the war, various temporary regulations dealing with the "mischief of spying" were passed, and the Government now felt that before those temporary regulations lapsed, they should be made a permanent part of the Official Secrets regulations.[33]

A handful of M.P.s were determined to oppose the sections that they considered threats to civil liberties. Sir Donald Maclean, Liberal member for Midlothian and leader of the non-Coalition Liberals who would find a place eleven years later in the National Government at the Ministry of Education, charged that the bill was a continuation of the "war habit." The act of 1911 ruled it an offense

> if any person for any purpose prejudicial to the safety or interests of the State approaches or is in the neighborhood of or enters any prohibited

> place within the meaning of this Act or makes any sketch, plan, model, or note which is calculated to be, or might or is intended to be, directly or indirectly useful to an enemy, or obtains or communicates to any other person any sketch, plan, model, article, or note, or other document, or information which is calculated to be, or might be, or is intended to be, directly or indirectly useful to an enemy.[34]

The original act obviously aimed at definite "spy work"; Maclean claimed that the new measure hit at legitimate functions of the press. In clause 2, section 2, the new act provided for an offense

> if any person retains for any purpose prejudicial to the safety or interests of the State any official document, whether or not completed or issued for use, when he had no right to retain it, or when it is contrary to his duty to retain it, or fails to comply with any directions issued by any Government Department, or any person authorised by such department with regard to the return or disposal thereof.[35]

The new act seemed to give the government the power to declare any document "prejudicial to the safety or interests of the State" and thereby keep the press from publishing or even possessing it. Hewart denied that the bill would diminish the freedom of the press, but the possibility was undeniably there. As Maclean pointed out, the bill would give the government a power of press censorship of unwarranted degree and would militate against the public service that the press could otherwise provide. The right to decide what was prejudicial to the state was to be left to the courts, and justice might be long delayed. The government could then control news even for purely political reasons, knowing that the delay involved in a court decision would be as effective as strict censorship.[36]

J. R. Clynes found in the bill what he considered to be a "totally new doctrine of the law." The terms of the official secrets bill would, he maintained, require "anybody proceeded against under it to prove himself innocent or else he is deemed guilty."[37] Clause 1, section 3 of the act read:

> In the case of any prosecution under this section involving the proof of a purpose prejudicial to the safety or interests of the State, Subsection (2) of Section one of the principal Act shall apply in like manner as it applies to prosecutions under that section.[38]

This part of the Official Secrets Act of 1911 read:

> On a prosecution under this Section, it shall not be necessary to show that the accused person was guilty of any particular act tending to show a purpose prejudicial to the safety or interests of the State, and notwith-

> standing that no such act is proved against him, he may be convicted if, from the circumstances of the case or his conduct or his known character as proved, it appears that his purpose was a purpose prejudicial to the safety or interests of the State.[39]

The letter of the 1911 act seemed to bear out Clynes's contentions and also to confirm Maclean's charge that the Government was offering the bill out of the "war habit." "Prejudicial to the safety or interests of the State" might bring the full range of social disorders under its meaning and give the government the power to strike at public expression through the press, thus constituting a veiled attack on the individual's rights of public information.

A further invasion of individual liberties was perceived in clause 4 of the bill, which gave the government the power to require upon orders of the Secretary of State the production of the texts of any telegram sent through the post office. Clause 4 provided that the Secretary of State could

> require any person who owns or controls any telegraphic cable or wire, or any apparatus for wireless telegraphy, used for the sending or receipt of telegrams to or from any place out of the United Kingdom, to produce to [the Secretary of State] or to any person named in the warrant, originals and transcripts . . . or apparatus, and all other papers relating to any such telegram as aforesaid.[40]

A final attack on civil liberties was perceived in clause 6 of the Official Secrets Act. It read:

> It shall be the duty of every person to give on demand to a chief officer of police, or to a superintendent or other officer of police not below the rank of inspector, appointed by a chief officer for the purpose, or to any member of His Majesty's Forces engaged on guard, sentry, patrol, or similar duty, any information in his power relating to an offence or suspected offence under the principal Act or this act . . . and, if any person fails to give any such information . . . he shall be guilty of a misdemeanor.[41]

The Attorney-General's assurances to the House were accepted, and the Opposition's protests were futile. The bill passed its second reading by a 143 to 34 margin. Only 177 members voted on the motion for the second reading, but the vote closely paralleled the party makeup in the House. Voting against the measure were 22 Labour members, 6 Asquith Liberals, 4 Independent Liberals, and 1 Scottish Home Ruler. Voting for the second reading were 32 Coalition Liberals, 100 Coalition Unionists, 7 non-Coalition Conservatives, 1 Independent, 1 Unionist Liberal, and 2 Labour members.

The coalition welded by Lloyd George in 1916 still seemed remarkably united.[42]

The motion for the second reading was the last time that the official secrets bill was tested in a division of the House. On 16 December 1920, the bill received its third reading. The Opposition, led by Lt. Com. J. M. Kenworthy, an Independent Liberal from Hull who would switch to the Labour party in 1926 and as Lord Strabolgi would serve as deputy leader of the Opposition in the House of Lords, especially feared the broad interpretations that could be given to parts of it. The words of clause 1 that read "or any other purpose prejudicial to the safety or interests of the State" were seen as having the widest possible meaning and as such seemed to threaten the liberty of the subject. Kenworthy's motion to leave those words out was not accepted. During the course of debate, which lasted until 4:30 A.M., Kenworthy proposed eleven separate amendments. Of these, three were withdrawn, seven were defeated without a division, and only one, calling for the substitution of the word *minefield* for *mine,* was accepted. The Attorney-General's minor amendments were, of course, easily passed. When it was finally given its third reading, there had been a number of changes in the wording, but the threats to civil liberties that the bill's critics had discerned remained intact.[43]

Most of the prosecutions under this act were in accord with the avowed intentions of the legislation. Such prosecutions were not rare; twenty-eight cases were recorded in the period from 1933 to 1938 alone.[44] There were several, however, that clearly did not fall within the limitations of intention pronounced in 1920. In 1932, the *Daily Mail* published wills of three famous persons—Sir John Rutherford, Sir William Pryke, and Mr. Leo Maxse—several hours before they were to be officially released. The leak was traced to a sixty-year-old clerk who had been employed at Somerset House since 1921 on a salary of three pounds per week. For this offense, he was dismissed and prosecuted under the Official Secrets Act of 1920. Although the clerk was seriously ill, the magistrate sentenced him to six weeks in jail. The reporter who received the information was sentenced to two months imprisonment. Appearing for the prosecution, Attorney-General Thomas Inskip, who had been a Conservative mainstay since being named Solicitor General in the Bonar Law Government in 1922 and who would eventually be named Lord Chief Justice in 1940, maintained that the defendants had "carried on this tampering with official sources of information to the prejudice of trade competition and corruption of civil servants."[45] The sentence was confirmed.

In 1915, Herbert Asquith, then Prime Minister, had made it plain that Cabinet members were subject to the terms of the Official Secrets Act of 1911. Although no prosecution has yet taken place against a former or serving Cabinet member, proceedings were initiated in 1934 to define the limits of the 1911 and the 1920 Official Secrets Acts. Opposition leader George Lansbury, founder and longtime editor of the *Daily Herald* and the first Commissioner of Works in MacDonald's second Labour Government, allowed his son access to papers relevant to the elder Lansbury's service in the Government. In this connection, Edgar Lansbury was convicted at Bow Street and fined ten pounds on each of two counts alleging that he had unlawfully received information contained in two memoranda issued to the Cabinet in 1930 and 1931. Thomas Inskip appeared for the prosecution and remarked, "In a matter of this sort concerning documents circulated to the Cabinet, the Official Secrets Act must either be, so far as possible, enforced or it must be treated as a dead letter."[46] In this case, it was enforced, and the younger Lansbury's biography of his father, in which the "official secrets" had appeared, was purged of its offending passages.[47]

In the late thirties, there were two other significant cases. In the first, the *Daily Dispatch* published a statement that a certain person was wanted by Southport police on a minor charge. A police officer went to the home of the reporter responsible for this news and demanded to know his source of information. The reporter refused to tell and was thereupon prosecuted under the terms of the Official Secrets Act for failing to give information to a police inspector. In *Lewis* v. *Cattle,* the High Court upheld his conviction.[48] The assurances that Attorney-General Sir Gordon Hewart had made in 1920 were belied. He had said, "Whoever may be the persons aimed at, they are certainly not journalists."[49] This proved embarrassing to him eighteen years later when he was Lord Chief Justice.[50]

In 1937, the National Council for Civil Liberties launched, jointly with the National Union of Journalists, a campaign against the misuse of the Official Secrets Acts. Particular attention was drawn to the case of Major Wilfred Foulston Vernon, a fifty-four-year-old technical officer who had been employed at the Royal Aircraft Establishment at Farnborough since 1925. Vernon had professed himself to be a Socialist since 1921 and was a member of the League of Nations Union. In the summer of 1937, Vernon went on leave to the Lake District, and on his return he was told that his cottage had been broken into by four men who claimed to be Fascists. The burglars were charged with the theft of Vernon's belongings, including some left-wing political books and pamphlets.[51]

The defendants claimed that the object of their action was to expose Vernon as a subversive and that they were not common burglars, a claim that might have been more believable had they not also taken such nonseditious items as the cutlery, a watch, some money, a telescope, and a traveling rug—the political significance of which could only be apparent to a Fascist who happened to also be a thief. The report of the case at quarter sessions, however, gave the impression that instead of the burglars being charged with theft, Major Vernon was under prosecution for his political opinions.[52]

J. Ford, who had been apprehended only twenty miles from Vernon's residence, had in his possession a sizable portion of Vernon's belongings, an imitation revolver, burglary tools, an aluminum "knuckle duster," and a Fascist flag. Nevertheless, Ford turned attention away from the burglary by stating that in 1934 he and Vernon had conspired to spread Communist propaganda among the troops at Aldershot, an allegation that Vernon vehemently denied. Ford's allegations had little relevance to the burglary (and the claim by an ex–Irish Republican Army man and a deserter from the British Army that he took the steps that he did "in the interests of his country" was, objectively considered, dubious), but it was Vernon who suffered. Shortly after the story of the stolen documents was revealed in the press, Vernon's chief superintendent wrote to him, "I am satisfied from documents found at your place that you have acted prejudiciously to the Service, and are therefore suspended."[53]

The jury, meanwhile, found the four defendants guilty of "larceny in a dwelling house," generally a serious offense. In spite of Ford's army record and the fact that another of the defendants had recently been convicted of an offense under the Public Order Act of 1936, the chairman of the jury said, "We are told that all four of you bear very good characters and at least two of you are in regular work. We are going to take the course of binding you over for twelve months."[54]

Among the papers stolen by the four Fascists were a few drawings and sketches relating to Vernon's work at the Royal Aircraft Establishment. The documents taken in the burglary came into the possession of the Air Ministry, which then prosecuted Major Vernon

under the Official Secrets Acts. The authorities presented Vernon with three summonses—two relating to the retaining of information and one relating to improper care of government documents. The wording of the Official Secrets Act of 1920 left little for the defense to do but plead guilty. D. N. Pritt, the Labour M.P. for North Hammersmith, represented the accused and was eventually able to get the penalty lowered to a fifty-pound fine. Vernon was dismissed from the civil service and remained out of the government until his election to Parliament in 1945.[55] This was just the sort of case that would appeal to Pritt, who has been described by Henry Pelling as "the inveterate fellow-traveler." Pritt's activities during the 1930s included everything from the Society for Cultural Relations with the Soviet Union to actively working for a common front between the Labour party and the Communist Party of Great Britain. He frequently served as a legal adviser to the CPGB at the same time that he was a member of the Labour party executive from 1937 until 1940, when he was expelled from the Labour party for denouncing the "imperialist war."

On 5 November 1938, the National Council for Civil Liberties and the National Union of Journalists cooperated in organizing a delegate conference on "Freedom of the Press and the Official Secrets Acts." The conference was attended by nine hundred delegates, representing about three hundred and fifty organizations. Major Gwilym Lloyd George, whose famous father had allowed him to accept a minor office in the first National Government but who was now firmly in the Opposition camp, was chairman of the conference. Among the principal speakers were three members of Parliament, Dingle Foot, M. Compton Mackenzie, and A. P. Herbert. Foot, a Liberal representing Dundee, was one of the famous sons of Isaac Foot and would go on to become the Solicitor General of the 1964 Labour Government. Mackenzie, an author and dedicated Scottish nationalist, had served as a literary critic for Lord Rothermere's *Daily Mail* and was at the time in the midst of his series of books known as *The Four Winds of Love*. Herbert, whose best-known legislation was the Matrimonial Causes Bill (the "divorce act"), represented Oxford University and was a writer of novels, poetry, essays, musical comedy, and opera libretti, and was a frequent contributor to *Punch*. Other speakers at the conference included L. C. White, assistant general secretary of the Civil Service Clerical Association, Kingsley Martin, editor of the *New Statesman and Nation*, C. J. Burdock, general secretary of the National Union of

Journalists, and R. Willis, secretary of the London Trades Council.[56]

Following the conference, a memorandum was presented to the Home Secretary demanding drastic reform of the Official Secrets Acts. The resolution read, in part:

> The only way of maintaining the freedom of the press and the liberty of the subject is by such amendment of the acts as will limit their scope to the purpose originally intended when they were passed by Parliament—safeguarding secrets vital to the state. The recent application of the Acts represents a dangerous intrusion into the liberty of the citizen, whose rights and privileges are the legitimate concern of the public press. It therefore urgently calls upon all national institutions and leaders of thought to press for an immediate change of governmental policy so that all possibility of what may amount to a dangerous form of censorship may be removed.[57]

As a result of this memorandum, a personal deputation to the Home Secretary, and general public outcry arising from the cases of *Lewis* v. *Cattle* and Major Vernon, the Government introduced an amending bill in February 1939.[58] The Official Secrets Act is still very much in effect, although the threat of prosecution has kept the actual number of prosecutions quite low, but the amended act, which restricted the power of interrogation to cases related to acts of espionage, represented a considerable victory for the National Council for Civil Liberties.[59] The comment printed in the *News Chronicle* shortly after *Lewis* v. *Cattle* is a fitting afterword to all the misapplications of the Official Secrets Acts:

> Doubtless the law is as the learned judges stated it. But so much the worse for the law. The sweeping provisions of the Official Secrets Acts date from the height of pre-war spy fever. They are intended to protect military and naval secrets and matters of high moment to the state. That they should be used as they have been in this case, to cover purely police information is a monstrous perversion of their purpose.[60]

The Civil Authorities Acts

The Civil Authorities Acts and the Special Powers Acts for Northern Ireland are two more instances of what opponents saw as the Government's willingness to abridge civil liberties. These two acts were passed in 1922 and 1933 respectively, and since they deal only with Northern Ireland are, strictly speaking, outside the scope of this study. They are pertinent, however. The act of 1922 was passed to give the government the power to rule by regulations issued by the Home Secretary without reference to the Northern Ireland Parliament. In the event of emergency, the governmental powers under the terms of this act were practically absolute.

The act had to be renewed annually, and the Government was eager to secure a more permanent form of control during emergencies. In 1928, in spite of the lowest crime rate in years, the act was renewed for five years, and in 1933 a further Special Powers Act was passed, ratifying and extending the powers of the 1922 law. These acts thus became part of the Northern Ireland constitution.[61]

The provisions of these two acts were in some respects similar to those in the Fascist countries on the Continent. The Home Minister of Northern Ireland was furnished with almost dictatorial powers, which he could delegate to any police officer. The acts gave unlimited powers of search and seizure, and the Home Minister was given the power to make new regulations defining new crimes at will. Habeas corpus might be suspended, and people could be arrested on suspicion only. Court cases could be heard *in camera*. These powers were intended to be exceptional powers used only in emergencies, but in practice they were employed not merely to prevent civil disturbances, but also to check the activities of labor, Communists, trade unions, Catholics, and nationalists.[62] The fears of such organizations as the National Council for Civil Liberties (NCCL), which frequently accused the National Government of Continental Fascist methods, were not unfounded in Northern Ireland.

In 1935, the NCCL sent a commission of inquiry to examine the purpose and effect of these Special Powers Acts. The published findings of this commission called attention to the repressive character of the Northern Ireland administration. The report was called "a staggering document . . . that must shake the confidence of anyone who values the traditions of British constitutional government."[63] Nevertheless, the Civil Authorities Acts remained in effect throughout the remaining interwar years.

The Emergency Powers Act, 1920

The war ended officially for Britain on 10 January 1920. The Defence of the Realm Act was automatically abrogated, and in the boom of the next few months there seemed little need for it. But in

April 1920, the boom began to collapse. Prices fell, unemployment rose, and labor became restless. The Government evidently wanted a pretext for reinstating some of the controls that had been adopted under the Defence of the Realm Act, and in October of that year it found one.

In July 1920, the miners of Great Britain put in a claim for more pay and a reduction in coal prices. The Government, in control of the mines, rejected those demands and a strike was set for 25 September. The miners turned for support to their colleagues in the so-called Triple Alliance—the transport workers and the railwaymen.

The support was not forthcoming, and on 16 October 1920 the miners, disunited and badly led, went on strike alone. The Triple Alliance opposed the strike from the beginning. The *Communist,* the official weekly organ of the CPGB, gave considerable support to the strikers and proclaimed, "Should the miners be defeated in this struggle, it will not be because of their own weakness as much as because of the treachery and betrayal by official Labour and the desertion of their colleagues of the Triple Alliance."[64] The "Datum Line" coal strike was eventually resolved by pay raises; in the meantime, the action of the strikers and the Communists had provided the impetus for the Emergency Powers Act, which passed through all legal stages in one week and became law on 29 October 1920.[65]

The emergency powers bill was a bill to "make exceptional provision for the protection of the Community in cases of emergency." According to the terms of the act, if it appeared "to His Majesty that any action had been taken or is immediately threatened by any person or body of persons of such a nature . . . as to be calculated [to interfere] with the supply and distribution of food, water, fuel, light, or other necessities, or with the means of locomotion . . . His Majesty may, by proclamation declare that a state of emergency exists."[66]

During such an emergency, wide powers, which would potentially affect the liberties of the subject in basic ways, were to be entrusted to the authorities. When the state of emergency had been declared, it was lawful for "His Majesty in Council" to make regulations for securing community essentials by order and to

> . . . confer or impose on a Secretary of State or other Governmental Department, or any other persons in His Majesty's behalf, such powers

> and duties as His Majesty may deem necessary for the preservation of peace, for securing and regulating the supply and distribution of food, water, fuel, light and other necessity for maintaining the means of transit or locomotion . . . and may make such provision incidental to the powers aforesaid as may appear to His Majesty to be required for making the exercise of those powers effective.[67]

In its original form there was also a time factor in the bill that seemed ominous to critics. The proclamation of the emergency had to be communicated to Parliament "forthwith," but if Parliament was at the time "separated by such adjournment or prorogation as will not expire within fourteen days, a proclamation shall be issued for the meeting of Parliament within fourteen days, and Parliament shall accordingly meet and sit upon that day" (clause 1, section 2).[68] In clause 2, section 2, the act provided that regulations made under the emergency powers "shall be laid before Parliament as soon as may be after they are made, and shall not continue in force after the expiration of fourteen days from the time when they are so laid unless a resolution is passed by both Houses providing for the continuance thereof."[69] Such emergency powers could, then, be in effect for as long as four weeks without parliamentary consent. Granting dictatorial powers to the government for a month would provide it with a tool of arbitrary repression, and the act was subsequently amended to provide for the calling together of Parliament within five days.

The efforts to amend the bill in the House of Commons to remove or regulate the sweeping powers granted to the government met with little success. The rapidity with which it moved through the legislative channels deprived opponents of the chance to organize effectively against it, but it is doubtful if they would have had much success in any event. On the division for the third reading, the Emergency Powers Act passed 238 to 58, with Labour providing most of the opposition.[70]

It was not long before the new act was used. In the depression of the winter of 1920–1921, coal prices fell rapidly. In February 1921, the Government gave back the mines to the private owners, who immediately announced a drastic reduction in wages. When the miners refused to accept them, the owners posted lock-out notices. The miners turned to the Triple Alliance once again.[71] On the day the work stoppage began, a royal proclamation was issued declaring a state of emergency to be in effect. Four days later, emergency regulations proclaimed that the Government had taken upon itself far-reaching powers. Troops were moved into the coalfields, and measures were taken to ensure the food supply. As it turned out, the Emergency Powers Act did not ruin the strike as effectively as did the failure of the Triple Alliance to rally. J. H. Thomas, then secretary of the National Union of Railwaymen, broke the solidarity of the alliance and the large strike was canceled. In Labour circles, the day became known as Black Friday.[72] Thomas, who had worked his way up from cleaner to engine driver on the Great Western Railway, had brilliantly led his union in the railroad strike of 1919. Although he considered himself a hard-bitten union man, his penchant for compromise and his love of office was evident during the collapse of the second Labour Government when he agreed to stay on as the National Government's Dominion Secretary.

The Emergency Powers Act was used twice more in the next five years, once by the first Labour Government, led by those who had fought it four years before, and once by the Conservative Government during the General Strike of 1926. In March 1924, the London tramwaymen struck for an eight-hour day and an eight-shilling-per-week increase. They were quickly joined by the busmen, and the Underground workers declared that they would go on strike within two days. The Government answered with the Emergency Powers Act. A Cabinet committee under Col. Josiah Wedgwood, Chancellor of the Duchy, considered using the army to operate the transportation system, a proposal not made public at the time and never adopted. But the emergency powers were in effect. With the General Council of the Trades Union Council (TUC) and the Executive Committee of the Labour party calling for a government takeover of the whole system, MacDonald was forced to reach a settlement that partly met the demands of the workers.[73]

In 1925, the owners of the coal mines across Britain gave notice that they would no longer be bound to the national wage agreement that they had made the previous year. The TUC strongly supported the cause of the miners, and Prime Minister Stanley Baldwin eventually was able to provide a temporary solution by granting a government subsidy to the industry. In May 1926, when the subsidy was due to expire, the mineowners demanded wage cuts, which were rejected by the workers and by the TUC.[74]

To support the miners, the TUC General Council decided on a policy called "coordinated action." This coordinated action involved the participation of the electricity, gas, transportation, steel, and printing industries and culminated in the General Strike of 3 May 1926.

The story of the General Strike of 1926 is too well known to need discussion here. On 1 May 1926, the same day that the conference of trade union executives had produced a plan of action, the Government issued a royal proclamation putting the Emergency Powers antistrike machinery into effect.[75] It was now an offense punishable by imprisonment to do "any act calculated to cause disaffection amongst the civilian population." The police were empowered to enter any place suspected of being used for printing, producing, publishing, or distributing any document calculated to cause disaffection among the police, troops, or even firemen. Police harassment may have been widespread, but only two convictions resulted. Mr. Shapurji Saklatvala, a Communist M.P. for North Battersea, was sentenced to two months in jail for a speech in Hyde Park, and a Labour member was sentenced to a two-month term for saying, "The Government is out to crush the workers."[76] The act was widely regarded as effective in dealing with the situation, and the crisis evoked a call for even stronger legislation to deal with labor disputes.

The Trades Disputes Act, 1927

Even before the General Strike, there had been Conservative pressure on Baldwin to change the law on trade unions. Once the General Strike began, he could no longer afford the luxury of inaction. A bill to deal with sympathy strikes was prepared by the Government even before the strike was over, but because of the high feeling that the strike had precipitated, introduction was delayed until 1927.[77]

The trades disputes bill of 1927 was perhaps the most violent issue of the decade between the Labour party and the Conservative party and was intensely disliked in working-class quarters. The tensions produced during the passage of the bill were such that James Maxton, a member of the Independent Labour party (ILP) from Glasgow-Bridgeton, called Attorney-General Sir Douglas Hogg "a blackguard and a liar."[78] Maxton, a dark, gaunt schoolteacher who had been imprisoned for seditious speeches in 1916 and who never tempered his words, had been elected chairman of the ILP only a month before the General Strike. The contrast to Sir Douglas Hogg, a stout Conservative who, as Lord Hailsham, would later serve as Lord Chancellor and War Secretary in the National Government, could hardly be greater. Maxton was suspended from the House for his attack on Hogg; however, his negative vote would hardly have dented the Government's 70 percent majority. The elections of October 1924 had resulted in an overwhelming Conservative victory; exploiting the Campbell case, and linking it to the big Red scare occasioned by the Zinoviev letter, the Conservatives had won 415 seats compared to 152 seats won by Labour and only 42 won by the Liberals. With solid support from the Conservative party, the vote on the Trades Disputes Act was 354 ayes to 139 noes.[79]

The broadest and most sensitive part of the Trades Disputes Act was clause 3, which concerned "prevention of intimidation." That clause gave the government power to detain arbitrarily anyone found in any vicinity involving any aspect of any actual or proposed strike. The clause declared it unlawful

> for one or more persons . . . to attend at or near a house or place where a person resides or works or happens to be, for the purpose of obtaining or communicating information or of persuading or inducing any person to work or to abstain from working.[80]

It was also made an offense to be present at or near such a place in such numbers as to cause in the mind of any person a reasonable apprehension of injury. This word *injury* could be interpreted to include injury in respect to business, occupation, employment, or other source of income and thereby went far beyond the question of personal safety and bodily health. In fact, it opened the door to police discrimination and bias and to improper pressure on police by employers.[81]

The Trades Disputes Act also included severe restrictions on the rights of civil servants. In clause 5, the bill denied them the right to belong to trade unions that were concerned with pay and working conditions unless such unions were exclusively composed of employees of the government. Specifically, the civil servants were not to be affiliated to the TUC or associated directly or indirectly with any political party. Before the act was passed, the Post Office Workers, the Post Office Engineering Union, the Civil Service Clerical Association, the Inland Revenue Staff Federation, and the Ministry of Labour Staff Association had all been affiliated.[82] As a result of the act, trade union membership declined from 3,352,347 in

1926 to 2,025,139 by 1928.[83] This loss did considerable damage to the Labour movement, but the act did increase working-class support for the Labour party by providing it with a significant grievance.

These acts provided a legacy of trade union repression to the National Government that was created in August 1931. The general implications of repression went beyond an attack on the Labour movement, however, and in the next decade, the Government added more acts to the list of legislation that contained inherent challenges to civil liberties. In the increasingly violent years of the next decade, the Incitement to Disaffection Act of 1934 and the Public Order Act of 1936 were passed. The timing, the passage, and the implementation of these acts reflected both the unique character of the National Government and the pressures under which it labored. These pressures can be better understood by an examination of the history and character of the two main extremist elements in British politics during the 1930s, the Communists and the Fascists.

Chapter 3

The Communist Party of Great Britain

As in many other European countries, the Socialists of Britain were badly split by World War I. The long-established Social Democratic Federation at first supported the war, while the new Socialist Labour party opposed it. When the October Revolution of 1917 occurred in Russia, the Socialist Labour party welcomed it as the first break in the front of the capitalist order. To apply bolshevik principles to England, four men, Arthur MacManus, Tom Bell, Jack Murphy, and William Paul, assumed leadership. In 1919 they published a tract entitled *Plea for the Reconstruction of Social Tactics and Organization,* which provided the basis for a new constitution drawn up by a special Socialist Labour party conference.[1] Meanwhile, the Social Democratic Federation had changed its name to the British Socialist party and had undergone considerable internal change. Those members who had supported the war had been forced out of the party in 1916.[2] With this faction ousted, the two major Socialist groups could develop along somewhat parallel lines.

One other major group of British Socialists was Sylvia Pankhurst's Workers Socialist Federation. Pankhurst, of the famous family of suffragettes, began direct correspondence with Lenin in July 1919. Her letter, telling him of the divisions within the party over the question of parliamentary participation, received his careful consideration. Unwilling to alienate any segment of the party, Lenin replied, "I am personally convinced that to renounce participation in the parliamentary elections is a mistake for the revolutionary workers of England, but better to make that mistake than to delay the formation of a big worker's Communist Party in England."[3]

With Lenin's position known, the Communist International issued an official summons to the various British Socialist groups to drop their differences and form a united party. The British Socialist party, which was the largest of the splinter groups and had the least to lose by unity, summoned a series of meetings between the various factions that extended from mid-June 1919 to spring 1920.[4] On 31 July 1920, 159 delegates attended the Communist Unity Convention in the Cannon Street Hotel. Albert Inkpin, acting secretary, opened the proceedings by recommending that Arthur MacManus, chairman of the Provisional Committee, be invited to preside. In his opening address, the new chairman appealed to the delegates to subordinate themselves to the work they had in hand, saying, "Any self-effacement would justify itself."[5] Later the delegates unanimously passed a resolution establishing the Communist Party of Great Britain with a program for the establishment of a soviet system, the dictatorship of the proletariat, and affiliation to the Third International. This reflected the will of Lenin, who wrote, "I consider it most desirable that a Communist Party be speedily organised on the basis of the decisions and principles of the Third International."[6]

The CPGB was thereby born, but it would be several months before all the various splinter groups accepted it as the only official Marxist party in Britain. The party lacked the drive and self-sacrificing spirit that was evident in some of the Communist parties on the Continent. It never attracted more than a few thousand card-carrying members, and although there were probably many more who sympathized with it, the party was rarely of political importance during the twenties and thirties.

The established parties, however, significantly feared the CPGB. In the early 1920s, the party emphasized political action to counteract governmental control over basic industries and governmental attempts to control the postwar wave of strikes. At the time of the formation of the CPGB, one observer concluded, "Britain is faced by universal unrest in the working class and by the demand that economic power shall be shifted from the owners of capital to the workers."[7] One delegate at the Communist Unity Convention claimed that the revolution was too near to try to convert the electorate to socialism, while another insisted upon "the historical and revolutionary value of guns in the hands of the working class."[8]

Such inflammatory statements did little to soothe the apprehensions of the propertied and conservative members of Parliament, including members of the Labour party. Lenin had insisted that the party not only should use the parliamentary system as a propaganda platform, but also should become part of the Labour party and support it as "the rope supports the hanging man."[9]

At the end of 1921 the Executive Committee of the Comintern specifically ordered the CPGB to "begin a vigorous campaign for their acceptance by the Labour Party." The CPGB thereupon withdrew its candidates from constituencies where Labour candidates had already been adopted. It was still possible for a Communist to be adopted as an official Labour candidate. The Labour party did not allow this situation to continue, however, and barred Communists from membership in 1924.[10] As J. R. Clynes said, "A communist is no more a left wing member of the Labour Party than an atheist is a left wing member of the Christian Church."[11]

The victory of the Labour party in the 1924 general election did not impress the CPGB. To them, it was only further evidence that the power of wealth in modern capitalism had been used deceptively against the workers. This had filled the House of Commons, according to J. R. Campbell, "with people whose connection with the constituents is remote and ephemeral, but who are bound by bonds of steel to capitalist economic interests."[12] Campbell's words were not a simple reaction to the Labour party's rejection of the CPGB. After 1923, the Comintern reversed its position on united fronts, and the British party, like other Communist parties in Europe, openly attacked the members of the Second International. Until 1929, when the Comintern was subordinated to the Russian party, such shifts in policy were numerous.

The Years of Stagnation

Until the General Strike of 1926, the growth of the CPGB was very slow. The party was subjected to several incidents of legal harassment, which in one case actually helped cause the downfall of the Labour Government. In July 1924, the *Worker's Weekly,* the official Communist journal, appealed to members of the armed forces not to obey orders when called upon to fire on strikers. Sir Patrick Hastings, the Attorney-General, authorized prosecutions on the basis of the 1797 Incitement to Mutiny Act.[13] (Hastings, a successful barrister and playwright who was considered by many to be a traitor to his class, later appeared for the defense in several actions taken against

Oswald Mosley and the British Union of Fascists.) On 5 August, the office of the *Worker's Weekly* was raided for evidence, and its editor, John Ross Campbell, was arrested and charged under the terms of the 1797 act. The prosecutions were withdrawn the next day, for reasons of political expediency.[14] The Government was defeated two months later on a motion of censure concerning its actions in the affair.[15]

One year later, twelve leading members of the CPGB were arrested and charged with "having on divers days since January 1st, 1924 unlawfully conspired together to utter and publish seditious libels and incite divers persons to commit breaches of the Incitement to Mutiny Act, 1797, against the peace of our Lord, the King, his Crown, and his dignity."[16] The prosecutor, Sir Travers Humphreys, averred that the CPGB was an illegal organization since it aimed to create antagonisms between classes and seduce members of the armed forces from their allegiance to the Crown. In their defense, the accused brought up the lenient way in which Sir Edward Carson and other leaders of the Ulster Rebellion had been treated in 1914. Although legally irrelevant, such comparisons were not lost on those who followed the proceedings.[17]

The examination of witnesses revealed that some had been instructed to dig up evidence for the prosecution. This included finding seditious passages in party pamphlets and periodicals, taking notes at party meetings, impersonating Communists to obtain information, and raiding the offices under the guise of a Fascist raid.[18] But there was never much doubt as to the result of the trial. The jury was absent for less than twenty minutes and returned a verdict of guilty. Five leaders were sentenced to twelve-months imprisonment because they had previous convictions. The other seven were offered a deal by the judge, who turned to them and said, "Those of you who will promise me that you will have nothing more to do with this association or the doctrines which it preaches, I will bind over to be of good behavior in the future. Those of you who do not promise will go to prison." To each of the seven the judge said, "Will you be bound over?" Each replied, "No, I will not!" and was given a six-month sentence.[19]

The sentences disrupted CPGB activity during the months immediately preceding the General Strike. The seven leaders who had been sentenced to six months were released just before the strike, and the others were released during the course of the miner's lock-out. Whether or not the Government was farsighted enough to keep the Communist leadership disrupted during the planning stages of the General Strike or whether it was a coincidence is still a matter of conjecture.[20]

Opinion on the prosecutions divided along predictable lines. On 1 December 1925, Ramsay MacDonald, disclaiming all Communist sympathies, introduced a resolution calling for a vote of censure against the Government for its prosecution of the twelve leaders. The resolution argued, "The action of the Government in initiating the prosecution of certain members of The Communist Party is a violation of the traditional British rights of freedom of speech and publication of opinion."[21]

The debate on the motion of censure lasted for over six hours and at times was quite bitter. The result of the vote on the motion was a foregone conclusion; the Labour Opposition had little success in swaying the opinions of the majority. The final vote against the resolution was 127 ayes and 351 noes.[22] The *Times* fully shared the opinion of the majority. It particularly objected to the line of attack that suggested that the statutes under which the prosecution proceeded were "obsolete" or "musty" and had been resurrected only for Government convenience. In a not too subtle reference to the leading exponent of this theory, Harold Laski, the *Times* suggested, "No man who [could] seriously put it forward is qualified to teach political science and history."[23] Laski, in addition to being a member of the executive committee of the Fabian Society (and eventually becoming chairman of the Labour party after World War II), was a professor of political science at the London School of Economics.

The CPGB was somewhat taken by surprise when the General Strike of 1926 began. Although its most prominent members were imprisoned, the CPGB adopted an extremely militant policy, and on the last day of the strike the Central Committee of the party issued a call against resumption of work. Such militancy was approved by some of the more embittered sections of the working class, and the CPGB membership roles increased dramatically. Before the strike, membership totaled about 6,000. By October 1926, according to the Eighth Congress Report, the membership had risen to 10,730, and Stalin was proclaiming the CPGB to be "one of the best sections of the Comintern."[24]

But from this point until the depression, there was a serious drop in membership. By October 1927, the membership was down to

7,377. By December 1929, it was down to 3,200.[25] Little progress could be made when most of the members of the CPGB were themselves unemployed. The total number of party members organized in factory cells was only 550, while the cells themselves numbered only eighty-two.[26]

The CPGB contested the election of 1929 in spite of a membership of little more than three thousand. Their platform for Britain was mild enough, calling for the right of the armed forces to form trade unions and political parties, for abolition of the death penalty, and for no use of the armed forces against workers in industrial disputes. It was the international platform, however, that showed the extent to which the CPGB was tied to Moscow. The party demanded the refusal to vote capitalist war credits, repudiation of all imperialist treaties and pacts including the Versailles, Locarno, and Kellogg-Briand pacts, exposure and repudiation of the League of Nations as a "capitalist war trust," annulment of the Dawes Plan, withdrawal of troops from the Rhine, China, India, Egypt, and all parts of the empire, full recognition and support of the Soviet Union, the publication of all secret treaties, and the establishment of a fighting Trade Union International as a weapon in the struggle against capitalism.[27] This lack of political subtlety showed in the polls and membership rolls of 1929.

At the Tenth Plenum of the Comintern in Moscow in July 1929, the relative independence of the CPGB executive was denounced. The Comintern performed, in effect, a coup d'etat from above. Harry Pollitt became the Comintern's man in London, and the old leadership of Inkpin and Bell was pushed aside.[28] The Comintern had been committed since its creation to a common policy of all sections, but since 1924 Stalin had been gradually forcing the national sections into subordination. This action represented the climax of his efforts.

The extent of submission to Moscow caused even more apprehension in the established parties. The new line emphasized "Class Against Class" and advocated militancy not only against capitalism but also against existing trade union machinery. In a minority movement, in fact, the CPGB established two breakaway unions. By such tactics, the Communists alienated themselves from that section where they could have expected most of their support. By their continued submission to Moscow, fears of a foreign government were added to the fears of a radical ideology.[29] Until the change in policy to the advocacy of united fronts, the "Class Against Class" policy meant only the elimination of the party from "any general influence whatsoever."[30]

The CPGB and the National Government

The CPGB witnessed no significant leap in membership, in spite of growing unemployment, until after the Labour Government fell in August 1931. The role of the New York bankers in the crisis seemed to confirm the Marxist view that international capitalism would find ways of undermining democratic policies. The party also benefited from a naval strike that took place a month later in Invergordon. The Invergordon Mutiny was not instigated by the CPGB, but the Government was content to claim Communist agitation as a leading cause, and the CPGB was eager to claim the credit. In the first few months of the National Government, however, the CPGB remained without political influence.

To the Communists, the depression was clearly the long-awaited, inevitable crisis in capitalism and was not simply due to any temporary accident of policy. It was "the inevitable outcome of the class ownership of the means of production, of the system of production for profit." Their solution was also plain: "Only the overthrow of capitalism, the driving out of the capitalists from ownership, the taking over and organising of production by the workers, can solve the crisis."[31]

By the general election in November, the membership had doubled. The number of members was still only six thousand, but most of these new recruits were unemployed and could not contribute dues to aid their candidates.[32] The CPGB contested, and lost, twenty-six seats. Only in eight constituencies did the Communist poll more than one-fifth the total of the Labour candidate.[33] Yet, according to R. Palme Dutt, writing in the *Daily Worker,* "The workers [have] lost confidence in the Labour Party, and seek elsewhere. . . . The Labour movement, the old Labour movement, is dying. The Worker's Movement, the independent Worker's Movement, is rising."[34]

In a sense, Dutt was right. Many *had* lost faith in the Labour party, and an independent worker's movement was rising. It was not, however, to the CPGB itself that many of the unemployed were turning, but to the National Unemployed Worker's Movement (NUWM). This organization, first formed in the early twenties, was led by Wal Hannington and S. J. Elias. Because both were active members of the CPGB, the NUWM was nearly a wing of the Communists. The CPGB, although benefiting surprisingly little in the way of membership, was able to attract a great deal of attention through the demonstrations of the NUWM.[35]

Demonstrations, which had been practically abandoned during the late twenties, grew tremendously during the thirties. Although the official Comintern policy directing the formation of "popular fronts" had not yet been born, by 1933 the CPGB was becoming more accommodating to non-Marxist groups. The rest of the British Left continued their struggle to find an "English way" short of a Communist revolution. Cutting across all doctrinal lines of the Left, the NUWM provided the first real test of the National Government's ability to maintain order within the bounds of previously respected civil liberties.

The largest NUWM rally was scheduled for Sunday, 25 February 1934. By Thursday of that week, hundreds of hunger marchers were pouring into London. The National Council for Civil Liberties, still in its infancy, sent representatives to act as observers during the demonstrations and to report on the conduct of both the marchers and the police.[36] The police were prepared to relieve marchers of their staves and walking sticks, but the peaceful marchers left them behind at St. Albans.[37] On the Friday night before the rally, Harry Pollitt and Tom Mann, two longtime Communist party leaders, were arrested on warrants obtained from the Glamorgan County police and were charged with sedition. Pollitt, a boilermaker who had opposed Ramsay MacDonald in the 1929 election, was arrested outside party headquarters. Mann was arrested at his house, which was subsequently searched by detectives.[38] According to Mann's wife, even the circumstances of the arrest were unusual. The *Daily Worker* quoted her as saying:

> A man came to the door saying that he was Mr. Keble, a journalist, and that he wanted to interview Tom about the hunger march. I asked what was the paper, but he couldn't name one. Tom was not at home, the man went away, but a messenger who came with a parcel told me that a strange man was hanging around the garden and a police van was at the "Black Horse." Then I knew what the "journalist" had come for.[39]

Both Pollitt and Mann were signatories of a petition requesting

MacDonald to receive a deputation of hunger marchers. But as the hunger marchers neared London, the Cabinet agreed that the Prime Minister should not receive any deputation from the marchers and that instead MacDonald should make some statement that such a meeting would only "encourage and recognize the exploitation for political ends" of the legitimate grievances of the unemployed. MacDonald was also to arrange for the Home Secretary to have the chance to say that the cooperation of the newly formed British Union of Fascists "was not desired."[40] The message delivered on behalf of MacDonald read:

> In reply to the letter sent through the National Congress and March Council asking the government to receive a deputation from the unemployed marchers, I have been instructed to say that I am unable to accede to your request. The deputation can do no service to the unemployed. The Communist purpose of these marches is common knowledge.[41]

The demonstration of the hunger marchers in Hyde Park proved to be entirely peaceful. About five thousand police had little trouble handling the crowd, estimated at over fifteen thousand.[42]

In the preliminary hearing for Pollitt and Mann, the prosecution defined sedition as

> all those practices, whether by word or deed, which fall short of high treason, but directly tend to have for their object to incite discontent or disaffection, to incite ill will between different classes of the King's subjects, create political disturbance or to lead to civil war, to bring into hatred or contempt the sovereign or the government, the laws of the constitution of the realm and generally endeavour to promote public disorder, or to incite people to unlawful associations or assemblies, insurrections, breaches of the peace, or forceable obstructions of the law or to use any form of physical force in any public matter connected with the state.[43]

This was not Mann's first appearance in court. He had been fined in 1902 for diluting beer, and in 1912 he had been sentenced to a short term for being a "disturber of the peace and an inciter of persons to take part in mass demonstrations calculated to involve the contravention of the Seditious Meetings Act of 1817."[44]

Pollitt claimed that his arrest had been merely an act by the Government to detain him from organizing the hunger marchers. According to a constable's shorthand notes, Pollitt had said in speeches at Treslow and Ferndale, ". . . There is only one course open to us—that is, revolution . . . . Make no mistake, mass attack of Carlyle's writings there is nothing that could be regarded as other than the product of a National Socialist mind.[4]

Although ignored by the Fascist researchers, a truer precursor to the BUF was the British Brothers League, founded in 1902. Essentially, this was a nationalist group organized under the motto England for the English. Although the membership rolls were based on the assumption that anyone who signed its manifesto was a member, the league boasted over forty-five thousand members. Originally directed only against destitute aliens, it soon degenerated into quiet anti-Semitism.[5]

The first movement to accept the name *Fascist* and acknowledge Italy as a source of inspiration was the British Fascisti of R. L. Lintorn-Orman. Lintorn-Orman, a twenty-six-year-old woman with a taste for mannish clothes, supposedly received the inspiration for the Fascisti while weeding the kitchen garden on her dairy farm.[6] The name was later changed to the British Fascists in order to avoid accusations that it owed loyalty to a foreign power. At first, Lintorn-Orman's group viewed fascism as an outgrowth of the Boy Scout movement. To them, both fascism and the scout movement upheld the ideals of brotherhood, service, and duty.[7] Actually, there was little Fascist content in the original ideology of the British Fascists. Cooperating with the Anti-Socialist and Anti-Communist Union, the Economic League, and the 1912 Club, even its high officials admitted that it was an adjunct of the Conservative party. By 1934, this group claimed six hundred and fourteen thousand members, but its modest headquarters and lack of branch organizations rather belied this claim.[8]

A second mainstream of fascism can be traced to Arnold Spencer Leese, a retired veterinary surgeon and specialist in diseases of camels who had spent most of his life in the Middle East. At age fifty, Leese retired from the army and went into his own particular brand of politics.[9] In 1924 Leese joined the British Fascisti and in 1928 became part of a splinter group that formed the National Fascist party. This party collapsed the same year due to financial difficulties and public ridicule occasioned by its officers' penchant for parading in front of the headquarters with drawn swords.[10]

The dissolution of the National Fascists led to the formation of the Imperial Fascist League, which was never more than a personal bodyguard for Arnold Leese. From the start its members wore black shirts and black pants. They originally used the fasces as their and force are our strongest weapons."[45] Pollitt presented three grounds for dismissal of the charges: first, he thought the shorthand ability of the officer who recorded his speech was questionable; second, he believed himself within the bounds of the law; and third, and perhaps most important, he claimed that the real political motives had not been brought out. Claiming that a deliberate distortion of his views constituted a frame-up, he mentioned that such action was sanctioned by Attorney-General Thomas Inskip, and that it was done

> . . . as a deliberate, provocative act, to try to provoke acts of disorder in London during the hunger marchers' demonstration. The London working class knew how to answer that by one of the finest exhibitions of solidarity and discipline, there was not one single prosecution for disturbance of the peace.[46]

The arrest of Mann and Pollitt on such charges was the result of inadequate existing legislation. The flimsiness of the charges was easily proved on the day of their trial, 4 July 1934, when both were acquitted of all charges. The defense proved that the officer who reportedly took the evidence down in shorthand was incapable of doing so. Obviously, someone in the police department had supplied the condemning evidence. The court threw the evidence against Mann out of court, and in light of that action, the prosecution withdrew its case against Pollitt. Commenting editorially, the *Guardian* warned, "The next time it may appear expedient to divert Communist leaders from a Hyde Park demonstration, a better excuse should be found."[47] The National Government, meanwhile, appeared to be working on just such legislation.

The Struggle for a Common Front

The growth of fascism on the Continent caused a shift in the policy of the Communist Party of Great Britain. By 1931, the CPGB was already alert to the dangers of fascism and warned, "The whole dominant tendency of British capitalism is now in the direction of fascism, the discarding of the old forms of parliamentary democracy, which is characteristic of a late stage of capitalistic development marked by capitalistic decay, and advancing class struggle."[48] The CPGB, therefore, was significantly antifascist before the British Union of Fascists was formed in 1932.

In early 1933, the Central Committee of the CPGB issued a call for the fullest possible support of the International Anti-fascist Congress projected for April of that year. As an immediate measure, it proposed convening mass demonstrations in London and in every provincial city in support of German and Austrian workers and against "attacks of the capitalists on the working class of Britain."[49] The official position was always clear: it warned that the forces of fascism would develop with great rapidity unless the workers succeeded in building up the widest possible fighting front. The movement to a common-front tactic was already visible in the Communist demand that the workers conduct "a ruthless struggle against the reformists who are endeavouring to break this unity."[50]

To the CPGB, the National Government was a more serious fascist enemy than the struggling British Union of Fascists. There was fascism in the "offensive of the National Government and the employers in Britain which is accompanied by increased police terror . . . . Everywhere in the capitalist world the ruling class is organising fascist bands and carrying on political banditism, torture of political prisoners, forging of documents, shooting down strikers, and the suppression of workers' organisations and the press."[51]

In March 1933, the first move to form common fronts was made, although of limited scope. The Comintern Executive instructed its national sections to approach the central organizations of the Second International with proposals for joint action and to "refrain from making attacks on Social-Democratic organisations." Within three days of the receipt of instructions from Moscow, the CPGB sent messages to the executives of the Labour party, the TUC, and the Independent Labour party (ILP).[52] A similar correspondence went on at the local levels.

For years the CPGB had been attacking the Labour party and the TUC, so it is not surprising that those bodies turned a deaf ear to the proposals. The TUC and Labour party leadership rejected this attempt at rapprochement and "affirmed [their] faith in the principles of representative democracy and socialism." Their declaration read, "If the British working class hesitate now between majority and minority rule, and toy with the idea of dictatorship, fascist or communist, they will go down to servitude such as they have never suffered."[53]

With the ILP, however, it was a different situation. The ILP had been in a period of slow decline, and in 1932, when it disassociated itself from the Labour party, this decline was hastened. The party fell in membership from 16,733 in 1932 to only 4,392 in 1935. The CPGB realized that if it could capture the ILP it would improve its own prospects of developing into a mass organization. Negotiations with the ILP went on for over a year. Fenner Brockway and James Maxton were in constant public correspondence with Moscow in an attempt to reconcile the differences between the two bodies. Brockway, who was the son of a missionary to India and who had been imprisoned as a pacifist during World War I, had been the organizing secretary of the ILP and was now serving as general secretary. In the end, the ILP's analysis that the Comintern was absolutely controlled by the Communist party of the Soviet Union proved to be a stumbling block. At the annual conference of the ILP during Easter 1934, the policy of "sympathetic affiliation" was defeated 98 votes to 51, and day-to-day cooperation with the CPGB, which had been in effect for a year, was also abandoned.[54]

The CPGB nevertheless continued its efforts at affiliation. A year later, at the annual conference of the ILP at Derby, James Maxton said that the possibility of a new workers' party being formed with the ILP and the Communist party at the central core was one "not of the far distant future."[55] The next day the conference voted to cooperate but not affiliate with the CPGB.

Cooperation with the other factions of the Labour movement, however, was never realized. In February 1934, the aging Arthur Henderson, then secretary of the Labour party and nearing the end of a political career that had seen him rise from being a Newcastle ironworker to being a member of the Cabinet, received letters from both the ILP and the CPGB suggesting that the British socialists should forget their differences and unite in resisting fascism at home and abroad. Henderson wrote to Fenner Brockway:

> Your suggestion for "an immediate consultation between the representatives of *all* sections of the working class" is one which in the considered opinion of the National Executive, would certainly not result in any agreed upon policy of "common action," in view of the fundamental differences which exist, for example, between the Labour Party and its associated movements on the one hand, and the Communist Party on the other hand.[56]

Henderson also wrote to Harry Pollitt of the CPGB, "In the opinion of the National Executive, it would be idle to ignore fundamental differences of policy and method which exist between the

Labour Party and the Communist Party and to establish a so called 'united front' behind which intensified Communist propaganda would be carried on against associated organisations."[57]

The National Joint Council of the TUC also considered the request from the CPGB for the formation of a "united front against fascism and war" in 1934. As before, it decided that there were no new circumstances that would permit them to depart from their established policies.[58]

Following the Seventh World Congress of the Communist International in Moscow in 1935, the first congress held since 1928 and the last to be held, attempts at forming a united front were redoubled. By this time, Russia had relaxed its executive control over the Comintern. Henry Pelling, in *The British Communist Party,* states that Stalin, in order to allay the fears of the British and French governments and to prepare them for an alliance with the Soviet Union, "relaxed the Comintern's detailed supervision of its national sections, secure in the knowledge that groups of his own tried henchmen were in control of each of them."[59] The resolution issued by the congress declared:

> Taking into consideration the constantly growing importance and responsibility of the Communist Parties . . . , taking into consideration the necessity of concentrating operative leadership within the sections themselves, the Seventh World Congress instructs the Executive Committee of the Communist International . . . to proceed in deciding any question from the concrete situation and specific conditions prevailing in each particular country, and as a rule to avoid direct intervention in internal organisational matters of the Communist Parties.[60]

The Comintern nevertheless spelled out that the national sections were to use this independence for the furtherance of common fronts. The Seventh World Congress placed at the center of the policy of the Communist parties the task of creating a "unity of action of the proletariat and a People's Front on a national and international scale against the offensive of capital, against fascism, for peace, and against imperialist war."[61] The Seventh World Congress declared:

> . . . The Communist International and its sections are ready to enter into negotiations with the Second International and its sections for the establishment of the unity of the working class in the struggle against the offensive of capital [and] fascism.[62]

These directives had an immediate effect on the CPGB. In the election of that year, all but two CPGB candidates withdrew after pledging to support Labour candidates. The Labour party showed little appreciation for this gesture, however, and bitterly contested the two seats for which the Communists did run. Harry Pollitt campaigned for a seat in East Rhondda and got 38 percent of the vote while Willie Gallacher, who had been jailed for inciting to riot during the Clyde Strike in 1919, actually won a seat in West Fife, which he kept for the next fifteen years. A number of local Communist councillors were also elected. In Rhondda, four Communist councillors were eventually able to obtain maternity clinics and worked to improve the conditions for nurses in the local hospital. In West Fife, the two Communist councillors had proved so effective that they were returned unopposed. By 1937, in fact, the Communist party had fifty-four representatives on urban district and county councils.[63]

As soon as the elections of 1935 were over, the CPGB officially applied for affiliation with the Labour party for the first time since 1924. The request was, of course, rejected out of hand, but the CPGB immediately began waging a campaign for affiliation at the Labour Party Conference of 1936. The extent to which the CPGB was willing to go in securing a united front is shown by Harry Pollitt's declaration in 1936 that the *Daily Worker* should be transformed "from a narrow party organ into the fighting daily newspaper of the united front . . . . Non-party people must be drawn on to the editorial board."[64]

A common front was never achieved, although considerable agitation for it continued throughout the rest of the decade. Besides the ideological differences, such a union would be of little practical value to either the Labour party or the TUC. For the ILP it could have meant rejuvenation, however, and therefore this was the only group that seriously considered it. The new image of the CPGB was nonetheless tremendously successful. While the Labour party executive pleaded with the rank and file to ignore Oswald Mosley's Blackshirts, the CPGB organized workers to march against them. In London's East End, site of the Blackshirts' most provocative demonstrations, it was to the CPGB that many people turned. To be sure, both the Labour party and the TUC passed resolutions condemning fascism, but it was members of the CPGB, independently free to carry on a campaign of working-class unity, who bloodied their shirts defending the East End Jews. There was no doubt considerable truth in Sir Anthony Eden's statement to German Foreign Secretary von Ribbentrop that England "had virtually no communists . . . except those whom Sir Oswald Mosley was creating."[65]

During this time the membership rolls increased dramatically. From less than 6,000 members in January 1935, the CPGB had increased to 7,700 by the time of the Seventh World Congress of the Comintern in July. In October 1936, membership stood at 11,500, and by May 1937, 12,250 belonged to the CPGB. Indeed, its membership continued to rise until 1943.[66]

Part of this increase can be attributed to the fact that communism suddenly became popular among middle-class students and intellectuals. The reasons for their sudden interest in communism varied, but Pelling's analysis, that their conversion was secured "by the apparent logic of international events, combined with feelings of social guilt thrust upon them by the depression," seems to explain the general attitude of many. Among the gifted writers attracted to the party's philosophy were Christopher Isherwood, Stephen Spender, W. H. Auden, and Cecil Day Lewis.

Designed to allay the fears of the Government concerning communism, the united front movement had somewhat the opposite effect because of the substantial growth of communism among the middle class. Kenneth Newton maintains that the middle-class members tended to be more concerned with the ideology of communism than working-class members. In 1931, Communist organizations were founded at Cambridge University, University College in London, and at the London School of Economics. Oxford's October Club, founded in 1932, boasted three hundred members by 1933. By 1938, one of every five students at Cambridge belonged to the Socialist Club.[67]

Many of the new members, however, were more anti-Fascist than they were Communist. Communism appealed to them as the only vanguard in an international fight against fascism. Furthermore, the new recruits, unlike earlier members, were often fairly well off. They could provide dues and subsidies such as the CPGB had never been able to accumulate. The *Daily Worker* expanded to a very respectable size. Left-wing and cultural journals, such as the *Week, Cambridge Left, Plan, New Verse, Storm, Controversy, New Writing,* and *Daylight* sprang up and flourished.[68] Most of the contributors to these publications were in their twenties or early thirties.[69]

In its opposition to the radical right, the CPGB could, for the first time, identify with and lead public opinion. J. M. Keynes reportedly said, "There is no one in politics today worth sixpence outside the ranks of the Liberals, except the post-war generation of intellectual communists under thirty-five."[70] It is no wonder, then, that many sections began to view with alarm the growth of the CPGB.

In 1934, the *Left Review* was founded under the auspices of the British section of the Writer's International and provided an outlet for young Communist writers. Well-known Fabians such as the Webbs, George Bernard Shaw, and H. G. Wells embarked on a love affair with the Soviet Union. The Webbs' book *Soviet Communism: A New Civilization?* appeared in 1935, and the 1937 edition significantly omitted the question mark from the title.[71] Innumerable novels appeared in which the hero, after a series of inner struggles, joined the Communist party on the last page.[72] Meanwhile, the Left Book Club had been launched by Victor Gollancz, the publisher, to provide left-wing publications at a cheap cost to their readers. Gollancz, Harold Laski, and John Strachey, none of whom were actually Communists, formed a panel to select the books. Strachey, who had been elected to Parliament at the age of twenty-eight and whose book *The Coming Struggle for Power* had captured the imagination of many of the leftist university students, helped insure that the Left Book Club would serve well the CPGB's effort to form a common front. Frequently regarded as a subversive organization, the club probably served as a safety valve for many of the intellectuals. "Reading is a substitute for action," wrote A. J. P. Taylor, "not a prelude to it; and the members of the Left Book Club worked off their rebelliousness by plodding through yet another orange covered volume."[73]

Beginning in 1936, however, hundreds of young idealistic Communists began to "work off their rebelliousness" in a different way. The civil war had broken out in Spain, and to many the struttings of the British Union of Fascists seemed minor compared to a genuine life-or-death struggle. As early as October 1936, a Tom Mann Centuria was serving on the Aragon front. Not all the British volunteers in Spain were Communists, as is evidenced by the existence of the Clement Attlee Brigade, but a good many were. By 1937, the *Daily Worker* published much more news on Spain and the international situation than on the necessity of forming a common front in Britain to stop Mosley or hold the National Government in check. By this time, the uniformed Fascist was off the British streets and seemed unimportant compared to his far-too-successful Continental counterpart.

Chapter 4

The British Union of Fascists

Fascist Precursors

The British have traditionally been suspicious of foreign institutions. After the British Union of Fascists was formed in late 1932, therefore, W. E. D. Allen, a former Conservative M.P. for Belfast West, set out to legitimize fascism by showing its roots in the British past. Allen, himself an Ulsterite, invoked the Ulster Volunteers and labeled Sir Edward Carson the leader of the first Fascist movement in Europe.[1] Anxious to gain a measure of respectability, the BUF embraced Carson, who had retired from active politics ten years before that organization was born, and called him their own. At his death, William Joyce, later the infamous Lord Haw Haw of World War II, wrote, "In bearing, will, act and thought Carson was a Fascist . . . . The Ulster Volunteer movement, Carson's own, was something more than a precursor of Fascism in Europe. It was the first real and tangible resistance that Liberal Plutocracy had to encounter in Britain."[2] Actually it was something less; it was just a national movement, occupying a position traditionally held by the British Right.

This was not the only distortion of the movement's genealogy. E. D. Hart, writing in the *Fascist Quarterly,* saw elements of fascism in Britain as far back as the 1820s. According to Hart, Charles Western and Thomas Atwood, who adopted the slogan Peace, Law, and Order, anticipated the methods of modern fascism in their efforts to revise the Corn Laws.[3] William Joyce later tried to extend the roots of fascism in another direction. Joyce wrote:

> Thomas Carlyle ranks first amongst British heralds of the Fascist Revolution. Other great thinkers who preceded him showed in their writings some of the main tendencies of Fascist philosophy; and in their number Shakespeare and Goldsmith contributed much; but in all the vast extent

emblem, but in 1933 they adopted the swastika superimposed upon the Union Jack.[11] The Imperial Fascist League defined fascism as the "patriotic revolt against democracy and a return to statesmanship" and hoped to impose a corporate state on England.[12] By 1934, its membership was estimated to total only about two hundred, and its headquarters consisted of two little rooms above a tailor's shop. Leese reportedly said, "I could have more, but I want them to represent an aristocracy of character."[13] Despite preposterous positions of Leese's such as calling for the shipment of all Jews to Madagascar, the German Nazi party did insert his pamphlets into its own when it propagandized in Great Britain.[14]

These early organizations never received much support or attention from the British public. Embarrassingly simpleminded, anti-Semitic, and irresponsible, they were never able to count a combined real membership of more than a few thousand.[15] Perhaps more than anything else they lacked a leader with the background and articulation to command respect. A leader, however, was about to emerge from a succession of frustrations that would result in the formation of the British Union of Fascists.

Oswald Mosley

Sir Oswald Mosley was born in 1896 and grew up in a relatively nonpolitical environment. Educated at Winchester and Sandhurst, he gained a reputation as a boxer and a fencer rather than as a scholar. During World War I, he served in the 16th Lancers and the Royal Flying Corps and, as a result of leg injuries, was left with a permanent limp. His parliamentary career began in 1918 when he was elected as a Conservative member for Harrow. At the age of twenty-three he was the youngest member of Parliament, and his height, his appearance, and his amiable mannerisms stamped him as a man to watch.[16] An outspoken defender of veterans' rights, Mosley was frequently at odds with the coalition Government.[17]

During the twenties, Mosley became a political chameleon. In 1922, he left the Conservative party and was reelected as an Independent Conservative. One year later he dropped the Conservative title and ran as an Independent. He did not join the Labour party until April 1924, some three months after that party formed a Government. In a style that served as a portent of things to come, he wrote to MacDonald, "You stand forth as the leader of the forces of progress in their assault upon the powers of reaction . . . . I ask leave to range myself beneath your standard."[18]

It was thought that the Labour party had gained a valuable recruit, in spite of his wealthy background and his marriage to Cynthia Curzon, the daughter of the Foreign Secretary. Such rapid conversions usually took several years, but Mosley became more socialist than most of the socialists, and his wife became greatly respected in the Labour movement. His Birmingham proposals, conceived in 1925, were a daring plan for public control of the supply of credit and currency through the nationalization of the banking system and the issuing of consumer credits to the unemployed.[19] Even the office of Prime Minister seemed to be within his grasp.

Mosley soon gathered around him some of the most outstanding people of the decade. Aneurin Bevan, Harold Nicolson, John Strachey, Allen Young, and Sidney and Beatrice Webb were all in frequent company with Mosley. The Webbs and Bevan, a coal miner of leftist sympathies who had just begun his remarkable parliamentary career in 1929, would remain in the Labour party. Nicolson, a writer, diplomat, and soon-to-be editor of New Party's newspaper, was a great personal friend of Mosley and his wife. Young, a Birmingham ILP organizer and economist, was Mosley's private secretary when Mosley was Chancellor of the Duchy, and Strachey was Mosley's parliamentary private secretary. Beatrice Webb, for her part, admired him very much but once remarked, "So much perfection argues rottenness somewhere."[20]

Mosley's plans for ending unemployment, which were evolved between 1925 and 1931 in collaboration with John Strachey and Allen Young, stamped him as "one of the major creative minds in modern politics."[21] Like John Maynard Keynes, he started with a problem which the laissez faire system could not solve and ended as a prophet of regulated capitalism. His success in devising good policies, however, was matched by his failure in implementing them. Continual frustration at the hands of men less imaginative but more patient than he drove him to extremism.

When the Labour party returned to power in 1929, Mosley was appointed Chancellor of the Duchy of Lancaster and was to assist J. H. Thomas with employment schemes. By 1930, unemployment had risen dramatically. Thomas attacked the problem with a fair degree of initiative, but its magnitude proved to be too much for him. Frustrated again, Mosley went over the head of Thomas and sent to

Ramsay MacDonald a series of proposals that came to be known as the Mosley Memorandum. But action on his proposals dragged. By April unemployment reached 1.7 million. The Cabinet finally rejected his memorandum, and on 20 May 1930 Mosley resigned from the Government.[22] Determined to bring "these grave matters to a test," Mosley appeared before Commons and moved a resolution calling for a new policy on unemployment based upon his proposals. He lost in the division, 210 to 29.[23]

In spite of the overwhelming defeat at the hands of his own party, the Mosley Memorandum was widely praised. Sir Anthony Eden, who after a remarkable career as Foreign Secretary would become Prime Minister himself in 1955, and who was hardly one to back a Labour proposal, wrote to the *Times:*

> Sir Oswald seems to have conceived a noble, and no doubt according to the accepted political standards of what are called "responsible statesmen," incredibly naive idea. He drew up and actually went so far as to present to his chief a memorandum which suggested that an attempt should be made to carry out at least some, if not all, of the pledges and promises by the exploitation of which the Socialist Party obtained power.[24]

For the rest of that year, Mosley tried to convert the Labour party to his point of view. Finally, on 27 January 1931, the Mosley Memorandum was considered again at a special meeting of the parliamentary Labour party. Here Mosley delivered one of the most magnificent speeches of his career, and had he not insisted on putting the issue to an immediate vote he might have rallied the bulk of the members present to his side. Harold Nicolson wrote that had Mosley been "less easily swept away by his own importance, he might have forced the Government to accept his terms. His error, at that crucial moment, deprived him of an unrepeated opportunity; and the country of a great Parliamentarian."[25]

But to Mosley this was the last word from the Labour party. The old political leadership must be replaced by something new. The Liberals had failed, the Conservatives had failed, and now the Labour party, in Mosley's judgment, had failed its crucial test.[26]

The New Party

Mosley's next step in 1931 was to found the New Party with Labour members such as John Strachey, Dr. Robert Forgan, and, of course, Lady Cynthia Mosley. Forgan was a quiet Scotsman who would later serve as the British Union of Fascists' director of organization and deputy director. He would later part company with Mosley over the issue of anti-Semitism. Lady Cynthia was, in this new venture, a tremendous asset to Mosley. Her grace and beauty would be greatly missed when she died of peritonitis in 1933. In all, five Labour members, a Conservative, and a Liberal shifted into the Mosley camp. The inchoate new party called for the recognition of the current crisis that faced Britain and demanded control of imports, national planning, and public works projects.[27] These plans originally had the backing of large numbers of Labourites, and Mosley hoped for a great deal of support.[28]

The New Party did attract supporters, but they constituted a rather mixed lot. Liberals, Conservatives, Socialists, and various intellectuals joined. Writers such as Osbert Sitwell and C. E. M. Joad actively worked in the party. Harold Macmillan, who would cap a parliamentary career that began in 1924 with the office of Prime Minister in 1957, admitted that he was tempted to work with the New Party, "for there were many of the points of [Mosley's] program which seemed to me at once reasonable and constructive."[29] Some of England's most prominent writers contributed to the party newspaper, *Action,* edited by Harold Nicolson.

The New Party claimed to come not to introduce utopia but to prevent the economic and social collapse that its adherents considered to be imminent. It was a party of young men; the average age of M.P.s who left the Labour party to join the New Party was only thirty-three. Together they dedicated themselves to a Mosleyite program of parliamentary reform, national planning, and the control of imports.[30]

The New Party sought, by applying "scientific method" to public affairs, to determine those things that needed to be done. The plea for public planning and public control was the guiding principle that ran through all proposals of the New Party. The government was to assist scientific research, give financial assistance to struggling industries, determine what new industries were to be established and where they were to be established, and make supervised loans to farmers. C. E. M. Joad stated the platform much more simply: "The situation is such that our immediate thought must be not how to enter economic paradise, but how to escape economic hell. We must plan not to introduce the millenium but to avoid the catastrophe."[31]

Mosley talked of contesting four hundred seats in the October 1931 general election, but that was wishful thinking. The New Party had marshaled its resources that spring to contest a by-election at Ashton-under-Lyne. Mosley appeared there in support of New Party candidate Allen Young. In 1929, the Labour party had easily won the seat. As the results were announced, and it became known that Young had not only lost, but had also drawn enough votes away from the Labour party candidate to enable the Conservative to win, the crowd angrily jeered Mosley. At this new high point of frustration, Mosley made perhaps his first real leap into fascism as he cried out, "These are the people who have got in the way of everybody who has tried to do anything since the last war."[32]

For the New Party, it was the beginning of the end. Mosley began to sound more and more like an Anglo-Mussolini, and the original supporters began to drift away. Those who stayed did so without enthusiasm. By September, the four hundred seats that Mosley had hoped to contest had been cut in half. When the election was held on 27 October 1931, only twenty-four candidates actually stood for the New Party. It polled 2 percent of the vote. Twenty-two of the twenty-four New Party candidates finished at the bottom. The record was even worse than that of the Communists.[33]

The Birth of the BUF

One year later the British Union of Fascists was formed. Britain was still in the depression, and Mosley was still trying to be the British savior. He forged the BUF out of remnants of the New Party's youth movement; although most of his New Party supporters had been alienated, he found a group of loyal recruits. In February 1933, the *Blackshirt* began to appear. Thus, the BUF was founded more than three months before Hitler's appointment as Chancellor in Germany and before the rise of Anglo-German tensions. Even as the BUF was born, the Communists began to attract many more members. This expansion in the size of extremist factions was presumably due primarily to domestic causes; foreign policy considerations were to come later.[34]

R. J. A. Skidelsky, in a penetrating article on the formation of British fascism, contends that the failures and the governmental inaction and hesitancy Mosley had experienced in the years prior to 1932 drove him to believe in the dynamics of fascism. He decided that power must be placed in the hands of a responsible leader and, with his belief in his own destiny, envisioned that leader to be himself. Analyzing the British political system, he decided that "both parties stand bound by the vested interests of the 'right' and the 'left' which creates them." The result, to Mosley, was compromise and indecision. "Somebody must be trusted," he warned, "or nothing will ever be done."[35]

Unlike the German NSDAP, the BUF was a child only of depression and not of military defeat. More than anything else, Mosley's modern and practical economic policies distinguished the BUF from its Continental counterparts in Italy and Germany.[36] But Mosley could not dissociate himself from the Continental Fascists. Brigitte Granzow, in *A Mirror of Nazism: British Public Opinion and the Emergence of Hitler, 1929–1932,* considers the eventual decline in Mosley's hopes for power in later years to be a result of the warning that the British public had taken from the destruction of German constitutionalism.[37]

It was for good reason, however, that the British public began to consider the BUF simply as a foreign transplant. The usual bag of tricks that characterized the Fascists on the Continent was imported to England. British Fascists wore black shirts, gave the Roman salute, marched around singing patriotic songs, and delighted in clicking their heels together. In spite of limited numbers, they rapidly made themselves known.

The Blackshirts were organized according to the leadership principle. Mosley saw himself as standing above the party, which was his creation, and controlling its destiny. To integrate the often-conflicting elements of the party under his control, Mosley used the military as a model. He leased the former Whitlands Teacher Training College in Chelsea and turned it into an administrative center. Black House, as the new headquarters came to be called, also contained dormitories for the paid Defence Force, together with a gymnasium, grounds for drilling, a canteen, and recreation facilities. The size of this Defence Force has been variously estimated to be between a few dozen and four hundred. Mosley maintains in his biography that these men paid for their keep and that the barracks were almost self-supporting, but former Blackshirts have stated that they received free lodging and free or subsidized board.[38] In addition, they were often given an allowance of about one pound per week, in exchange for which they performed janitorial duties or acted as guards, messengers, stewards at meetings, or newspaper peddlers.[39] Part of the finances came from dues and newspaper sales, but a large part is thought to have come from Mosley's pocket. Sir John Simon stated in Parliament that the BUF did receive some aid from Italy.

The creation of such a force gave Mosley much of the attention that he needed. BUF publications showed Blackshirts standing at attention or in drill formation looking resplendent in their black uniforms. By 1934, the BUF had even purchased four "specially constructed" vans, which the public was quick to see as armored cars. Home Secretary Sir John Gilmour said in answer to a question of the House that the Government was aware of these vans "for the conveyance of speakers to and from the meetings" but denied that they were "armoured cars in the sense of carrying arms."[40] (Indeed, it turned out that they were only stock commercial vans with wire over the windows.[41]) Later that year the Gloucestershire branch of the BUF organized a flying club with 250 members and five airplanes. In the House of Commons this was referred to as the creation of a Fascist air force.[42] The existence of such paramilitary activities did little to inspire confidence in the National Government's competence to uphold public order.

In January 1934, the BUF gained a powerful, although temporary, ally. Lord Rothermere, press baron of the *Daily Mail*, the *Evening News*, the *Sunday Dispatch*, and the *Sunday Pictorial*, informed his two-and-one-half-million readers that the BUF was purely British. In a leader entitled "Hurrah for the Blackshirts," he claimed that in Italy and Germany "the people feel such pride and confidence in their rulers." To Rothermere, who had dabbled in right-wing politics before (as in 1929 when he joined with fellow press baron Lord Beaverbrook to found the short-lived Union Empire party), it was essential that a "party of the right with the same directness of purpose and energy of method as Hitler and Mussolini have displayed" be returned in the next general election.[43]

Rothermere was obviously more interested in strong conservatism and anticommunism than he was in fascism per se and only wanted to use the movement to support his own position. During the next six months there were numerous articles on Mosley and the Blackshirts, all tending to show that Mosley's fascism and Rothermere's idea of conservatism were compatible.[44] Randolph Churchill highly complimented Mosley when reporting for the *Daily Mail*.

Covering a Mosley address at Leeds, Churchill wrote, "Sir Oswald's peroration was one of the most magnificent feats of oratory I have ever heard. The audience which had listened with close attention to his reasoned arguments were swept away in spontaneous reiterated bursts of applause."[45]

It was during this period that the BUF reached its peak in terms of membership and in the scale of its activities. In June 1934, the violence that accompanied the Olympia rally and the fears engendered by the "night of the long knives" in Germany caused the growth of the movement to slow, and membership finally began a slow decline. The size of the membership is hard to determine, for Mosley refused to reveal membership lists even to his closest associates. The movement's own membership figures were highly exaggerated to give the maximum impression of strength. Press estimates in 1934 and 1935 put the membership at between seventeen thousand and thirty-five thousand. In September 1934, American correspondent Leo Rosten, writing in *Harper's Magazine,* stated, "Today Oswald Mosley may safely be said to have a following of over 100,000 members."[46] Dr. Robert Forgan, the former deputy leader of the party, claimed a maximum membership of forty thousand. By 1937, membership was estimated to be eleven thousand by former party official John Beckett. A. K. Chesterton, a cousin of the popular writer G. K. Chesterton and a superpatriot who would leave the BUF in 1938, join the army and fight fascism in Italy at the age of forty, and in 1954 found his own League of Empire Loyalists, estimated only three thousand active members in 1938, and the Home Secretary announced in 1940 that only one thousand active members of the BUF remained.[47]

B.U.F. Platforms and Policies

What alternatives did Mosley propose for Great Britain? Upon the founding of the BUF, Mosley published his program for economic reform in his book *The Greater Britain.* According to Mosley, the government and the "old gang" were bound to collapse, Fascists and communists would clash, and the Fascists would emerge to solve the crisis. The only alternative to this chain of events was to give power to the Fascists so that they could prevent the otherwise-inevitable collapse.[48] Early literature appealed for members to read

The Greater Britain as a blueprint for the Fascist cause. Anti-Semitism was yet unmentioned, as the five early platforms of the BUF called for (1) Britain First—The Fascists would reorder Britain instead of waiting for "backward countries" to advance. To do this, Britain would have to send for her "men of action." (2) Wake up Parliament—The Fascists would turn Parliament "from a talkshop to a workshop." A Fascist Government would only submit measures to the Parliament for a yes or no vote. (3) Revive industry—A Fascist Government would make protection conditional on good wages to the worker and low prices for the consumer. (4) Stop class war—A British Fascist Government, like those on the Continent, would make trade unions and employers "joint directors instead of the two general staffs of opposing armies." (5) Kill D.O.R.A.—The Defence of the Realm Act was no longer in effect, but it did provide Mosley with an excuse to call for personal freedom and national revival. There would be, of course, a mass organization of the populace, but within this regimentation, Mosley promised private liberty.[49]

In a form letter of 7 November 1932, Mosley appealed for cooperation from those "who have long believed in fascism, but have been disappointed by the lack of progress and want of constructive policies in former fascist organisations." Included in the appeal were membership and dues forms, which called on the prospective member to pledge his "life and energies" to the Fascist cause and to pay one shilling per month.[50]

The new fascism, wrote Mosley, would come through the "instrument of steel," as he called his new movement. "Its leadership may be individual, or in the case of the British character, a team with clearly allocated functions and responsibilities. In either case, the only effective instrument of revolutionary change is absolute authority."[51] This absolute authority was dictatorship "in the modern sense of the word, which implies government armed by the people with complete powers of action to overcome problems which must be solved if the nation is to live."[52] "Under a Fascist Dictatorship," wrote William Joyce, "Britain shall veritably live as an organic unity. Those who would have her exist as a dismembered corpse in the dissecting room of democracy have had their day."[53]

For those less enthusiastic converts who did not wish to read *The Greater Britain,* Mosley published a smaller handbook called *Fascism in Britain*. Here he identified fascism as the "system of the next stage of civilisation." Noting the causes of the economic breakdown, Mosley called for the Fascist remedy of a corporate state in which "every member of that body acts in harmony with the purpose of the whole under the guidance and driving brain of Fascist government."[54]

Mosley also called for the building up of the home market and the consolidating of both buying and selling organizations abroad. This would lead, he believed, to the development of a corporate empire that would coordinate the various corporate states of the dominions and colonies. All of this would eventually bring world harmony, for "fascist organisation is the method of world peace among nations bound together by the universal fascism of the twentieth century."[55] The relationship between Britain and her empire was deplored by the BUF. William Joyce wrote, "The final fact is that we must get rid of politicians or get rid of India."[56] There was only one conclusion for Joyce to draw. "Fascism," he decided, "is true imperialism."[57]

Mosley's theories for the future British Fascist state were frequently at odds with other, often more Continental, plans put forth by underlings such as William Joyce and Alexander Raven Thomson. Frequently the left hand seemed not to know the right hand's activities. While Mosley spoke of a grandiose Investment Board in the National Corporation, Raven Thomson wrote of a tightly limited board. While Mosley attempted to play down the idea of a rigid dictatorship, Joyce propagated it.[58] Such conflicting pronouncements left the true BUF position extremely vague. In any event, hypernationalism was supposed to make up for any gaps that appeared in the general program of action. In *The Greater Britain,* Mosley said that if the policy of the BUF could be summed up in two words, they would be "Britain First."[59] Mosley acknowledged that the BUF was essentially a national movement, but the concept of Britain First did not preclude international cooperation with other Fascist states.

The general foreign policy of the BUF was based on a platform of European peace through British support of Italian and German fascism. Although the BUF paid homage to Hitler and Mussolini, it did not take orders from abroad. In 1935, when the Abyssinian crisis occurred, the BUF began a campaign summed up by the slogan Mind Britain's Business. During the next few years, even though the BUF praised Hitler and ever more closely emulated the NSDAP, it did not become its agent. When war broke out in 1939, Mosley instructed all BUF members to do nothing to impede the war effort or to help any enemy power.[60]

The intense nationalism called into being an equally intense show of patriotism. The BUF flag was almost always attended by the Union Jack, and there were frequent reports of Blackshirts attacking people for not standing during the national anthem. Mosley's own pronouncements on patriotism and national service indicate the general theme of all BUF flag-waving rhetoric:

> We seek, in fact, to establish a new morality of service to the nation. The winning of a system so opposed to that which prevails today, of course, means a revolutionary change. But Fascist revolution is a national revolution, not the struggle of class or faction for mastery. For the first time, revolution is combined with patriotism. We join a love of king and country with the determination to build a country so great that it is worthy of that love.[61]

The first issue of the *British Union Quarterly,* which appeared in 1937, showed the degree to which the BUF was in the mainstream of Fascist thought as an international movement. Among the more eye-catching articles were an essay on Olivera Salazar, a color story on Hitler's Berchtesgaden, an interpretive history on "Stalin, Robespierre, and the Red Napoleon," an article by Vidkun Quisling entitled "A Nordic World Federation," and an incredible review of Ezra Pound's latest book, *Jefferson and/or Mussolini,* which over forty publishers had refused to print.[62]

The BUF also had taken the Nazi road on the Jewish question. In 1936, the *Fascist Quarterly* had proclaimed:

> Fascism challenges every concept and every "principle" of the bourgeois-democratic world. The Blackshirts challenge above all the ACCEPTANCE OF DECADENCE which forms the psychological background of all bourgeois *laissez-faire* tolerance, broadmindedness, liberalism, and pessimism.[63]

There was little "tolerance, broadmindedness, or liberalism" in the *Fascist Quarterly*. It was full of the usual potpourri of anti-Semitism, praise for the Continental Fascists, and articles such as an attack on the New Deal called "The Judaic-Communist Movement in the United States."[64] But these official publications only recognized the move toward anti-Semitism that had begun two years earlier.

In his autobiography, Mosley wrote, "I never attacked the Jews as a people."[65] Mosley's claims, of course, depend upon his own definitions of anti-Semitism. There had been no mention of Jews when the BUF was formed. There were increasing incidents between Jews and Blackshirts in 1933 and 1934, but it was not until October 1934 that Mosley specifically began to attack the Jews. There were, of course, persistent anti-Semites within the movement, and this in part influenced Lord Rothermere to drop his support of the Blackshirts. The loss of his support, and the general unpopularity of the BUF in the wake of the Olympia meeting, caused Mosley to turn to Hitler's scapegoat. As Robert Benewick wrote:

> Mosley had to construct a rationale to account for the failure of his movement, and at the same time to justify its continued existence and hold the allegiance of his followers. The Jews were a tangible outlet for frustration. Unlike the "Old Gang," and "the communists," they could be located geographically, for many had settled together in particular sections of urban areas. As far as the prejudiced and resentful were concerned, the Jews were also physically identifiable. And since they were conspicuous in some trades and professions, if only as a minority, malcontents, whether working or middle class, could focus their aggressions on them.[66]

The exact reasons varied with the individual concerned, but in any event, anti-Semitism came to be a large part of BUF policy after 1934. In his Albert Hall speech of that year, Mosley reversed his earlier condemnation of Hitler's anti-Jewish activities, explaining that the Jewish population of Germany was three times that of England and hence a much larger problem. He still insisted, however, that he only attacked the Jews as representatives of international finance and promised, "Those Jews who were prepared to put the interests of Britain before those of Jewry need have no fear of fascism at all."[67] From this point onward, the BUF allowed its resident anti-Semites, such as William Joyce and John Beckett, considerably more freedom to attack the Jews.

In the next three years, BUF attacks on Jews grew more vicious. A. K. Chesterton published a nasty pamphlet containing news clippings edited to make the Jews appear to be draft dodgers and Communists.[68] A. Raven Thomson, in *Big Fish and Little Fish: Finance, Democracy, and the Shopkeeper,* proclaimed that fascism advocated "a movement empowered by the people to crush the alien usurer, and to allow British people to develop the national characteristics of private and independent enterprises, free from the tyranny of big business and capitalist combines."[69] Mosley often referred to the "alien sweepings of the gutter" and promised that fascism would deal "with the great alien financiers of the City of London who use the financial power of Britain in the interests, not of this country, but of foreign countries."[70] At Leicester, on 14 April 1935, Mosley said:

> For the first time I publicly challenge the Jewish interest in this country commanding commerce, commanding the press, commanding the cinemas, dominating the City of London, killing industry with sweatshops. These great interests are not intimidating, and will not intimidate the Fascist movement of the Modern Age.[71]

A short time later, the *Blackshirt* reported that Mosley had received a message from Julius Streicher, the founder of *Der Sturmer* and a violent anti-Semite, saying, "I greatly esteem your message in the midst of our hard struggle. The forces of Jewish corruption must be overcome in all great countries before the future of Europe can be made secure in justice and peace."[72]

In April 1933, Mosley paid a visit to Mussolini and declared that the BUF was in no way anti-Jewish, and went on to say, "Hitler made his greatest mistake in his attitude towards the Jews."[73] To say that Mosley's greatest mistake was in the acceptance of Hitler's position may be academic; however, Mosley began to imitate Hitler more than Mussolini. If he was not at first an anti-Semite, there is little doubt that many anti-Semites saw the BUF as the logical home for their own prejudices.

In turning a large amount of their energies to the Jews, however, the BUF sacrificed a great deal of their national appeal. For those in the East End who were unemployed and imagined the Jews to be holding their rightful jobs, the issue might have been real, but for those in the provinces who were interested in economic recovery the Jewish issue had little meaning. As economic conditions improved, therefore, the BUF strength became highly localized. Although spent as a sincere national threat by the end of 1934, the presence of these pockets of strength was a consistent nuisance when brought into contact with the Jewish and Communist elements of London's East End.

When the National Government of Stanley Baldwin finally acted to quell the mass disturbances between these elements, Home Secretary Sir John Simon admitted, "Immediate crying need for some of this legislation is really only felt in a very limited number of constituencies."[74] The mass disturbances and public disorders, however, produced a clamor for legislation that affected the entire country. Just as the ebbing and flooding of public disorder affected the police departments of London and Manchester, so too did this uneven activity of these two counterforces dictate the political actions of the National Government.

Chapter 5

The Incitement to Disaffection Act

In April 1934, the National Government introduced what was to become the Incitement to Disaffection Act. In light of the increased growth of the Communists and Fascists, many people anticipated that the Government was acting to insure public order. But the Incitement to Disaffection Act did not aim at reducing political tension or securing order; instead, it was designed solely to protect the armed forces from Communist propaganda.

Communist propaganda was distributed frequently among members of the armed forces. There were no laws to prevent such a practice, with the exception of the musty Incitement to Mutiny Act of 1797. Incitement to disaffection was considered to be a far milder offense than incitement to mutiny, however, and the Government was reluctant to use the extreme measures of the 1797 act. The Incitement to Disaffection Act made illegal the distribution of literature and other actions that might cause disaffection among the members of His Majesty's forces.

It is a reflection of the conservative composition of the Government that while fascism was growing rapidly the Government introduced a measure directed against the Communists. The fear of leftist elements, as indicated by the legislative reaction of earlier governments, remained constant and exaggerated. In substance, the act was merely legislation to protect servicemen from sedition, but the language of the original bill had extensive implications of threats to civil liberties. It was bitterly opposed in many quarters as an unwarranted invasion of individual rights, and seven months passed before it became law. The clear and present danger necessary to produce an atmosphere in which such legislation could easily be passed was lacking. In contrast to late 1936, the National Government could not provide clear proof of the need to sacrifice civil liberties for internal order.

The National Government

In order to understand the character of the Government that introduced the incitement to disaffection bill in 1934, it is necessary to understand its origin. The National Government was born out of the crisis of August 1931. Unable to resolve the necessary budget cuts needed to satisfy New York banking interests, the second Labour Government was deadlocked. On 24 August 1931, MacDonald met with King George V. With the King's blessing, the Prime Minister met with Stanley Baldwin and Sir Herbert Samuel to form a National Government of individuals and not parties for the sole purpose of settling the financial crisis. A few hours later, MacDonald met with his ex-Cabinet. As he went around the table asking them to serve the new Government, only J. H. Thomas, Lord Sankey, who had gained fame as the chairman of the Coal Industry Commission in 1919, and Philip Snowden, the old-time socialist who was now serving as the Chancellor of the Exchequer, agreed to stay with him. The inglorious end of the second Labour Government called forth a mass of denunciations that are still appearing today. Foremost among these charges was that a "banker's ramp" had led to Ramsay MacDonald's "great betrayal." J. R. Clynes called the formation of the National Government "a sequel of political desertion and realignment that has no parallel in modern history."[1] Oswald Mosley, in the midst of forming the New Party, said:

> The spokesmen of the late Labour Government proclaimed that the present crisis was that collapse of capitalism which they had long prophesied with religious fervour. When the great moment came, they had the whole resources of the State at their command. The day dawned, but Labour resigned. What would you think of a Salvation Army which took to its heels on the day of judgment?[2]

Conservatives flocked under the wings of MacDonald. Many, no doubt, considered it an honorable way to serve the Government in surmounting the crisis. G. M. Young, in his biography of Baldwin, called Baldwin's acceptance of a position below MacDonald "a gesture of magnanimity which the country would appreciate and understand." But it was more than that. In joining the National Government, which would inevitably be in effect a Conservative Government since the Liberal party was small and only three Labour ministers had agreed to follow MacDonald, Baldwin insured that a sizeable number of his followers would attain office. Furthermore, he could have political power without its inherent responsibilities and avoid "the labours which he always tried to evade, of mastering papers, of answering arguments, above all of giving decisions."[3]

In the new Cabinet, Baldwin became Lord President, and although MacDonald held the office of Prime Minister, Baldwin, as leader of the largest block of Government supporters, could dictate policy if and when he desired. The three holdover Labour ministers, Snowden, Sankey, and Thomas, kept their old jobs as the Chancellor of the Exchequer, the Lord Chancellor, and the Lord Privy Seal. Besides Baldwin, the Conservatives in the new Cabinet were Sir Samuel Hoare at the India Office, Neville Chamberlain at the Ministry of Health, and Cunliffe-Lister at the Board of Trade. All three were Conservative party loyalists. Cunliffe-Lister, who would be created Viscount Swinton in 1935, had been the president of the Board of Trade in Bonar Law's Cabinet. Hoare served as a Conservative M.P. for Chelsea from 1910 until 1944 and would serve as Foreign Secretary, First Lord of the Admiralty, Home Secretary, and ambassador to Spain before being created Viscount Templewood in 1944. Chamberlain, soon to be known for his appeasement policies, was, although unloved, one of the stronger men in the Cabinet. The two Liberal representatives were Herbert Samuel, the Home Secretary, and Lord Reading (Rufus Isaacs), Asquith's Attorney-General and Lord Chief Justice, and former ambassador to the United States and viceroy of India, who took over at the Foreign Office.

The formation of the National Government shattered Liberal and Labour party cohesion. On 28 September, the Labour party expelled all its members who were associated with the Government. This drove the National Labour members further into the arms of their Conservative allies and also relieved the uneasiness that existed in the Conservative party concerning MacDonald's reliability.

In early October, the National Government fought for a "doctor's mandate" in a general election. A. J. P. Taylor aptly described it as "a blank authority for the National Government to do whatever they could agree upon."[4] On 27 October 1931, after a campaign that featured bitter and vicious assaults on his old colleagues by Snowden, the election took place. The Conservative party won 473 seats, National Labour 13, and the National Liberal party 35, for a Government total of 521. With the support of certain independents, the

Government could command a total of 556 votes. The dissident Liberals returned 33 members, and the Labour party dropped to 46, with only George Lansbury remaining of the senior members and Clement Attlee and Stafford Cripps of the minor leadership. Both Attlee and Cripps had been in the second Labour Government, Attlee as Chancellor of the Duchy and Cripps as Solicitor-General.

The election results were confusing. Although the Liberal party had increased its number of seats, it had won fewer votes and, by joining the National Government, had also lost its independence. The Labour party had also lost votes and had lost more than a proportionate number of seats and much of its influence. On the other hand, it had demonstrated a good deal of unity and independence. The Conservative party was clearly in the driver's seat, as is apparent from J. C. C. Davidson's remarks in a letter sent to his uncle in South America. Davidson, who was Chancellor of the Duchy in the new National Government, had been chairman of the Conservative party from 1927 until 1930. "In effect," he wrote, "the British nation had done through the ballot box what Continental countries can only do by revolution. We have a Dictatorship and the Conservative Party has sufficient Members of Parliament to give it a majority over everyone else, including Socialists, Liberals, and the MacDonald group, of 326."[5]

Many voters of the Labour party succumbed to the appeal of patriotism that MacDonald made for his "doctor's mandate." The whole Opposition dropped to fifty-six, of whom six were ILP members of James Maxton's group and four were Independent Liberals, which really meant Lloyd George and his family representing rural Welsh constituencies. Labour party representation in the House of Commons was less than it had been after the Khaki Election of 1918 and only four more than in 1910.

The new National Government continued under the partnership of MacDonald as Prime Minister and Baldwin as Lord President. Snowden, as Lord Privy Seal, went to the House of Lords, and Neville Chamberlain took over at the Exchequer. Lord Reading surrendered the Foreign Office to Sir John Simon, and Herbert Samuel remained at the Home Office. The Cabinet was enlarged to its normal size of twenty members. There were four Labour members, with Thomas and Sankey retaining their former posts. Five Liberals held office, three from the official party and two Simonites. Significantly, there were eleven Conservatives in the Cabinet. It was not an inspiring Cabinet, and was perhaps most notable for its omissions such as Winston Churchill, Lloyd George, and Austen Chamberlain.

The personalities involved were not dissimilar in spite of the diversity of party labels. Neither MacDonald nor Baldwin ever provided dynamic leadership. The former's inability to present a clear image made him an ideal representative of such a coalition, while the latter had always given the impression of being a dull but reliable Englishman. Furthermore, the National Government seemed to have the stability of a Tory board of directors. Almost all the great corporate interests had directors in Parliament, among them Stanley Baldwin (steel trust), Neville Chamberlain (Imperial Allied Chemicals), and Sir John Gilmour (Caledonian Railway Co.).[6]

Within a year after the general election of 1931, there was little "national" left in the Government. The tariff policy caused Snowden to resign and undertake a bitter attack on MacDonald. Liberal ministers Herbert Samuel and Archibald Sinclair also resigned, as did Liberal under-secretaries Lord Lothian and Isaac Foot. Sir Donald Maclean, also a Liberal, died and was replaced at the Board of Education by Lord Irwin, a Conservative. Sir William Jewett, the Labour Attorney-General, resigned and was replaced by Conservative Sir Thomas Inskip. MacDonald, Thomas, Sankey, and Simon stayed on. In fact, Thomas could say, "We are a National Government composed of all parties, but we are much better than we are given credit for. There are more differences exhibited in speeches for outside consumption than we see inside."[7]

The Conservatives never had doubts as to which party really controlled the country. At the Annual Conservative Party Conference at Bristol in 1934, Sir Edward Grigg, M.P. for Altrinchan who despite being Lloyd George's private secretary in 1921–1922 was a recent convert to the Conservative party, startled his colleagues by flatly stating that a "National Government cannot be 100 per cent Conservative. Liberal Nationals and National Labour men cannot be regarded as only figureheads on the bows of the ship to amuse the dolphins." It was the first time during the conference that anyone had remotely suggested that the National Government and unqualified Toryism were not interchangeable terms. Despite Grigg's argument, the Conservatives seemed to want just such an arrangement—a National Government with a wholly Tory policy. The delegates passed Grigg's motion to direct propaganda toward retaining "the interests and loyalty of all who supported the National Government at the last election," but also passed a resolution commanding the Conservative party leaders to "maintain intact within the limits of National Government the policy and traditions of the Conservative Party."[8]

In foreign affairs, the performance of the National Government was already drawing harsh criticism. The Manchurian crisis had taken place when the Government was barely a month old. As Foreign Secretary, Sir John Simon did little to strengthen the League of Nations when, after months of bickering with American Secretary of State Henry L. Stimson, he allowed the Japanese aggression to go unchallenged. Britain was experiencing an unprecedented wave of pacifism and the National Government swayed with the tide. Disarmament talks were held in 1932 and 1933, but when Hitler withdrew from the Disarmament Conference at Geneva the chances of disarmament were dead. As Hitler tightened his hold on Germany and Mussolini began to cast covetous eyes on Ethiopia, Britain seemed to be paralyzed without a foreign policy.

By 1934, when German rearmament had been greatly accelerated, Britain had reached its high point in disarmament. Almost alone, Winston Churchill actively decried the trend. His demands for increased air power were met with calm assurances from Stanley Baldwin. In April of that year, Dollfuss was still alive in Austria, Mussolini had not yet mobilized his armies, and the German official policy was still relatively tame. But there was widespread uneasiness in Europe, and the National Government hardly stood as a bulwark of collective security. Without strong leadership, the National Government never realistically faced this, its most important, challenge.

The principal agent for legislation and enforcement of civil liberties was the Home Secretary. The Home Secretaries for the entire life of the National Government were in the 1931 Cabinet. Herbert Samuel had been Home Secretary under Asquith and a high commissioner in Palestine in the twenties. A cultivated orator and philosopher, he stepped down a year later when he could not support the Government on its tariff policies. He was replaced by Sir John Gilmour, a Conservative and former Secretary of State for Scotland, who had been mildly successful as Secretary of Agriculture. Gilmour remained as Home Secretary until Baldwin reorganized the

National Government in June 1935. Sir John Simon, Foreign Secretary from 1931 to 1935, succeeded Gilmour and was Home Secretary at the time of the East End civil disturbances. H. Montgomery Hyde once called him "the greatest lawyer in the country, possibly in the English speaking world."[9] Simon had entered Parliament in 1906 as a Liberal for Walthamstow. In 1911, at the age of thirty-seven, he became the youngest Solicitor-General in modern times; two years later, he sat in the Cabinet as Attorney-General. Generally regarded as an unfortunate choice for the Foreign Office because he was often too willing to see both sides of the question, Simon was once described by Baldwin as having a "Rolls-Royce brain without a chauffeur."[10]

The National Government retained token representation of all parties until Chamberlain absorbed them into the purely Conservative Government of 1937. Sir John Simon and the name *National* were all that remained after that date. Baldwin and MacDonald changed places in 1935, but this had little effect on the temper of the Government. Labour made a significant comeback in the general election of 1935, but Baldwin's Government could still claim a majority of 247 over the Opposition. With its overwhelming numerical superiority, the National Government could be assured that almost any legislation for which it asked would be passed by Parliament. The incitement to disaffection bill, however, gave evidence that the Opposition could still make its presence felt.

Introduction of the Bill

The incitement to disaffection bill made its first appearance in the House of Commons on 10 April 1934. Labeled bill #95, it was submitted by the Attorney-General and supported by the Solicitor-General, Sir Donald Bradley Somervell, Sir Bolton Eyres Monsell, Sir Philip Sassoon, and Duff Cooper in order "to make better provision for the prevention and punishment of endeavours to seduce members of His Majesty's Forces from their duty or allegiance."[11] In addition to Inskip and Somervell, this was a staunchly Conservative group. Monsell had been chief Conservative whip from 1923 to 1931 and was now First Lord of the Admiralty. Sassoon was under-secretary for air and the son-in-law of Baron Rothchild, while Cooper, who had helped save Baldwin's Conservative leadership in 1931, would later be rewarded with the office of War Secretary in 1935.

Defending the bill, Attorney-General Thomas Inskip claimed that the chief offenders had been driven underground and that "a somewhat sly and almost skulking breed of inciters has come into existence . . . too sly or cowardly to put their names and address to the literature which they are in the habit of producing."[12] He read from a pamphlet called *Soldier's Voice,* dated May 1932:

> Let us use the knowledge of arms which they give us, when the opportunity presents itself, to overthrow their rule, and in unity with our fellow workers, to establish free socialist Britain.

Inskip also quoted from the *Red Signal* of October 1932:

> They will not put a gun in your hands. Take it, and study the arts of war. This knowledge is essential for workers in order to fight against the capitalists of their own countries, in order to put an end to capitalism.[13]

The Attorney-General said that such leaflets were printed in different languages and distributed on parade grounds, dance halls, and cabarets. Soldiers or sailors were often surprised to reach into their pocket and find that someone had slipped them a seditious document.[14] Inskip presented the bill as a minor one to facilitate the apprehension and prosecution of those falling under the definition of incitement to disaffection.

At the time of the introduction of the bill, Inskip estimated that nearly fifty thousand copies of seditious documents had been produced and distributed among His Majesty's forces. In 1932, according to Inskip, there had been seventeen subversive pamphlets of differing titles distributed in twenty locations. In 1933, there had been eleven pamphlets in fourteen places of distribution. Most of these were heaved over barracks walls or pressed into servicemen's hands in public places.[15] If the distributor of such literature were apprehended, however, the only law under which he could be tried was the 1797 act. The Government wanted to introduce a bill that could allow for magisterial treatment of the distributor, who was usually paid only a few shillings to spread other people's sedition.[16]

The Incitement to Mutiny Act had made it an offense to seduce from his duty and allegiance to the King any person serving in His Majesty's forces. This was essentially the first clause of the bill under consideration. Prosecutions under that act had taken place only a year before in the trial before Old Bailey of four Communists who had been charged with distributing leaflets at the Newport barracks. In the trial, the presiding justice insisted that it was ridiculous to look upon these as political persecutions.[17]

At the time of the passage of the 1797 bill, and again in 1817, when an antisedition bill was passed, England faced perilous situations. In 1797, the Nore Mutiny had galvanized the Government into action. Inciting troops to mutiny had not been a crime before, but it now became a felony "maliciously and advisedly to seduce" any serviceman from his duty and allegiance. The act was intended to be temporary and was allowed to lapse in 1805.[18] In 1817, the Liverpool Government, faced with extensive civil disturbances, revived the 1797 statute and raised the penalty for conviction.[19] Other measures were passed later to accomplish the same purpose, such as the Army Act of 1881 and the Naval Discipline Act of 1866, which were extended to the Air Force by Orders in Council in 1913.[20]

The 1797 act was based on the assumption that the mutiny at Nore was politically inspired when in fact it seems to have been concerned with arrears in pay. The Act of 1817, providing punishment for seditious acts against the constitution, defined them to include demands for universal suffrage, annual meetings of Parliament, and the vote by ballot.[21] There were, however, no officially instigated prosecutions under these acts between 1804 and 1912.[22]

Put forth as a procedural bill, the incitement to disaffection bill was seen by the Opposition in a different light, as was soon obvious. Many members of the Labour party thought that it was aimed at them. They realized that if the army were called out during a general strike, any Labour party pamphlet attacking capitalism could be interpreted as an attempt to seduce. It was party policy to protest future wars for capitalist interests against working-class interests. John Lawson, the Labour member for Chester-le-Street, whose social attitudes owed more to Methodism than Marxism, noted that the Attorney-General's examples of sedition were obscure pamphlets. Labour demanded to know why the Government was wasting time on such matters while "the gentlemen who march about the streets" wearing black shirts were being ignored.[23]

Harold Laski found the first part of the bill "astonishing" and questioned the meaning of "endeavours to seduce," but there was little in the first clause that seriously challenged the civil liberties of the people. Clause 2, however, caused more apprehension. Section 1 read:

> If any person, without lawful excuse, has in his possession or under his control any document of such a nature that the dissemination of copies thereof among members of His Majesty's forces would be an offence under section one of this Act, he shall be guilty of an offence under this Act.[24]

This released a torrent of related questions inherent in the language of the section. Just what was "without lawful excuse" when Englishmen had been accustomed to freedom of the press? In one's library, seditious material could exist with "lawful excuse," but if a person had such literature on his body, the law was left open to charge him with *intent* to commit disaffection. How, then, did one transport it, if at all; and where could one keep it? The bill seemed to leave it up to the person found in possession of seditious material to satisfy the court as to his lawful excuse for possession. In this respect it was similar to the Official Secrets Act of 1920.

Section 2, clause 2 also seemed a novel interference with individual rights, but Inskip claimed precedents. The section read, "If any person does or attempts to do, or causes to be done or attempted any act preparatory to the commission of an offence under section one of this Act, he shall be guilty of an offence under this Act."[25] The Attorney-General pointed out that section 7 of the Official Secrets Act of 1920 contained precisely the same provision.[26] But what was committing an act preparatory to a crime? Was buying matches preparatory to committing a crime of arson? Was buying a ticket to Aldershot preparatory to inciting His Majesty's forces there? One could see in this a type of preventive detention that would violate the ancient rights of habeas corpus.

As Gwilym Lloyd George pointed out in debate, even the definition of the word *seduce* was open to interpretation. Seducing could be defined as "stirring up or fomenting discontent against the government and the disturbing of public tranquility as by inflammatory speeches or writings."[27] Any government could use such a definition to its own political advantage. Eleanor Rathbone, Independent member for the Combined English Universities, whose liberal sympathies ranged from family allowances to defense of women's rights in India, also challenged Inskip on his definition of seditious literature. A tenacious fighter for the underprivileged who was quick to see class bias in the government, Rathbone questioned him as to whether a mere treatise on pacifism would fall under the definition of seditious literature found in the bill. Inskip answered her in the official language of the bill that a document "intended and brought into existence with a view toward seducing" would be determined by the courts.[28] To leave the question of whether a pamphlet was seditious to the magistrate was, as Isaac Foot (the Liberal M.P. for Bodmin, chairman of the Parliamentary Temperance Group, devout Methodist, and father of famous sons) said, "like calling in plumbers to deal with problems of psychology."[29]

Section 3 of clause 2 caused the greatest immediate concern. The power given to the justice of the peace and to the police at the expense of the privacy of the individual was obvious.

> If a justice of the peace is satisfied by information on oath that there is reasonable ground for suspecting that an offence under this act has been committed, he may grant a search warrant authorising any constable named therein to enter at any time, if necessary by force, any premises or place named in the warrant, and to search the premises or place and every person found therein, and to seize anything found on the premises or place or any such person which he has reasonable ground for suspecting to be evidence of the commission of such an offence as aforesaid.[30]

It reminded many of the odious "general warrants" of days gone by. But Inskip defended this part of the bill, protesting that it was not at all like a general warrant and maintaining that the clause was practically in the same words as the search provision in the Official Secrets Act of 1911. He also took great pains to point out that that act had been passed during an era of Liberal supremacy.[31]

Ever since *Entick* v. *Carrington* in 1765, no magistrate had had the power to grant a warrant for the general search of premises unless stolen goods were expected to be found. In defending the clause, the Solicitor-General pointed out that there were already in existence sixty-eight acts of Parliament dealing with everything from cruelty to animals to explosive substances under which search warrants could be issued. He insisted that the Englishman's home had remained his castle and little public inconvenience had resulted.[32] The earlier provisions for search, however, were far less wide than those proposed in the incitement to disaffection bill.

Another inherent defect in the original bill was the quasi-judicial power it gave to the constable and the justice of the peace. With no time limit and no place limit to their powers, no one could be considered immune. Furthermore, the interpretations left to the justice of the peace were potentially dangerous. An extremely conservative justice would have the power to condemn anything remotely left of his views. The constable, on entering any premises, had the power to take whatever he saw fit. Clearly, with no guidelines established, the bill could turn into a license for police or government or even private harassment. The constable was given the power to use force, making it theoretically acceptable to dynamite a structure containing suspected seditious works. Rathbone commented that under such provisions large numbers of searches could take place and that that portion of the bill tore "a large hole in British Liberties through which an elephant may get through . . . . The purpose of the bill is aptly described by its title—Incitement to Disaffection Bill. I can imagine no bill which is more likely to be an incitement to disaffection than this."[33]

Clause 3, section 1 existed as another significant attack on civil liberty. By setting the fine at no more than fifty pounds and imprisonment at no more than three months, it would deprive the accused of a trial by jury and would be a potentially dangerous weapon in the hands of a government that wanted to use preventive detention against political enemies. Inskip promised to amend it to provide for the allowance of a jury trial. Section 2 of that clause contained a measure of doubtful legality that read, "Where a prosecution under this Act is being carried on by the Director of Public Prosecutions a court of summary jurisdiction shall not deal with the case summarily without the consent of the director."[34] The director of public prosecutions could, subject to political motivations, deprive a British subject of his right to a trial by jury.

These and other objections were raised on the day of the presentation of the incitement to disaffection bill. In the course of time, more threats were found. Labour members were quick to point out that Ramsay MacDonald would have been prosecuted under the terms of this act during World War I. Furthermore, if anyone still had copies of his speeches, they could be liable to prosecution. When the Conservative Home Secretary had introduced a criminal justice bill in 1924 that contained search warrant clauses similar to the one involved in the current bill, Ramsay MacDonald had called it "the most pernicious proposal that has been made in modern times for the undermining of popular liberty."[35] Faced with his earlier words, the Prime Minister was notably silent about the new bill.

As the Solicitor-General pointed out at the end of the first day of debate, however, almost to a man those who spoke out against the bill also condemned the practice of incitement to disaffection. He went on to say:

> I do not deny for a moment that a considerable number of speeches have been made by those unfavourable to this Bill, but one must look a good deal deeper than that, and those who have followed this Debate will, I believe, agree with me that no argument of substance has, on examination, been produced against this Bill.[36]

The Opposition, however, thought it had produced several arguments of substance against it. A. V. Dicey had clearly established the legal implications of such a position when he wrote, "Anyone will see at once that the legal definition of seditious libel might easily be so used to check a great deal of what is ordinarily considered allowable discussion, and would, if rigidly enforced, be inconsistent with prevailing forms of political agitation."[37] Under rigorous interpretation of the law, it was seditious to stir up ill will between classes, and it was clear that much Labour party literature would fit in this category.

On the day after the second reading, a leader in the *Guardian* questioned the bill and the Government's intentions. Noting what it thought was the "fascist temper" of the bill, the newspaper said it "makes it easier to send people to prison for their opinions, widens the scope of political offence, and greatly increases the power of the police to interfere arbitrarily with the domestic liberties of the individual."[38] Professor Harold J. Laski, quoted in the *Guardian*, called it "highly dangerous" and questioned the meaning of phrases such as *endeavours to seduce* and *without lawful excuse*. He concluded, "The powers sought are so wide and vague that in time of public commotion it gives practically a free hand to the judge." Clement Attlee was quoted as saying, "Politically the Bill is foolish . . . . It marches disturbingly with all the other repressive symptoms of the times."[39] John McGovern, ILP member for Shettleston, the outspoken Glaswegian who had been forcibly ejected from the House in 1931 in connection with a free-speech campaign and who had recently led a hunger march from Glasgow to London, charged that it was another attempt to give the Government complete power over civil action. He suggested that there was now no need for Mosley's Blackshirts, as the National Government was using legislative machinery to accomplish the same ends and also had "entered office on the passions, fears, and prejudices of the people at the time of emergency."[40]

The reasons for the introduction of the bill at this time were indeed somewhat unclear. A naval correspondent for the *New Statesman* thought that the inspiration for the bill came mainly from the Admiralty, and that the impetus sprang from the naval strike at Invergordon in 1931.[41] But this mutinous behavior was evidently not sparked in any important way by sedition; it arose from wage demands. Most of the married sailors of the lower deck had purchased goods on the installment plan and had their pay carefully budgeted. When the Government reduced their pay, they started a demonstration. The Admiralty (which one writer has said was "always the most inept of government departments in its handling of public relations"[42]) let the matter get out of hand. There was great solidarity among the sailors of the whole Atlantic fleet as they sang, "The more we are together the happier we shall be."[43]

Another possible reason for the bill's introduction at this time was to put a stamp of legality on actions such as those of the Metropolitan Police Force in 1932. The National Unemployed Workers Movement had organized a hunger march, which was to converge on London. The proposed march made such a stir that certain elements called for the arrest of the leaders. Eventually a warrant was issued for the arrest of Wal Hannington on a charge of inciting disaffection among the Metropolitan Police Force in violation of the Police Act of 1919. He was arrested immediately before the demonstration on evidence obtained from shorthand notes taken by police officers covering one of his speeches. When Hannington was allowed to return to work at the NUWM headquarters, he was greeted by the sight of several police officers hauling away ledgers, receipts, and other documents. No documents were examined on the spot and no list of documents taken was produced. This harassment considerably disrupted the work of the NUWM.

An officer of the NUWM, Sidney Job Elias, instituted proceedings against Police Commissioner Lord Trenchard and the two police officers principally involved. The defense emphasized that the papers had been seized "for the purposes of examination and investigation in connection with the arrest." Mr. Justice Horridge, who had been a Liberal M.P. for East Manchester in the Asquith government and would retain his position as judge of the King's Bench until his eightieth year, ruled, however, that the police had seized and removed the documents without any legal justification, and awarded damages to the plaintiff. It was therefore clear that although it was defended by the Home Office, the search had been illegal. But the court went a step further when it ruled that while the police seizure of documents without examination might be illegal, if the documents in question were evidence of a crime committed by the defendant or by any other person, the illegality of the seizure was made legal because by chance those documents were found to be evidence of a crime.[44] This decision formed the basis of *Elias* v. *Pasmore,* January 1934.

As a result of the search of Wal Hannington's papers, letters were found from Elias. The letters, written while Elias was on a trip to Russia, contained plans for the organization of hunger marches. He was sentenced to two years imprisonment for inciting to disaffection.[45] The decision was upheld in *Elias* v. *Pasmore,* which for the first time recognized as valid a search that resulted in the discovery of documents not in the possession of the person named in the warrant, containing evidence of an offense committed by any person, even though the search and seizure were illegal as regards other documents discovered on that occasion.[46]

There were yet other views on the genesis of the bill. Some thought its purpose was to find a scapegoat for the nation's ills. Lawson remarked on the day it was introduced, "If there is any disaffection in the Army, Navy, or Air Force, it is because many have enlisted when unemployed and because they have fathers and brothers in the country who have been idle for so long that they are almost rotting physically because of that unemployment."[47]

The CPGB ironically saw the bill as a means for the National Government to prevent the servicemen from learning the extent of the war preparations, the economic rivalries between the capitalistic states, and the real reason why the workers were being asked to "shed their blood." The *Daily Worker* warned, "Here is one of the biggest attacks yet made on the rights of working class organisation, one of the biggest single moves to fascism in this country."[48]

The real motives of the bill were never revealed to either the Opposition or the majority of the bill's supporters. Although it appeared to have been hastily drafted and presented, it had actually had its beginnings more than six months before it was introduced. On 9 October 1933, the First Lord of the Admiralty had made a verbal report to the Cabinet stating that Communist "agents" had in their possession a pamphlet that they intended to issue to the fleet. The "agents" themselves were not further identified. The pamphlet, according to the Admiralty, contained a gross incitement to mutiny. The state of the law was such that nothing could be done to stop the issuance of the pamphlet. TheHome Secretary informed the Cabinet that this was a question of long standing and that a bill had already been drafted to cover such situations. The Cabinet therefore resolved that Sir John Gilmour should distribute the draft as a memorandum.[49]

Nine days later, the Cabinet saw the draft incitement to disaffection bill for the first time. It appeared as a joint memorandum from the Home Secretary, the First Lord of the Admiralty, the Secretary of State for War, and the Secretary of State for Air. In its original form, the bill contained alternative provisions to meet an eventual decision whether the bill should or should not apply to civil servants. The majority of the Cabinet agreed that the bill should apply only to the defense services.[50] As late as February 1934, however, Gilmour was still trying to get the police covered by the act. In a secret memorandum to the cabinet, marked "to be kept under lock and key," Gilmour insisted that there were no adequate safeguards to prevent the dissemination of documents that could cause disaffection among the police and that no provision for the right to search for such documents existed. He confided, "A good deal of information has come to light which suggests that the public service contains at least a portion of men who could not be relied on to withstand attempts to undermine their loyalty, and . . . there can be no doubt that the risk of such attempts is a serious one."[51]

Five days after this meeting, considerable criticism of the extension of police powers within the bill took place within the Cabinet, but since Gilmour himself was not present, this aspect of the bill was not resolved. In the next few months, the Home Secretary would be at great pains to explain that the incitement to disaffection bill was not a "sedition" bill, but as late as the end of February the title of the bill was "The Incitement to Sedition Bill." In his "most secret memorandum," Gilmour had maintained that it was most desirable to use this "sedition bill" to extend the powers that already existed under the Police Act of 1919 and that it was appropriate that any measure dealing with attempts to seduce members of the defense services should also apply to the police.[52] Gilmour hoped to do this under section 3 of clause 2 of the draft bill, which provided that anyone who "attempts to do, or causes to be done, any act preparatory to the commission of an offence under the foregoing provision of this section shall be guilty of an offence under this act," and as such would be an extension of those offenses under the Police Act of 1919.[53]

But at the next meeting, the rest of the Cabinet objected to Gilmour's plan. They claimed that the Cabinet would thereby be extending considerably the field of search. Furthermore, it was suggested that the extension would subject the bill to criticism and might "jeopardize the passage of a measure which was much needed for the defence services." MacDonald appealed to Gilmour to leave the police out of the bill, and Gilmour finally agreed to do so with the understanding that if events should make it necessary, he would retain the right to reopen the question.[54] With this last departmental hurdle cleared, the Cabinet, on 21 March 1934, authorized the introduction of the bill into the House of Commons and invited the Attorney-General to consult with the parliamentary secretary of the treasury to arrange for an early date for its introduction.[55]

It is apparent from Cabinet discussions that the Government did not comprehend the seriousness of the objections that would arise to the bill. The Opposition, however, saw it as a definite attack on the Left. There is no evidence that the Government intended to use the bill to attack the labour movement, but the CPGB was correct in claiming that the bill was aimed largely at them. Mosley felt that, whatever the outcome, the bill could only benefit his movement. If the bill were passed, part of his England First program would be fulfilled. If it were not, and in the unlikely event that Labour would be able to make it an issue on which to defeat the Government, Mosley hoped that all the defeated Conservatives would join his party for a strong Opposition. But the history of the bill belied his calculations.

The circumstances surrounding the bill were to put the National Government in a most unfavorable light. Its frequent reversals of position on provisions of the bill created an aura of distrust in the Government. This distrust, together with the Government's failure to take action against the British Union of Fascists, resulted in one of the greatest campaigns against a single piece of legislation in modern British history.

As the bill was read a second time and sent to a committee, various civil liberty groups across the country began to work against it. It was an accepted dictum for these groups that "discretionary authority on the part of the government must mean insecurity for legal freedom on the part of its subjects."[56] To lessen this discretionary authority, then, became the task of Opposition within Standing Committee A and of all those private citizens who would rally and march in the next six months.

The Incitement to Disaffection Bill in Committee

Standing Committee A normally redrafted legislation and considered amendments that had been proposed during the second reading of any bill. The composition of the committee closely paralleled respective party strength within the House of Commons. In addition to the regular members of Standing Committee A, ten additional members were appointed by the chairman, Thomas Cape, Labour member for Workington. Cape had been a pit boy at the age of thirteen, and by the time he was thirty-eight was president of the Cumberland Miner's Association. With a confidence arising from sixteen years service in Commons, he appointed the Attorney-General and the Solicitor-General as well as outspoken critics of the bill such as John Lawson and James Maxton.[57] On 8 May, the committee began consideration of the incitement to disaffection bill. As a first concession, Inskip agreed to include the words "maliciously and advisedly"—the exact words used in the Mutiny Act of 1797—in a description of the offense. This was requested by Dingle Foot, Liberal member for Dundee, because he deemed it unfortunate if the Government were to pass a law more stringent than that of the panic year of 1797.[58]

Inskip had decided that the bill could indeed use a little patching. He deleted the vague "without lawful excuse" from clause 2 and substituted "with intent to commit or to aid, abet, counsel, or procure the commission of an offence under Section One of this Act." This removed one of the more astonishing aspects of the bill by transferring the onus of proof from the defendant to the prosecution.[59]

In the first meeting of the committee, Maxton voiced the fears of many of his colleagues. Noting that neither the ILP nor the Communist party were illegal organizations, he questioned the interpretation that could be given to the bill. It was the political creed of any Communist to preach revolution. Such efforts on the part of a Communist could be legal or illegal, and Maxton demanded a clearer interpretation than the muddy descriptions given by Inskip. He also spoke out about the inevitable confusion and obscurity of any sedition legislation. The trouble with it, he said,

> . . . is that everything is so vague. It usually means that some poor devil who is unknown, who has no public standing, and who uses words carelessly, gets run in, while the clever politician carries on the same kind of agitation and gets away with it.

Maxton moved that the committee amend the bill to exempt from penalty "an article in the newspaper," since any soldier could read seditious material in the newspaper. His motion was defeated, along party lines, 23 to 3.[60]

The committee met on Tuesdays and Thursdays for the next two months. In the 29 May meeting, Lawson asked for a provision stating that a person should not be guilty of sedition "by reason only that he has expressed or published an opinion." He was supported by W. H. Mainwaring, Labour member for Rhondda, a former miners' agent and now lecturer at Labour College, who claimed that every pacifist clergyman could come under the letter of the bill as it then stood. This amendment was unceremoniously defeated 28 to 4.[61]

It is not necessary to list all the amendments proposed by the Opposition and defeated along party lines, generally by a margin of about six to one. Most of the amendments were designed to add safeguards to the bill to protect the civil liberties of subjects. In the meeting of 31 May, Inskip admitted that much objection had been raised against clause 2 but argued that his suggested amendment, which replaced "without lawful excuse," had satisfied both Sir William Holdsworth and Professor Brierly, well-known jurists at Oxford. Holdsworth, according to Inskip, had said that "the amendment made the section comparatively unobjectionable." Brierly had noted, "If this Bill is necessary at all, no objection is now to be raised against this section since the intent has to be proved by the prosecution."[62]

The endorsements were obviously unenthusiastic, but Inskip felt it necessary to use them. He was well aware of the unfavorable propaganda that was circulating. One pamphlet, issued by the No More War Movement, warned its followers that if the incitement to disaffection bill were passed, books that showed the realities of war, such as Remarque's *All Quiet on the Western Front,* would be considered seditious literature and that the government would use the bill as a weapon against anyone "of any sort who turns his face against war or . . . preparation for it." In the face of this propaganda, Inskip said that it was not aimed at the expression of opinion or the holding of antiwar views, that he himself had similar views concerning war, and that such propaganda was "not founded on good sense or honesty."[63]

In the stormy but productive meeting of the committee on 5 June, Inskip was again questioned as to the Government's purpose for the bill, and again he turned to the threat of the Comintern. Without becoming further elucidated on the origin of the bill, the Opposition turned once more to its contents. Eventually the Opposition was able to convince Inskip to withdraw the portion that dealt with acts "preparatory" to the commission of an offense.[64]

Some of the dangers in clause 3 were removed during June. Eleanor Rathbone had pointed out the inconsistency of protecting the armed forces from sedition while failing to protect the magistrates and public officials who would deal with such offenses. There was nothing to prevent a magistrate from being converted to Fascist sympathies and using his newfound convictions to persecute Socialists, Communists, or even Jews.[65] Speaking for the Government in the absence of the Attorney-General, Solicitor-General Somervell said that the Government would accept an amendment providing that no officer below the rank of inspector could make the search and that the search warrant would have to be signed by two officers instead of one.[66] This would not protect the magistrates from sedition, but it would make it more difficult for them to force their opinions on others.

For a time there was even the hope that the Government would drop the bill altogether. In a letter to G. A. Sutherland, the principal of Dalton Hall in Manchester, Inskip wrote that he would give full attention to all of the objections to it "if it is to be proceeded with."[67] Most were sure that Inskip only pursued the passage of the bill because of his position. The Admiralty wanted the bill, it was thought, and Inskip was merely doing his duty as Attorney-General. The "if" made it appear that he had found a way out.

Inskip's less-than-enthusiastic attitude about the bill arose in the face of continuing bitter attacks against it in committee. In the 26 June session, Maxton sarcastically commented that some of the members of the committee had "stood on the public platforms and said the Englishman's home is his castle. Now their attitude is that the Englishman's home is to be the recreation ground for the police force." He particularly objected to the words *at any time* appearing in the search clause. "Why the passion for the midnight search?" he asked. "I honestly believe that it is derived from reading detective and crook stories and going to the pictures and seeing American gangster films."[68]

The power of search was amended somewhat, but only along governmentally suggested guidelines. The Government offered an amendment that added the following limitation: "provided that a search warrant shall only be issued in respect of an offence suspected to have been committed within three months prior to the laying of the information thereof."[69] This token gesture toward the protection of civil liberties did not, of course, quell the anxieties of the Opposition.

By 10 July, most of the committee members wanted it finished and pushed downstairs. Inskip had magnanimously promised not to employ closure, but he made no protest when one of his supporters succeeded in getting that motion before the chair.[70] Still open to amendments, he agreed to allow the three-month sentence to be extended to four months to allow for trial by jury for those accused. He also agreed to reduce the maximum penalty from fifty pounds to twenty pounds.[71]

All during the committee meetings, the status of the bill remained tremendously important to its opponents. Although there was an occasional lack of quorum, it was not due to the absence of the Opposition. Maxton protested before Commons that his committee had to meet on the same day as the Commons debate on the shipping industry, which concerned his constituents. Although the House of Commons voted down his request for rescheduling, it was an indication of the great interest in the bill.[72]

On 17 July, Standing Committee A voted to return the incitement to disaffection bill, as amended, to the floor of the House of Commons. It would wait downstairs until the reassembly of Parliament after its summer recess. The vote for reporting the bill was ayes 23, noes 3.[73] Considerable changes had been made, but not enough to suit the opponents of the bill, who were voicing their disapproval all over Britain. Vocal public opinion had been instrumental in getting the bill amended as much as it was, and attention was now turned to a last major thrust before late October, when the bill would receive its last reading.

Public Pressure Against the Act

The Government had not provided clear proof that the bill was worth the loss of liberties it seemed to entail. Unlike 1936, when the Home Department would point to virtual civil war in East London, the public could see no need for this bill. Walter Bagehot had written in *The English Constitution,* "Parliament by its policy and its speech well embodies and expresses public opinion. I own, I think it must be conceded that it is not equally successful in elevating public opinion. The teaching task of Parliament is the task it does worst."[74] His analysis may be judged correct in relation to the incitement to disaffection bill. In amending the bill, Parliament probably represented the views of the vast majority of public opinion; the Government's efforts to teach the public that it was harmless had little effect. In this case, it was Parliament that was taught. When the bill was finally passed in November 1934, the leftist *New Statesman and Nation* correctly remarked that the public reaction to the bill showed that "a popular agitation, if intelligently led, has still power to affect a reactionary government." The *New Statesman* reasoned that the whole bill might have been a "try on" by Scotland Yard and the service departments that slipped through the Cabinet in an absence of mind, but it was certain that pressure against the bill in the House of Commons alone would never have been sufficient to procure such extensive amendments. The magazine gave credit to Sir William Holdsworth, independent Labour, Liberal, and Conservative politicians, church dignitaries such as the bishop of Birmingham, writers such as H. G. Wells and E. M. Forster, and the Society of Friends. It especially praised the National Council for Civil Liberties.[75]

The *New Statesman* could also have given credit to itself. Shortly after the bill had been introduced, the magazine denounced it as "a dangerous measure" and warned that the door would be opened to the prosecutor "to use acts in themselves quite harmless for ends in fact quite remote from their intention." This would give the Government new weapons against "extremist" political organizations.[76] That fear was in the minds of other publishers as well. Stanley Unwin, whose firm had published the English translations of Marx and Engels fifty years before, warned in a letter to the *New Statesman* that if the incitement to disaffection bill were passed there would be few intelligent men who could not be prosecuted. Unwin cried out, "Milton! Thou shouldst be living at this hour!"[77]

Within forty-eight hours after the publication of the bill, the National Council for Civil Liberties circulated an analysis of the provisions it considered dangerous. Within fifteen days, it had called a delegate conference of more than forty societies, followed by a mass meeting at Kingsway Hall under the chairmanship of the dean of Canterbury and supported by numerous political, scholastic, pacifist, and industrial societies. Eventually, the NCCL organized all of the principal districts of London into area committees, which operated in turn through borough committees, by which an extensive campaign against the bill was waged.[78]

Throughout Britain other groups began to form. On 6 May, a large protest meeting against the bill was held at Oxford. Men such as Dr. Henry Gillett, D. N. Pritt, John Lawson, Sir Michael Sadler, an Oxford professor and writer who was a leading scholar on the British educational system, Gilbert Murray, the Regis Professor of Greek at Oxford and chairman of the League of Nations Union, and a host of other intellectuals voiced violent opposition to the bill, which Professor Holdsworth described as "contrary to the spirit of criminal law."[79] The president of the National Union of General and Municipal Workers, J. R. Clynes, himself a former Home Secretary, told members of his union that the incitement to disaffection bill would drive discontent below the surface and added, "We don't want a growth of secret societies in this country."[80] A group of members of the Society of Friends, appointed by its executive committee, arranged to meet with Inskip to present a resolution concerning liberties involving freedom of religion.[81]

Discontent with the bill was also spilling across the Midlands. P. M. Oliver, a barrister-at-law who had been a Liberal M.P. for Blackley of Manchester during both Labour Governments, spoke before a rally at the Manchester Liberal Federation and called for a defeat of the bill to show a world "overcome by tyranny" that Britain would not give up her cherished freedoms. Gwilym Lloyd George, the principal speaker of the rally, summoned up memories of his father's radical days and called for the government to drop the bill and concentrate on some of England's other problems.[82] Three weeks later J. R. Clynes drew up a manifesto entitled "What Is The Motive?" Clynes's interpretation, delivered to a Labour party rally in Manchester, argued that the bill was a concentrated effort on the part of the National Government to crush the workers and insinuated that the Government was ready to stimulate Blackshirt attacks against them.[83]

Throughout the unions, strong views were heard against the bill. D. N. Pritt said:

> The true reason that this bill is sought to be passed into law is because it can be used to do all the things I say it can be used to do by powerful influences behind the government who do not want people going about stirring up peace. There are such things as people who place documents . . . . This Bill might be described as the industrious bobby's open sesame. In a moment of panic or any anxiety, in the preparing for war, this Bill will be used against everyone and anyone; printers, newsagents, and distributors all come within its scope.[84]

At the May 1934 meeting of the General Council of the TUC, a strong resolution condemning the bill was passed. Calling for MacDonald to withdraw it, the General Council placed on record "their strong opposition to the Government's Incitement to Disaffection Bill, now before Parliament, believing that it constitutes a very grave threat to those liberties of the subject that have been won over many generations of struggle. In view of the Council, the Bill is a grave danger to the principle of democracy."[85]

Raising the specter of fascism soon became a common tactic in the Left's opposition to the bill. Not only would the bill impose heavy penalties for working-class antiwar propaganda among troops, but it would also aim to stop revolutionary agitation and propaganda of any kind.[86] P. O. Gordon-Walker, tutor of Christ's Church who later ran the Commonwealth Relations Office in the Attlee Labour Government and who would serve for three months as Foreign Secretary in Harold Wilson's 1964 Cabinet, said:

> In general it appears to me to be a Bill with a Fascist outlook. It proposes steps which are fundamentally the same as those which have already been taken in Germany . . . . I think the government must have been very frightened to take such a step . . . . Although when it was first announced it was said to be a move against the Communists and Fascists, it is obvious that the Fascists will be the last people to be attacked.[87]

The CPGB began a tremendous campaign against the bill. Shortly after the bill was introduced, the *Daily Worker* commented, "The National Government, while talking about its love for freedom, is steadily developing the state in a Fascist direction." The *Worker* also argued, "Here is a test of all those who have been declaring their abhorrence of Fascism. If they really abhor Fascism, then they must build the United Front against this Bill."[88] The CPGB later called for a great May Day demonstration against the bill. Meanwhile, the Bradford Trades Council demanded that the TUC should organize a one-day general strike protesting the bill.[89]

By the end of May, this public clamor had reached the House of Commons. Major James Milner, Labour member for Leeds, a prominent solicitor and parliamentary private secretary to the Minister of Agriculture during the second Labour Government, asked Inskip how many protests against the bill he had received. Inskip admitted that he had received a large number, but hastened to counter that most of them were machine made and that he had "some of the Roneo-produced instructions to send these letters." Milner challenged the lightness with which Inskip took this reflection of popular sentiment and maintained that strong feelings against the bill existed all over the country.[90] Solicitor-General Somervell fielded a similar question on 4 June. He replied that the Attorney-General had received 161 resolutions of protest, but quickly added that it was the Government's policy to judge the protests on quality rather than quantity and that "the largest bulk of them [were] based upon complete misunderstanding of the purposes and provisions of the Bill."[91]

The resolutions adopted throughout the nation had one thing in common: they wanted the bill dropped or radically amended. On 9 May, the officers of organized peace movements within the churches published the following manifesto:

> The undersigned, who are ministers in other Christian communions, desire to record publicly their unity with the representation to the government, which, they understand, members of the Society of Friends are making against the Incitement to Disaffection Bill, as an invasion of religious and civil liberty . . . . We feel constrained by the Christian Gospel to use our own full influence against war and war policies, and actually to serve the cause of peace and reconciliation.[92]

Resolutions came from secular sources in an even steadier barrage. The Liberal Women's Conference expressed "its determined opposition to the Bill and [called] upon all Liberals to oppose it by all means in their power."[93] At the National Liberal Federation, Sir Charles Hobhouse, a former Liberal M.P. who had been Chancellor of the Duchy and Postmaster General in the Asquith Government, moved a resolution requesting all Liberal members of the House to resist the incitement to disaffection bill.[94] The National Union of Railwaymen denounced the measure as "a most serious and unjustified attack upon the traditional liberties of the people."[95] The Lancashire, Cheshire, and Northwestern Federation of the League of Young Liberals passed a resolution that the bill was "likely to menace individual freedom."[96]

The leading organization opposing the bill, however, was the National Council for Civil Liberties. It had been founded in early 1934 in order "to coordinate the efforts of a wide range of political and other organisations whose activities, though directed on specific issues to a common end, were generally unrelated and too often at cross purposes."[97] Back in April, while still in its infancy, the group passed a resolution at a mass meeting called with other groups to protest the incitement to disaffection bill. The resolution read:

> . . . This meeting protests against the Incitement to Disaffection Bill and demands complete withdrawal of the Bill. It calls on all organisations here represented to use every effort to mobilize public opinion against such encroachments on liberty, and to throw their efforts into advertising the public meeting which the Council for Civil Liberties is organising for May 16th.[98]

E. M. Forster, the famous author, chaired this conference, which represented thirty-six separate organizations.

Public demonstration against the bill increased dramatically in June, possibly because of the increased public awareness resulting from the Olympia Meeting Hall incident of 7 June. Two days after that meeting, over fifteen hundred delegates, representing trades councils, trade unions, and all schools of liberal opinion, attended a conference in Memorial Hall in London. The meeting, convened by the NCCL and the London Trades Council, was chaired by W. H. Thompson. A. M. Wall, secretary of the London Trades Council, called on the conference to unite together "in order to defeat the reactionary aims of the Government."[99]

On 24 June more than ten thousand people, called together by the NCCL, assembled in Trafalgar Square to protest against the bill. Contingents representing all political parties marched in from suburban districts. The speakers included representatives from the Labour party, the London Trades Council, the ILP, the CPGB, the Liberal party, the Society of Friends, the National Association of

Schoolmasters, the National Women's Liberal Federation, the Suffragettes, the International Labour Defence, and the National Union of Journalists.[100]

If the CPGB had not been successful in organizing a united front against fascism, it had at least participated in one against the incitement to disaffection bill. W. N. Warbey, speaking for the ILP, said, "We must realize that if this bill is to be fought adequately we have to have the backing of all the organisations, political, religious, and otherwise throughout the country." Seymour Spon of the London University Club pledged, "The Liberal Party will do its utmost to defeat the most monstrous bill ever attempted to be put on the statute book." J. R. Campbell of the CPGB warned, "Fascism as we know comes in two ways. Sometimes up the street with bands and banners and dressed in black shirts. But it can come in a more insidious way, through a gradual undermining of the liberties of the working class."[101]

The 24 June rally passed a resolution demanding the complete withdrawal of the bill, saying that the action of the Government was "in direct opposition to the expressed will of the people." The meeting also went on record as viewing "with disgust the growing tendency of repressive measures directed against individual liberty, both in this country and abroad."[102]

Meanwhile, the NCCL was carrying on a lively exchange with the Attorney-General. Inskip, whom J. C. C. Davidson described as "an able man" but "somewhat ponderous and not very active in decision making," became the Government's chief defender of the bill.[103] On 8 June, he wrote to Ronald Kidd, secretary of the NCCL, "I am bound to say that the suggestion that this bill is aimed at working class organisations is simply untrue."[104] Kidd answered this letter with a long and detailed analysis of the bill, pointing out those sections that could be interpreted to adversely affect the working class. Kidd also quoted the statement by Ramsay MacDonald, made years earlier, that "an Army is always a powerful weapon in the hands of Governments to destroy the chances of Labour in a hard fought industrial dispute"; Kidd added that although the NCCL did not wish to endorse this "extreme attitude," it did wish to point out that throughout British history "the power in the hands of the executive has always been regarded as a potential threat to the liberty of the people."[105]

This exchange had been prompted by Kidd's letter in the *Specta-*

tor charging Inskip with "misstatements which are highly reprehensible to the crown."[106] The exchange continued for several weeks until D. N. Pritt, a vice-president of the NCCL, intervened for Inskip, telling Kidd that Inskip "would never intentionally make a misstatement or leave an important misstatement uncorrected."[107] Nevertheless, Kidd wrote to Inskip on 23 July, "We consider that the method in which the Disaffection [bill] was presented to the House of Commons was one of the worst examples of that new despotism of the bureaucracy."[108]

The hostility between Inskip and Kidd was apparent when a ten-member delegation of which Kidd was a member met with Inskip to protest the bill on 30 July. E. M. Forster, president of the NCCL, introduced the deputation, and C. E. M. Joad lost little time in attacking some of the more questionable features of the bill. Milner Gray, of the National Liberal Federation, who had been an M.P. from 1929 to 1931 and had served as parliamentary secretary to the Minister of Labour, told Inskip, "You have a Government with a tremendously overwhelming majority of one party elected on a non-party ticket carrying a measure which deeply offends the susceptibilities of the other two parties."[109] Throughout the lengthy discussion, there was obvious tension between Inskip and Kidd. Reacting to Kidd's insinuation that the bill would be used for political purposes, Inskip said, "If I wanted to harass my political enemies I should give directions for their houses to be searched in order to find whether they were in possession of official secrets and I can guarantee I can put my fingers on a dozen opponents of the Government who have official secrets in their houses."[110] And at the end of the meeting, he concluded, "Mr. Kidd and I have met face to face. If he can regard me with less disfavour than he has done in the past, our meeting will not have been wholly wasted."[111]

Personal animosity may have cooled somewhat, but the NCCL was still violently opposed to the bill. Shortly before Parliament reassembled, Kidd wrote to Inskip that the "whole idea" of such a bill was objectionable and told Inskip that the NCCL had passed a resolution calling the bill "an extremely sinister measure." "Not only is there no evidence of disloyalty amongst the armed forces," the resolution continued, "but it is quite contrary to the spirit in which the National Government made its appeal to the people in the last election."[112]

There was also correspondence between the NCCL and Downing Street. In a letter to MacDonald's secretary, Kidd asked if he were "aware that this Bill, capable of such repressive and tyrannical application in the hands of a reactionary Government, is closely paralleled in modern Continental legislation?" Kidd continued:

> The Attorney-General has assured us in the House that there is no great or alarming degree of disloyalty among the troops, yet he sees fit to introduce, and the Prime Minister to defend, the introduction, in a time of peace, of a measure which might possibly be excused in a time of war and grave national emergency. I invite you to say whether it does not appear that a Government which so closely follows the precedents laid down in Fascist countries may be encouraging the very tendencies which your letter suggests it is the Prime Minister's wish to prevent.[113]

By the end of July, Inskip had received nineteen resolutions of protest addressed to him by organized groups. He was quick to point out that all of the protests he had received were based on a complete misunderstanding of the bill.[114] The summer recess was at hand, and it seemed that most of the protest against it was also in recess. The American correspondent Leo Rosten observed that the Attorney-General was reluctant to push the bill and suggested that it would be dropped because of widespread public opposition.[115] But the opposition now began to marshal their forces for an all-out offensive in the fall.

In October the NCCL scheduled a new series of rallies for the days just before the reopening of Parliament. At this time, the Executive Committee of the National Peace Council resolved, "Amendments made to the Bill since its introduction do not touch the fundamental objections, namely that it confers dangerously wide powers of prosecution to search which make possible drastic interference to promote 'peace' opinion." Dr. E. W. Barnes, the modernist bishop of Birmingham who had gained fame as an outspoken defender of the theory of evolution, said, "The Bill is needless. It is unworthy of statesmen. It is foolishly provocative and it is dangerous to freedom." Finally, E. M. Forster concluded, "The Bill is un-English. It is an attempt to Continentalize us. Our so called National Government is trying to do an unnational thing, and I don't believe the nation will stand for it."[116] At a Fleet Street protest meeting of 18 October, H. G. Wells concluded, "There is something greater than Communism, greater than anything else in the world, and that is the freedom of the human mind. The Sedition Bill may not go as far towards complete suffocation as Russia, or towards violent persecution as in Germany or Italy, but it goes pretty far."[117]

In Manchester, almost three thousand people marched to Platt Fields to demonstrate against fascism and the incitement to disaffection bill. About thirty speakers appeared before the rally, among them the historian A. J. P. Taylor, Aneurin Bevan, the Rev. Thomas Shimwell, canon of Manchester, and Arthur Greenwood, who had served in the second Labour Government as Minister of Health and was now widely regarded as a possible successor to George Lansbury as chairman of the Labour party. Taylor claimed that the bill was a war measure in deliberate preparation for the next European war. Canon Shinwell said, "Where the spirit of the Lord is, there is liberty," and he failed to find the spirit of the Lord anywhere in the bill. Greenwood said, "If a nation could rely only on fighting services that were kept in ignorance, that nation deserves perdition."[118]

There was wide feeling that the bill was another reflection of the Fascist forces that were prevalent in contemporary Europe. Bevan warned that the BUF was too dangerous to be ignored and that in Germany none of the political leaders approved of Hitler until he was strong enough to take power. "If we allow it," he continued, "a time will come here when Mr. Baldwin will step aside and Mr. Sir Oswald Mosley will step in . . . . While we are looking at Hitler and Mussolini, the National Government is carrying out a fascist programme under our eyes."[119] Aneurin Bevan also joined the mass demonstration against the bill at Trafalgar Square. Here members of the Labour party, the trade unions, the ILP, and the CPGB sat together in opposition to the bill, in spite of the fact that only days before, the Southport Conference of the Labour party had condemned Labourite flirtations with radical parties.[120] But in the struggle against the incitement to disaffection bill, they felt comfortable on the same side. In the September issue of *Labour,* the editorial pledged, "The Trade Union and Labour Movement will continue relentlessly to fight this amazing attack on the liberty of the subject."[121]

The Trafalgar Square demonstration was held on the Sunday before the bill was to go before Commons for its third reading. Nearly four thousand people marched to the square, and by the time the thirty speeches organized by the NCCL had been given, the crowd had grown to nine thousand. Banners proclaimed, "Your Liberty or the

Sedition Bill—One Must Go.'' The only major disturbance took place when a vanload of Blackshirts shouting insults careened into the crowd.[122]

Opinions at the rally differed. Canon Guy Rogers, the rector of Birmingham and chaplain to the King, said that he refused to associate himself with those who attributed deliberate wickedness to the Government, but said, ''Though I do not think it is a wicked bill, I am convinced that it is a stupid one.'' Bevan, on the other hand, insisted that it was part of a long history of attacks against democracy starting with the Trades Disputes Act of 1927 and continuing with the reorganization of the Metropolitan Police, the attack on cooperative societies, and the unemployment act that was pending in Commons.[123]

On 30 October a mass lobby in Parliament was organized with the slogan Unite to Smash the Sedition Bill.[124] Called together by Ronald Kidd and the NCCL, the protesters filled the halls of Parliament.[125] Some still hoped that the bill would be dropped; others hoped for amendments to kill several of its more dangerous portions. The third reading was to take place later that week, so if the opposition to the bill were to make an effective last stand, it would have to be in the next two days.

The Passage of the Bill

By 23 October, it was possible to foresee how the bill would fare in the House of Commons. Amendments in committee had made the bill more consistent with British liberties, but two major problems remained: the wide powers given magistrates to interpret sedition and the wide powers of search. To opponents of the bill, only its defeat would be satisfactory; but the Government had far more than enough votes to insure passage of the measure, so their concern was to get it amended. Three minimum safeguards seemed necessary. First, the words *duty or allegiance* should be replaced by *duty and allegiance*. This would legally narrow the offense. Second, protection should be given from loss or damage that might occur during the search. Finally, search warrants should be issued by a judge in chambers rather than by two justices of the peace.[126]

In an open letter in the *Times* to a critic of the bill, Inskip cited two reasons why the bill was introduced. He insisted that it was not a sedition bill, and went on to say that the sole effect of it was "(1) to make fresh and, as I think, better provision for the trial of persons charged with attempting to seduce a soldier or sailor from his duty or allegiance; and (2) to prevent the persons who engage in this underhand business from carrying out their designs."[127]

The House was full on the first day of debate, which was scheduled for two days. To avoid a long night session, MacDonald agreed to allow a third day.[128] Defeated in committee in their attempts to regulate the powers of search granted in the bill, its opponents resumed the attack in the House of Commons.

The Labour M.P. from Colne Valley, Edward Mallalieu, who had been parliamentary private secretary to Sir Donald Maclean when the latter was president of the Board of Education, moved that a new clause providing more exact directions for the search be drawn up. His amendment required the party undertaking the search to call upon two disinterested parties to witness the search and assist in the making of a list of items seized. Countering charges that there was no precedent for such an amendment, Mallalieu cited a similar provision in the India Criminal Code of 1898, which was then in effect in a large part of the empire.[129]

Mallalieu's amendment was discussed in the House for about three hours. Most of the discussion came from opponents of the bill; very little was said in defense of it. But Government supporters sent the amendment to an ignominious defeat. Eighty-one M.P.s (including tellers) voted for the amendment; twenty-three Liberals, fifty-four Labourites, two Conservatives, and two Independents. Although most of the Conservatives were unenthusiastic, it was obvious that any discussion on amendments that the Government did not favor was a waste of time.[130] And the Government did not want to waste time. It was feared that unless the bill followed a strict time schedule it would not get through the House of Lords by the prorogation on 16 November.[131]

During the next two days several other major amendments were similarly defeated. Major Milner's, requiring that "no legal proceedings shall be instituted under this act without the consent of the Attorney-General," was defeated 305 to 73.[132] McGovern's, presented to the midnight crowd at the end of the first day, would have inserted the words "by a pamphlet or paper specifically prepared for that purpose" in clause 1. It was defeated 219 to 32.[133] Dingle Foot's amendment to leave out section 1 of clause 2, which would have challenged the whole purpose of the law, was defeated 271 to 67.[134]

But on a motion to insert "a judge of the high court" into section 3, clause 2, in place of two justices of the peace, the Opposition had more success. The amendment was accepted by the Government, and the House agreed to it without a division.[135] Further amendments clarifying language or making the bill consistent with accepted amendments were dealt with in a similar manner.

On the day of the vote, Eleanor Rathbone summed up the constitutional arguments of the Opposition. All the rights of Englishmen, she said, were subject to limitations; but no fresh limitation on liberty should be accepted by Parliament unless its need had been strictly defined and proved. The only real justification for such limitations would be evidence that particular rights either infringed on the rights of others or injured the public in general. "Our objection to the bill," she concluded, "is that neither of those things have been proved."[136]

Shortly thereafter, the Solicitor-General moved that the incitement to disaffection bill be read a third time. He opened with a long defense of the bill in which he described its original intent and his reasons for supporting it, then warned against leaving the stable door unlocked until the horse had been stolen.[137] At four o'clock on the afternoon of 2 November, the incitement to disaffection bill was read for the third time.[138]

There remained the formality of sending the bill to the House of Lords. There, on 6 November, the Lords read it for the second time without a division. Viscount Hailsham, the leader of the House, characterized it as the most misunderstood and misrepresented bill he could remember, with the possible exception of the trades disputes bill of 1927. But even in the House of Lords there was considerable opposition. The very leftist Lord Strabolgi suspected "a sinister motive" for the bill. Lord Reading, the one-time Liberal Chief Justice, questioned again its whole purpose, as did Lord Allen, a complex and fascinating personality who had helped organize the No-Conscription Fellowship in 1914, had been imprisoned for refusing induction, had once led the ILP but had supported MacDonald after the formation of the National Government, and had been created a peer for his loyalty. Lord Ponsonby, a former Liberal who had served as Chancellor of the Duchy in the second Labour Government and who was now the leader of the Opposition in the House of Lords, said, "The House now knew that the bill was the result of partial hysteria on the part of the Government as to the danger of communism and partly of mistrust and want of confidence in the forces of the crown."[139] However, the bill easily went through the House of Lords committee on 8 November.[140]

Lord Ponsonby announced shortly before the third reading that he and his supporters would not vote against the bill because they thought it was not their function to reject any measure passed by the majority of representatives in the House of Commons. Nevertheless, he described it as "ill devised, badly constructed, and wrongly drafted."[141] On 13 November, the Lords sent a message to the Commons saying that they had agreed to the incitement to disaffection bill "without amendments."[142]

Shortly before proroguing the third session of his thirty-sixth Parliament, King George V gave his royal assent to the Incitement to Disaffection Act.[143] It was now the law of the land.

Significance of the Act

The Incitement to Disaffection Act is still on the statute book. Eleanor Rathbone's fears in 1934 that the bill would result in a "smelling out of witches and a search for revolutionaries" did not materialize.[144] There have been no excessive use of powers and no cries of curtailed liberties.[145] Only one prosecution has taken place under the act. In 1937, a Leeds University student of "extreme political views" was sentenced to twelve months in prison.[146] He had engaged a Royal Air Force pilot in conversation in a restaurant, and in the course of it he had suggested that the pilot steal an RAF airplane and fly it to Spain to help the Spanish Republican Army. The extraordinarily severe sentence was imposed as a "public warning." The severity of the sentence aroused strong protests throughout Britain, and it was eventually reduced to a few months.[147]

One much-discussed item had remained unchanged throughout the debate. With passage, it introduced a new offense into law. This item was the word *or*. In clause 1, the bill called for a penalty for persons endeavoring to seduce a member of "His Majesty's Forces from his duty or allegiance." It was pointed out in Commons that this was different from the Mutiny Act of 1797, which read "duty and allegiance."[148] The distinction was not trivial. One could keep a soldier ten minutes past his leave time and seduce him from his duty, but that would hardly seduce him from his allegiance. Under the act, it became technically criminal.[149]

Numerous assurances were given by the Prime Minister and the Attorney-General that the act was not directed against minority political parties, but assurances have no standing in law. In time of national emergency, panic, or hysteria, wide powers might be used against any group whose activities were unwelcome to the Government. The Opposition was certainly correct in claiming that the act was a potential instrument of oppression. That potentiality was not realized, if the number of prosecutions under it is a sure guide. But the act may have deterred what could now be judged seditious propaganda and may also have indirectly censored the press. A printer naturally avoided printing anything that might be considered seditious if it fell into the hands of servicemen. A number of incidents took place shortly after the passage of the act in which printers refused to print antiwar material. In one case, the *Friend,* the official organ of the Quakers, appeared with a blank space and an editorial note that the printer had been afraid of the consequences of publishing a letter from a Quaker dealing with the ethics of military service.[150] A pamphlet reporting the resolutions of a unity conference between the CPGB and the ILP was censored by its printer, Marshalsea Press, with potentially illegal passages replaced by asterisks.[151] A pamphlet ridiculing the law called *That's Sedition—That Was* was issued with a glued-in warning on the title page that "no member of H. M. Forces should come into possession of this pamphlet."[152]

One way to handle this problem was suggested by Reginald Reynolds, the general secretary of the No More War Movement. He proposed that every piece of literature published by his group bear the following warning:

> In view of the vital necessity of His Majesty's Forces being kept uninformed, no copies of this publication should be distributed to any member of the Navy, Army or Air Force. Police in plain clothes take this at their own risk and are advised not to read it. The Movement can not hold itself responsible for any damage done to the ignorance of members of the Forces wearing civilian dress who obtain information under false pretenses.[153]

The Incitement to Disaffection Act remained an active political issue for the next few years. At the 66th TUC Congress, A. G. Walkden of the General Council, who returned to Parliament in 1935 as a Labour M.P. for South Bristol, praised the opposition of George Lansbury and the parliamentary Labour party.[154] A year later, at the 67th Congress, a resolution was passed calling for repeal of the act, warning that working-class soldiers should be in touch with and not turned against the rest of the working class in time of crisis.[155]

In early 1937, the NCCL, together with the Haldane Club, attended an International Conference on Civil Liberties in Paris. There Sir William Holdsworth, K.C. and professor of English and Law at Oxford, said:

> The fact that such a bill could be introduced by the National Government, and still more by the fact that such a Government should be surprised at the storm of indignation from persons of all parties which it has aroused, is a very disquieting feature of the political mentality of the present day . . . . This Bill shows that there is some danger that with the help of Parliament, the conception of the rule of law, and of liberties guaranteed by a supreme law, will disappear . . . . This tendency to circumvent the rule of law and to represent it as an out of date conception, is dangerous.[156]

More than anything else, the Incitement to Disaffection Act was a product of its time, when bolshevism appeared to the Government to be more dangerous than fascism. In less than two years, however, as the Blackshirt attacks on East End Jews grew more and more bold and as Hitler reoccupied the Rhineland, new legislation would be aimed at the extreme Right, culminating in the Public Order Act of 1936. Until then, the violence between opposing extremists would continue.

Chapter 6

Olympia

Robert Benewick, a careful student of British fascism, has called the BUF demonstration at Olympia Meeting Hall on 7 June 1934 the "watershed" for the movement.[1] It was also significant in other ways as well: it determined the National Government's policy on public disorder, and it was the occasion of the British Communist party's first large anti-Fascist demonstration. It served, too, to focus the public eye on a domestic conflict that had until then not made sensational headlines.

The Metropolitan Police knew well in advance of the massive rally that was planned and also of the anti-Fascist demonstration. No one, however, foresaw the extent of the disorder that ultimately occurred. Nevertheless, from the pattern of violence that had begun to grow in early 1934, such disorder might have been anticipated. The materials for an explosion had long been visibly present.

The BUF had existed only five months when violence broke out during Mosley's speech at Manchester's Free Trade Hall in March 1933. Upon the eviction of a heckler by Fascist stewards, there were several minor scuffles. A *Manchester Guardian* reporter claimed that he saw rubber truncheons used by the BUF stewards. In the end, as half of the audience sang "God Save the King" while the other half sang the "Red Flag," police broke up the meeting and sent the Blackshirts home.[2] It was this meeting that set the pattern for future BUF rallies as Mosley increasingly called attention to his Defence Force stewards, who were only too anxious to be provoked into action. In October of that year, violence occurred on a minor scale at Belle Vue park in Manchester and at the Oxford Town Hall.[3]

Mosley was determined to have free speech, but on his own terms. Speaking in Birmingham in January 1934, Mosley declared:

> We, too, should betray our country if we did not challenge the old parties with a new creed and a new policy of action . . . . We claim the right of

> free speech. No one will be interfered with by the Fascist Defence Force, who gave that free speech. But we are determined to have free speech, and we are organised to get it.[4]

The bullying and brazen attitude of the Blackshirts was procuring some of the publicity that they sought. Some people saw them as the underdogs and as defenders of underdogs generally. On 18 February 1934, nineteen Blackshirts were arrested on the charge that they "unlawfully did conspire together to effect a public mischief in obstructing the removal of certain pigs and cattle lawfully impounded under distress for the tithe." The Blackshirts had dug trenches, felled trees, and thrown up barricades around the livestock to prevent them from being impounded to pay off the poor farmer's debt.[5] Over fifty policemen were used to break up the demonstration. At their trial, the Blackshirts were summarily scolded, released, and bound over to keep the peace. The defense had pleaded, "Every one of these young men is a man of the highest possible character . . . . The organisation has been and is today against any possible breach of the law."[6]

As the days grew longer and the weather warmer, more meetings moved outdoors, and mass gatherings replaced local rallies. The Communist Party of Great Britain, in the process of attempting to build a united front against fascism, increasingly demonstrated against the Mosley gatherings. E. Woolley, a reporter for the *Daily Worker,* reported that he was attacked while attempting to cover Mosley's Albert Hall speech of 22 April. Although the press credentials of the *Daily Worker* were legitimate, he was pushed out of the hall into an area where several police were standing. A Blackshirt whom Woolley identified as a former Communist struck him in the face, causing blood to flow from his nose and mouth. Demanding that the police inspector charge the Blackshirt with assault, Woolley reported that he was met with general laughter from all the police.[7]

In Manchester the next month, the Hulme Anti-fascist Campaign Committee confronted a BUF meeting at the Hulme Town Hall. The principal speaker, William Joyce, reminded the anti-Fascist forces of the public meetings laws and reasoned that the Fascists were not breaking up the committee's meetings. Nevertheless, as a group of between fifty and sixty people stormed the speaker, violence erupted, and in the resulting turmoil two Blackshirts were injured.[8]

In London, each side took delight in describing how (although the other side had started the disturbance) it had gotten the best of the fight. On 14 May, the Fascists had been driven out of Finsbury Park in London's East End by a large group of Communists. In a manner suggestive of street gangs, the Fascists returned three Sundays later to renew the fight. This time they were practically escorted by the police, and did succeed in holding a one-hour meeting in spite of renewed violence. The position of the CPGB was that even though the meeting had been held, the "workers had their revenge and before the battle was over, more than one Fascist had to be carried to the armoured car, where a group of Blackshirt women gave first aid."[9]

After this "Second Battle of Finsbury Park," the *Daily Worker* published a letter it claimed had been "found in Finsbury Park after the Fascists had been driven out." The letter, supposedly sent from BUF headquarters to all London district chapters, read:

> As you are doubtless aware, we are holding a Fascist rally at Finsbury Park on Sunday, June 3, at 11:30 A.M. We have been informed by the local police that we might expect a very serious disturbance in this connection from the Communist Party, who have sent an all London call to their various members. I would greatly appreciate your assistance in the form of sending out as many stewards as is in your power.[10]

The CPGB used this police warning to claim that the police were backing the Fascists. The next issue of the *Blackshirt,* however, seemed to put the police on the other side. The role of aggressor was assigned to the Communists. The Fascist voice complained:

> The police authorities do not intervene until they are compelled to do so and hitherto they have shown a studied indifference to the threats that are being repeatedly made against the Blackshirts. Finsbury Park has recently been the "battleground" on which Blackshirt speakers have been attacked, and that such attacks have been deliberately planned is revealed in the boastful manifesto recently drawn up by the North London Committee of the CPGB.[11]

The Olympia meeting was scheduled to be far larger than any previous BUF rally. The *Fascist Week* proclaimed three weeks before the meeting that it promised "to be a landmark, not only in the history of fascism, but also in the history of Britain." The BUF paper continued, "Requests for tickets are coming from all parts of the country, from all classes of the community. The letters reveal a desire to hear the Fascist creed expounded by Oswald Mosley, recognised as the greatest orator in Britain today."[12]

The CPGB, meanwhile, had become increasingly alarmed at the

growth of the BUF. The *Daily Mail* of Lord Rothermere, which hailed Mosley as "perhaps the greatest political teacher we have produced in our history," had served to place a veil of respectability over the movement. The *Guardian* warned, "Sir Oswald is making headway, as Lord Rothermere wants him to do, by attracting Tory die-hards and creating a new Tory party of intolerance and reaction."[13] The counterdemonstration of the CPGB at Olympia would do much to strip away the illusions of those Tories who wished to use Mosley as a stalking-horse.

The whole week before the Olympia meeting, the *Daily Worker* reported growing numbers of organizations pledged to join the anti-Fascist campaign. The Catering Branch of the Transport and General Workers, the Kensington Branch of the Union of Post Office Workers, the Chiswick, Fulham, and Chelsea United Front Committees all ignored Labour party and TUC admonitions to stay away from the meeting and publicly called for their members to join the counterdemonstration. Five days before the meeting, the *Worker* proclaimed that the counterdemonstration against Mosley "promises to be the biggest ever held in London." Even machine minders of the Rothermere *Daily Mail* and *Evening News* decided to join the demonstration, supported by the Printing and Allied Trades Antifascist Movement.[14] Two days before the meeting, the *Daily Worker* published a map showing how to get to Olympia.[15]

On the day of the meeting, the East End of London was chalked white with anti-Fascist slogans and exhortations to join the counterdemonstration. The police had issued orders that no processions would be permitted on Kensington High Street and Kensington Road, the main streets leading to Olympia, because such processions would cause obstructions. The *Worker* predicted, "London workers will show tonight that they are not one whit behind the workers in the provinces in their hatred for fascism and their readiness to fight against it."[16]

The CPGB proved to be highly successful in disrupting the meeting and discrediting the BUF. They printed counterfeit tickets to create a tremendous bottleneck at the entrance to Olympia Hall. Those who did gain entrance stationed themselves at strategic spots within the building. Anticipating a repetition of the violence at Finsbury Park and elsewhere, the CPGB thoughtfully established first aid stations in nearby houses. As the appointed time drew near, there was the usual pushing, parading, and banner-waving that always accompanied such occasions.[17]

The meeting began, thirty-five minutes late, with all the theatrical components of Mosley's Continental counterparts. While the crowd waited for Mosley's stylishly late entrance, the band played various patriotic rousers. Finally, the lights dramatically flickered, an arc lamp swung down an aisle lined with uniformed Blackshirts, and Mosley appeared in a maze of Union Jacks and BUF banners. Many in the audience stood to join the Blackshirt salute and to chant "Hail Mosley."[18] The scene would have made Joseph Goebbels proud.

The rest of the meeting is not quite so simple to recount. Almost as soon as Mosley began to speak, heckling started. Mosley dramatically paused while spotlights were centered on the areas of the disruption. Uniformed stewards moved to eject the hecklers, several fights broke out, and for the next two hours the hall was filled with outbursts from protesters followed by violent ejections. The police, with no instructions to enter, remained outside the hall as interested spectators.

Conflicting reports concerning the nature and the extent of the disorder made it difficult to evaluate what happened, and the Olympia meeting soon became an object of public dispute. Immediately after the fracas, Geoffrey Lloyd, Conservative from Birmingham and parliamentary private secretary to Stanley Baldwin, reported:

> I saw with my own eyes case after case of single interrupters being attacked by ten to twenty fascists. Again and again, as five or six fascists carried out an interrupter by arms and legs, several other Blackshirts were engaged in kicking his helpless body . . . . I have no hesitation in saying that this was completely unnecessary, and that for Sir Oswald to talk of free speech is sheer humbug. His tactics were calculated to exaggerate the effect of the most trivial interruptions and to provide an apparent excuse for the violence of the Blackshirts. I came to the conclusion that Mosley was a political maniac, and that decent English people must combine to kill his movement.[19]

W. J. Anstruther-Gray, a young Conservative M.P. for North Lanarkshire who would become Secretary of State for Scotland in the Chamberlain Cabinet, testified before the House of Commons that while he saw the necessity of evicting interrupters at political meetings to maintain free speech, he failed "to see the necessity for this brutality which is so foreign to the British race. In my opinion, the wearing of political uniforms is definitely provocative. Something must be done to prevent a recurrence of last night's disgusting behaviour."[20]

The newly formed National Council for Civil Liberties undertook a full-scale investigation. Witnesses reported seeing men being carried upside down while getting kicked in the face, being pushed off the balcony, and being beaten senseless with chairs. Furthermore, the Blackshirt violence was often carried on to the delight of the Fascist partisans. One witness, Mrs. Naomi Mitcheson, reported that she saw several scenes of violence, and when she could stand it no longer she turned to the man next to her and said, "You call yourself a gentleman? Do you enjoy this sort of thing?" The man turned around and replied, "Yes, I do. I am enjoying myself. Do you want some of it yourself?"[21]

But not all saw the same thing. Major Francis Yeats-Brown, a conservative-minded author best known for his book *Bengal Lancer,* wrote to Ronald Kidd, secretary of the NCCL, asking if that body was considering evidence "with regard to the brutal assault on Stewards by those who came armed to break up the meeting."[22] Kidd answered him saying that he would be "glad to know any authenticated case of brutal assaults on stewards," adding that if Brown could give the names of any other witnesses, the NCCL would be "very glad indeed."[23] Brown's letter, in fact, seems to be the only pro-Fascist account of the meeting officially submitted to the NCCL, although pro-Fascist reports of Olympia were actually quite numerous.

Predictably, the official positions of the CPGB and the BUF were totally different. The *Blackshirt* reported that there were several attacks on Blackshirt stewards and on Blackshirt women and that the use of razors by the Communists was common. A. K. Chesterton reported that both the occasion and its marshaling were triumphant, and William Joyce was "overcome with sentiment . . . for the magnificent work of the Fascist Defence Force at Olympia." Mosley assured his legions:

> . . . The Blackshirt spirit triumphed at Olympia. It smashed the biggest organised attempt ever made in this country to wreck a meeting by Red violence. Blackshirt spirit and discipline triumphed over Red violence and protected a good audience from mob terror. That achievement has found great response in the heart of the British proper. Overwhelming evidence of public backing and sympathy has already reached me. Olympia marks another milestone in the fascist advance.[24]

Just before the Olympia meeting, Julius Streicher had said, "The baptism which the Mosley movement has already received in bloody battles in public halls and streets assures it a happy future, provided it continues on its way without compromise."[25] In the wake of the Olympia meeting, the official Nazi newspaper, the *Volkischer Beobachter,* acclaimed "the energetic defence of the Blackshirts in a bloody battle."[26] Mosley's most influential backer at home, Lord Rothermere, wrote in a leader in the *Daily Mail,* "The right of free speech was at stake, and it was firmly upheld . . . . Sir Oswald Mosley at his meetings has only expressed—with one or two exceptions—views which are identical with those of the robuster minds of the Conservative Party. Like them, he stands for law, order, free speech, and English methods."[27]

In a BBC broadcast the next night, Mosley charged that opponents who accused the Blackshirts of deliberate brutality in ejecting the "Reds" were telling "deliberate lies." Then, after stating that the brutality did not take place, Mosley defended it: "Would you have handled these 'Reds' more gently when you had seen your men kicked in the stomach and your women with their faces streaming with blood?" As his "very definite proof" that the Fascists were innocent of instigating violence, Mosley charged, "For over three weeks certain communist and socialist papers have published incitements to their readers to attack this meeting."[28]

The Communists denied that they had attacked the meeting but were anxious to claim a major portion of the credit for disrupting it. They staunchly maintained that theirs had been a peaceful demonstration and that violence could only be laid on the doorstep of the BUF. The CPGB considered it a magnificent victory in spite of their casualties. The *Daily Worker* proclaimed, "The great Olympia counter-demonstration of the workers against Blackshirts stands out as an important landmark in the struggle against Fascism in this country."[29]

The National Government could not afford to ignore the conflict now that it had been brought so glaringly into the light. The energy needed to overcome the inertia of the National Government would, however, be a long time in building. Even on the day of Olympia, MacDonald had said, "Normally this country will accept no dictatorship and no tampering with the liberties of a democracy, but in times like these, a National Government with Labour adequately represented in it, is the safest bulwark against dictators."[30] In spite of his optimism, the National Government could only point to the ill-defined incitement to disaffection bill, then in committee, as a legislative example of action to secure internal order.

Parliamentary Reaction to Olympia

On the Monday following the Olympia meeting, Mr. Anstruther-Gray asked MacDonald if the government would "give an early date for the discussion of measures to avert this menace to public order and good will?" MacDonald passed the buck to Gilmour and told Anstruther-Gray that the matter could be raised before the Home Secretary on the day allocated to the vote on the supply bill, set for Thursday of that week.[31]

By this time there had been several appeals for legislative action. A *Guardian* leader, printed five days after the Olympia meeting, spelled out the direction such legislation would have to take.

> If additional legislation is called for, it would be simple to frame it so that it should neither be nor appear to be directed against any particular party, group, or organisation. It would apply to all alike whose methods, in the wearing of uniforms, in military marching, in conduct of public meetings, constitute a proved threat to public order. It need not even be based on any assumed threat to the constitution or civil liberties. It could be much more obviously based on a considered extension of the law of public nuisance. A public nuisance is defined in law as "such an inconvenient or troublesome offence as annoys the community in general." That seems to us as good a definition of the social effect in England of the impact of these foreign importations as can be given.[32]

The same day, Gilmour reported to the House of Commons on the general state of public order. He told the members that the present policy with regard to public meetings was based on the recommendations of the Departmental Committee appointed by Herbert Gladstone in 1909. In accordance with that attitude, it was not the ordinary procedure of the police to deal with public meetings held on private premises. Furthermore, he pointed out that the police had no legal authority to enter the premises of such meetings unless asked to do so by the promoters or when they believed that a breach of the peace was being committed.[33] Many of his listeners had already concluded that an alert constable could have detected a breach of the peace at Olympia.

With regard to those disturbances, Gilmour reported, "The British Union of Fascists informed the Commissioner that the Fascists did not require the assistance of the police inside the building and at no stage was any request made for police to enter the meeting.''[34] On one occasion, a small party of uniformed policemen entered the precincts of Olympia, though not the meeting itself, on being told that there was a man who required attention. Gilmour stated that the 760 police detailed to Olympia were essentially concerned with crowd and traffic control. He concluded:

> Scenes of disorder on a scale which we have recently witnessed cannot be tolerated and . . . if they continue it may be necessary to arm the executive authorities with further powers for the purpose of preserving public order. I am not concerned today to apportion the blame between the Fascists and Communists. It is the function of the Government to preserve law and order. They would be failing in their duty if they allowed any faction, either of the Right or the Left, to disturb the public peace, and they are certainly not prepared to allow their responsibilities for the maintenance of order and the preservation of our free institutions to be usurped by any private and irresponsible body no matter what be their avowed aims or objects.[35]

The police force was at this time in the midst of a reform movement. Hugh Montague Trenchard, who had received a baronetcy for his service in World War I and was known as the ''father of the Royal Air Force,'' was now commissioner of police. Trenchard's reforms included better statistical analyses, and Gilmour had earlier reported that, according to figures supplied by Trenchard, no person had been injured at Fascist meetings in 1932. During 1933, however, ten persons had been reported injured, and during the first few months of 1934, forty-eight people had been reported injured. These cases, however, were only the ones reported to police, and the actual number was probably considerably higher.[36]

Estimates of the number of people injured at Olympia varied considerably. Mosley testified under oath two years later that a small number of Blackshirts had been injured seriously and that one hundred were treated by doctors.[37] But in his 1968 autobiography, Mosley cited a long list of Blackshirt casualties and stated, ''No evidence was produced of similar injuries among the opposition or of any serious injuries at all.''[38] Two days after the meeting, the *Times* reported that one doctor claimed to have treated between sixty and seventy people at Olympia, none of whom were Blackshirts.[39] Gilmour told Commons that fourteen people, including one Blackshirt, had been treated by hospitals.[40] Only thirty-six persons were arrested at Olympia, however, on charges ranging from insulting words to assault. Of this number, only five were known to be Fascists.[41] To many members of Commons, it seemed clear that more forceful action would have to be taken.

Exactly one week after the meeting, the topic of Olympia was aired in a full debate of the House. At one point, Isaac Foot quoted Mosley's statement at Olympia that "it is in the Blackshirt's power today to stop any socialist meeting in the country any night we choose."[42] Several members from the other side of the House interrupted with cries of "Hear! Hear!" Foot said Lord Trenchard had reported instances in which Fascists had broken up meetings. On 24 November 1933, members of the BUF had broken up a meeting of Arnold Leese's Imperial Fascist League; later they had tried to break up a meeting of the British Anti-war Movement.[43] If Olympia marked a serious escalation of violence in breaking up meetings, as most members feared it did, free speech in public meetings was in grave danger.

Another member interrupted Foot's speech with a call to "let them fight it out"—a sentiment widely held throughout the country. Foot replied that if they "only broke each other's heads" it would not matter so much, but that a certain principle of social life was endangered. Foot argued that if the principle that no man be allowed to take the law into his own hands remained valid, it was still more important that organizations not be allowed to do this. "There is a temptation to turn to the Blackshirt movement as something that will crush Communism," Foot continued. "I believe that what has happened of late has done more than anything else to create sympathy with Communism."[44] He was thankful for Olympia in one sense, however, because it had "revealed our danger . . . like a flash of lightning that has lit up the political landscape."[45]

The Labour party and the Liberal party were solidly behind Foot's sentiments. James Maxton, the firebrand of the ILP who had been in recent contact with the CPGB, also endorsed Foot's stand. Maxton thought Mosley's motive was to hold the National Government and all parliamentary institutions up to public contempt. "His desire at the moment," said Maxton, "is to show that he can maintain law and order more effectively, more efficiently, and do the strong man better than those people who have been publicly appointed to do that job."[46]

All parties in Parliament decried the violence at Olympia, but there remained a certain measure of ideological kinship to the particulars involved. Captain Terrance J. O'Connor, Conservative member for Nottingham Central, who had been looking out for Conservative interests in Parliament since 1924, admitted that some Conservatives were in sympathy with Mosley because they could not "resist some satisfaction at seeing the biter bitten for once." O'Connor himself found it difficult to "believe in this new found enthusiasm in the party opposite for free speech" and contended that "a Communist is only a logical Socialist." To this, Aneurin Bevan shouted, "And a Fascist is a logical Tory."[47]

But O'Connor also expressed the keynote of concern for the majority of the members when he said:

> Democracies are going down like nine-pins all over Europe, largely because the right of free expression of opinion has been denied to democracy. We have to preserve that right if we are to see democracy survive, and in order to do that we must be vigilant and, in an extreme case such as this, learn its lessons and take in time the steps necessary to maintain our position as the greatest democratic country in the world.[48]

The members generally agreed on the need to preserve order and free speech, but they were by no means unanimous in their condemnation of fascism. When Will Thorne, who had begun work as a twine spinner at age six and now at age seventy-seven had represented his district of West Ham for twenty-eight years, charged that the majority of the Fascists were "armed with some very dangerous implements," several members interrupted with cries of "Oh! What about the Communists?" Furthermore, when Thorne demanded that the BUF be declared an illegal organization, several cries of no came from the Government benches. M. W. Beaumont, Conservative member for Aylesbury, once hailed as the "first parliamentary fascist convert," even asked Gilmour to ensure that any party, however distasteful its views may be, would have "a chance of presenting its case to the public and [be] enabled to attend meetings without organised opposition and molestation."[49] This, of course, was what Mosley had been calling for all along.

The long debate on Olympia ended amid Gilmour's hints that action would be taken and legislation was imminent. The next day the *Guardian* reported that legislation would shortly be introduced and would be in effect before the next large BUF rally, which was being proposed for White City Stadium in August. The House of Commons and the people of England sat back and waited for the Government's bill. It would be a long wait.

Meanwhile, the events of Olympia were having repercussions in London's East End. The disruption of the meeting had been largely the work of the CPGB, and now the party began to reap the rewards. The Jewish population in the East End saw the CPGB as the stoutest opponent of fascism, and many Jews rallied to the party. One of the first to join after the Olympia meeting was Phil Piratin, who eventually became a Communist M.P. for Mile End.[50] With rumors of legislation in the air, the *Daily Worker* charged that the National Government was making use of Olympia to "fashion a club which will be used with more deadly effect against the workers, at the same time that it evolves guarantees to provide for Blackshirt protection against the wrath of the masses who are refusing to allow Mosley's gangsters to carry on."[51]

A short time later, Baldwin, addressing a Conservative rally in Derbyshire, warned of the increasing tendency to take sides in the Fascist-Communist disputes. "If you do have this country divided into two private armies," Baldwin said, ". . . you will have then the raw materials for what we have not had for three hundred years, and that is civil war."[52]

In June 1934, then, all the necessary elements for legislation concerning public order were present. The general public was clamoring for such action. Parliament had expressed its desire for it. The National Government had promised it. But instead of action, there occurred a legislative hiatus. Instead of providing a new bill, the National Government continued its push for the one that had been introduced suddenly in April. Talk centered around Olympia and the whole problem of public order; action centered around the vaguely worded incitement to disaffection bill.

Chapter 7

After Olympia: The Hiatus of Public Disorder

In the aftermath of the Olympia meeting, the Blackshirts, little noticed before the meeting, now stood prominently in the public eye. For most people they were associated with the Olympia violence and became a symbol of "un-British" politics. The question of a ban on uniforms was first broached in Commons on 20 February 1934, when the Home Secretary said that the matter was being given "serious consideration," although Lord Trenchard, commissioner of police for Metropolitan London, had urged the government to take legislative action in the autumn of 1933.[1] At the time of Gilmour's first introduction of the subject, the *Guardian* observed that the Fascists had "undoubted gifts for making a public and provocative nuisance of themselves, to put a legal stopper on this part of their little game would be a timely move in the general interest . . . . The Salvation Army should be the only S.A. Squad which our people should be able to join."[2]

The next day, Foreign Secretary Sir John Simon, who would succeed Gilmour as Home Secretary in June 1935, said in a speech in Glasgow that there was "a special objection" to political uniforms. "The existence of one private and unauthorised force," he said, "inevitably tends to call into existence another. If people start expressing political ideas not only by the color of their shirts but also by their physical force there will be more colors than one. We may end by finding ourselves black and blue in the scuffle."[3]

Existing Regulations on Drilling and Political Uniforms

To the man who walked through Chelsea and saw the Blackshirts drilling and marching around Black House, the BUF might have seemed nothing short of a standing private army. Besides the facts that the Blackshirts created a vast public nuisance, called for additional constables to be called up while others were diverted from their regular duties, and caused needless expense to the taxpayers, such a standing army was also illegal. In *R*. v. *Little and Dunning, ex parte* Wise (1910, 74 J.P. 7), the magistrate was upheld in his action of issuing a warrant for the preventive arrest of the defendant, who had led one march that had resulted in a riot, to desist from making a similar demonstration. The King's Bench Divisional Court upheld this decision. In other words, the government had legal means to stop large-scale demonstrations and processions such as marching Blackshirts on parade.[4]

The most definite law that could have been applied against Mosley's army was the Unlawful Drilling Act of 1819, which prohibited "all meetings and assemblies" without the authority of the Secretary of State for training, drilling with weapons, or practicing military exercises. In the leading case relating to drilling, *Redford* v. *Birley, 1822,* Justice Holroyd had said that, in his judgment, "if the object of the drilling is to secure the attention of the persons drilled to disaffected speeches, and to give confidence by an appearance of strength to those willing to join them, that would be illegal." Furthermore, the Bill of Rights of 1689 prohibited a standing army from being raised without the annual consent of Parliament. The Army and Air Force Annual Act of 1933 recognized this and plainly stated, "The raising or keeping of a standing army within the United Kingdom in time of peace, unless it be with the consent of Parliament, is against law."[5]

The application of such laws, however, always depended upon the definition of "standing armies." C. E. Lewis, legal advisor for the BUF, claimed that the Blackshirts were not an army, did not even have arms, and were not engaged in unlawful drilling. They were merely organized in ranks of three or four so that they could march in parade with "ease and regularity." Lewis insisted that the black shirt was not a uniform, that people wore it only if they wanted, and, in any event, that it did not produce violence. To prove his case, Lewis noted that the BUF averaged about one thousand meetings per week; considering that Trenchard and Gilmour could only point to thirty-three Fascist arrests since the organization had been founded, this was only one police court case for every 2,836 Blackshirt meetings.[6]

Mosley defended the use of colored shirts and special salutes against criticism that they were a foreign transplant. He said that socialism came from nineteenth-century Germany and liberalism from eighteenth-century France (and conservatism from "the Stone Age International"). Mosley defended the use of political uniforms by saying that it broke down all class barriers and defended the salute as the oldest salute of European civilization.[7] Mosley's BUF biographer, W. E. D. Allen, wrote:

> In no respect was Mosley's instinct more correct than in the decision to adopt a significant uniform. . . . The Blackshirts have done more to bring the reality of Fascism in Britain home to the man in the street than all the concentrated propaganda which has been put out by Party headquarters.[8]

Although there were laws against illegal drilling, there was nothing illegal—apart from a law relating to elections—about wearing uniforms in public for political purposes. The only law that applied was the Uniforms Act of 1894, section 2, which made it unlawful for any person not serving in His Majesty's forces "to wear without permission the uniform of any of these forces, or any dress having the appearance or bearing of any of the regimental or other distinctive marks of any such uniform."[9] This certainly did not apply to the BUF, for one could not mistake the Blackshirt for a member of His Majesty's forces. The marching Fascists nevertheless did give all the appearances of military force, and certain parts of the population disliked it.

At the annual meeting of the TUC Advisory Council on 4 May 1934, a strong stand was taken against paramilitary activity:

> This conference views with alarm the drilling of certain sections of the community with a view to effecting by violent means political change and the suppression of the liberties of the people and democratic government by consent. . . . The General Council are requested to demand from the Government an unequivocal declaration that such drilling is illegal and will be suppressed without regard to those who may be responsible for such drilling.[10]

Early Government Action on Public Order

The National Government had not entirely disregarded the problem despite its appearance of apathy. Even before Olympia, the question of public order and political uniforms was being discussed in the Cabinet. On 23 May 1934, Gilmour presented a secret memorandum designed to solicit views on the problem of political uniforms. He stated that it was obvious that an organization like the BUF,

> . . . though it may for the time profess an intention to achieve its objectives by constitutional means, might, if it developed sufficiently in numbers and influences, feel itself strong enough at some future date to adopt other methods . . . . I have looked at the problem more from the purely police point of view and recent developments make it clear that the Fascists are responsible for a substantial amount of disorder . . . . There can be no doubt that the wearing of uniforms is an important factor in the problem. It intensifies the aggressive behaviour of the Fascists and gives to what would otherwise be harmless evolutions a semi-military appearance which causes considerable resentment. It also gives to their assemblies a coherence and discipline which, in the event of a clash, greatly increases the difficulties of the police.[11]

Gilmour claimed that a law against political uniforms would greatly aid the police, but he did not at that time submit any definite proposals to the Cabinet. He stated that although the press generally clamored for such action, it appeared to him doubtful that the House of Commons would support the imposition of any restrictions. He said that he was confirmed in this view by the attitude of the House when, on 16 May, it refused without a division to allow Commander Locker-Lampson, Conservative M.P. for Birmingham and former Secretary at both the Home Office and the Foreign Office, to introduce a bill for just such a purpose. Gilmour suggested adopting a wait-and-see attitude.[12]

A week later, he wrote another memorandum for the Cabinet asking the views of his colleagues concerning the wearing of political uniforms. It was specifically stated at this meeting that, although any legislation would have to be of general application, it would primarily be directed against the BUF, "the only organisation to which any immediate practical problem existed."[13] The Home Secretary repeated his contention that it was clear from the police point of view that the Fascists were responsible for a substantial amount of disorder and that "there can be no doubt that the wearing of uniforms was an important factor in the problem." Gilmour suggested that he would arrange a question in the House of Commons, in reply to which he would make it clear that the Government did not "intend to allow any political organisation, right or left, to act in such a way as to be a menace to public order and that if future developments should make it necessary they would submit to Parliament such proposals as they thought appropriate." The Cabinet agreed to approve his approach but directed that in replying to questions in the House he should "lay emphasis on the law and order aspects of the problem and the additional duties that [were] being placed on the police, rather than on the actual wearing of political uniforms."[14] Before the question was put, however, the violence at the Olympia meeting had created a new situation.

After the Olympia meeting of 7 June 1934, the customary pace in the Home Office was replaced by a rush of legislative action. The need to control political uniforms, instead of receiving occasional mention, now became the dominant topic of Cabinet conversations. At the first Cabinet meeting after Olympia, the furor displaced foreign affairs as the top item on the agenda. The Home Secretary presented a note on the preservation of public order, in which he asked the ministers their views as to the desirability of (a) legislation to strengthen the powers of police concerning entry to a public meeting where disturbances were anticipated and (b) legislation to regulate the wearing of uniforms by political bodies. Gilmour mentioned in the course of discussion that drilling could actually be prevented under the Military Drilling Act of 1819 but that he was reluctant to take action under so old a statute.[15] No doubt his experiences with the Mutiny Act of 1797 reinforced his reluctance.

One question that was to lead to difficulties in interpreting the Public Order Act when it was finally passed two-and-one-half years later was raised even in this early stage—what constituted a political uniform? Attorney-General Thomas Inskip said that a clause could be included in any legislation enabling the magistrate to decide whether there had been a breach of the law, since prosecution would be instituted by the director of public prosecutions. He added that the police attached "the greatest importance" to prohibiting the wearing of uniforms. Political uniforms added greatly to their difficulties, he said, since men in uniform were able to recognize each other at once and it was therefore much harder for the police to break them up.[16]

Gilmour's report was an accurate reflection of the attitudes and existing powers of the National Government concerning political uniforms and public order. He said that the Government would have to be prepared to deal with the problem of preserving free speech by preventing or checking the practice of organized interruptions and disorder. There were also the problems of preventing bodily assaults at public meetings, whether those most to blame were interrupters or stewards, of preventing the formation of private armies, and of preventing any unofficial organization, whatever its political complexion, from "arrogating to itself the functions which belong to the police."[17]

The Home Secretary foresaw general agreement that such bodies ought not usurp the powers of the police, but thought that it would be

> . . . represented that, if the police are unable to deal effectively with people who organise disorder for the purpose of preventing speakers at public meetings from getting a hearing, then it is inevitable that bodies like the Fascists will take the law into their own hands and will use excessive violence, claiming that they have in view the object of securing the right of free speech.[18]

The position of the police, Gilmour explained, was that they had no right to enter public meetings held on private property unless they were invited to do so by the promoters of the meeting or unless they knew that a breach of the peace was being committed. Police had a duty to enter a building if disorder had taken place, but not merely because they thought that disorder might occur. With the growth of the Fascist and Communist organizations, both reluctant to have police at their meetings, the Home Office considered it necessary to strengthen the powers of the police to permit them to enter a meeting whenever the chief constable had reason to suspect that disorder would occur. There would be difficulties, as Gilmour recognized, but he said flatly that the Government could not defend its present position. Therefore, he recommended legislation enabling the police, whenever there were grounds for apprehending serious disturbances, "to make arrangements for the purpose of uniformed officers in the building—whether the promoters of the meeting do or do not ask for police assistance."[19]

The mere strengthening of police powers to enable them to enter a meeting hall would not deal with the central problem, which was, of course, the training of private bodies to act in concert to enforce their purposes by violence or intimidation. Gilmour labeled such bodies "inconsistent with our free institutions" and said he was convinced that there was no method of dealing with them except by legislation. He considered allowing private bodies to exercise military functions to be "tantamount to the abdication of authority by the

Central Government." He closed his strongly worded note by saying:

> Unless I can announce during debate that the Government recognizes that the existing law needs strengthening . . . I see no adequate answer to the very grave criticisms which will no doubt be raised against the very ineffective measures which . . . alone are available for dealing with disorders which we have witnessed and are bound to recur, perhaps on an intensified scale.[20]

There was general agreement in the Cabinet that it was desirable for the police to have all the powers that were necessary for the preservation of public order, but at the same time it was felt that legislation dealing with political uniforms required further consideration. The Cabinet therefore agreed that the Home Secretary in his appearance before Parliament the next day was to confine himself to a description of the events at Olympia, point out the limitations in the current powers of the police, make it clear that the Government wished to avoid any infringement of the liberty of the subject, and convey a hint that the desirability of obtaining futher powers was being carefully examined. Gilmour was also instructed to circulate a memorandum at the next weekly Cabinet meeting on all aspects of his proposals.[21]

In Commons the next day, most of the members seemed of the same mind as the Home Secretary. Geoffrey Lloyd, Liberal member for Ladywood, Baldwin's parliamentary private secretary and an eyewitness to Olympia, suggested that the Government devise a law to provide that for any meeting "at which there was good reason to apprehend disorder on a scale sufficient to prevent free speech," the police should be present in sufficient force at the beginning of the meeting.[22] This was remarkably similar to Gilmour's own proposal before the Cabinet. With regard to the question of private armies, Gilmour himself remarked, "It is contrary to all democratic ideas and customs; it is contrary to the traditions of our country that we should allow the usurpation of power by any body other than the State."[23]

The impact of the Olympia meeting upon the members of Parliament has already been noted. When Commons adjourned after the long debate of 14 June, prompt legislative action seemed certain. The Labour party and the TUC, however, felt that the Government's attitude on the day of the debate had been unsatisfactory. A deputation, consisting of the full General Council of the TUC and the Executive of the Labour party, called on the Home Secretary within two weeks. Upon being introduced by Clement Attlee, Arthur Conley, the chairman of the TUC, and Walter Citrine, then in the middle of a twenty-year term as general secretary of the TUC, joined two former Labour M.P.s, W. R. Smith (Norwich) and Joseph Toole (Salford) in expressing their grave concern over the Olympia disturbance and trying "to impress upon the government the extreme danger of allowing the militarization of politics to become an accomplished fact."[24] A contrast was drawn between the effective steps taken by police authorities at Fascist meetings at Manchester and the inaction of the Metropolitan Police in the face of violence at Olympia. The deputation also emphasized the importance of maintaining freedom of speech and the need for impartiality on the part of the police and the judiciary. As minister responsible for the administration of law and order, Gilmour was specifically questioned on the legality of forming uniformed bands as a political force.[25]

The deputation had expected that the legislation hinted at so positively during the week following Olympia would already have been introduced. The Home Secretary explained the delay by saying what he had been saying before Olympia: the Government was determined not to tolerate disorder from any quarter, and it was reviewing the whole legal position with regard to the preservation of order at public meetings.[26] Gilmour assured the delegation that the matter was under "very earnest consideration," but the question of new legislation was surrounded with difficulties, and time was needed for further investigation. The deputation gave Gilmour numerous documents they had collected that illustrated the aims and activities of the BUF.[27]

This was the last significant effort by the Opposition to force the Government to initiate action for the preservation of public order until another outbreak of violence in October 1936. Gilmour assured the deputation that their views had been noted and would be considered. It was also intimated that the Government intended to consult the party leaders in the House of Commons prior to submitting legislation to Parliament. Consultations consequently did take place with the parliamentary Labour party, but they produced no measurable results.[28]

Three weeks after Olympia, a large BUF rally was held in Sheffield. Several thousand anti-Fascists held a counterdemonstration nearby. There were a few minor interruptions during Sir Oswald's speech, but the event passed without violence. Mosley fielded questions, some of which were quite hostile, without the aid of Blackshirt stewards. The police kept order outside the hall. Six men were taken into custody, but no wholesale arrests occurred.[29] The desire to "do something" after Olympia was no longer quite so noticeable.

By July it appeared that a proposed BUF rally in the White City Stadium, which earlier had been touted as the follow-up to Olympia, would not be held. Instead, Gilmour reported to the Cabinet that he had reason to believe that the Fascists would hold a meeting in Hyde Park or Trafalgar Square and observed, "It would be easier to deal with them in the open."[30]

A week later, the Home Secretary submitted a report to the Cabinet on the possibility of establishing more solid guarantees of public order. Gilmour quoted an act that had recently passed in the Swedish Riksdag. This act, to go into effect on 1 August 1934, made in unlawful (a) "to form or to take part in an organisation which according to its declared purposes is intended to serve as a defence corps for a political party or similar group, or which in view of its structure, operation or activities, must be considered as intended to constitute an instrument of force of such character as a body of troops or the police," and (b) "to arm, lease premises to, or support such an organisation with money or otherwise." Gilmour said, however, that he doubted

> . . . whether it would be practical or would serve the purpose in view to propose legislation in this country on exactly the same lines as the Swedish laws. What seems to be wanted is rather a provision aimed at the same evils—namely, the formation of a body of persons who are drilled or trained physically for political purposes, including the purpose of performing functions which properly belong to His Majesty's Forces or the police.[31]

On 18 July, the Home Office submitted to the Cabinet a secret memorandum representing the views of the chief officers of police, as well as a separate memorandum from the commissioner of police, in which he stated his views of the general situation and indicated the steps that he judged should be taken. After discussing several aspects of the problem, the Home Secretary gave a summarized list of proposals that he recommended for adoption. These were (1) that the police should be given the power of entry into public meetings held on private grounds whenever the chief constable had reason to believe that disorder was likely to occur, (2) that the Home Secretary be permitted to prohibit concentrations of persons outside areas in which they reside if he was satisfied that such a concentration would lead to disorder, (3) that chief constables be empowered to prohibit open-air meetings that were likely either to interfere with public authorities or to result in clashes with rival meetings, (4) that chief constables be empowered to prescribe the route of processions, (5) that it should be an offense to be in possession of offensive weapons when taking part in a meeting or procession, and (6) that it be an offense for any person in pursuit of a political object to form any body of persons into an organization of military character.[32] Most of these provisions were incorporated into the Public Order Act of 1936.

Gilmour pointed out that Belgium had followed the Swedish example and had recently passed a law concerning the wearing of political uniforms. He said that he thought British public opinion was prepared for the view that the wearing of political uniforms was a matter for action by the Government, the police and local authorities, and that, while the utmost freedom of speech should be permitted, the challenge to government by movements similar to the Blackshirts would not be tolerated.[33]

It had been the BUF that had precipitated the call for legislation, but the Cabinet was equally concerned about the CPGB. This organization, however, had no defense force, no uniformed stewards, and very little violence at their meetings. Indeed, when the subject of a uniformed Red Guard came up several months later, it was almost unanimously rejected by the party. Gilmour nevertheless insisted that his proposals were aimed not only at the BUF, but also at the Communists.[34] It was obvious that any legislation introduced by the Government would have some provisions affecting the extreme Left, even when it had not precipitated the disorder. The Government still seemed to fear bolshevism more than the Nazi terror.

The Urgency Fades

Just six weeks after Olympia, ardor for the proposals to maintain public order was beginning to cool. The White City Stadium rally was definitely rescheduled for Hyde Park, and the Blackshirts seemed to be behaving themselves. Mosley was doing his best to restrain his stewards, instructing them to turn disrupters over to the police. The anti-Fascists, both Communist and non-Communist, changed their tactics and concentrated on demonstrations outside the meeting halls.[35] The National Government, never disposed to quick action, began to procrastinate.

On 19 July, furthermore, the BUF lost its only important ally within the public press. On that date, the *Daily Mail* carried a statement by Lord Rothermere in which he repudiated the aims and policies of the BUF. Rothermere disagreed with Mosley on four counts. First, he thought that a movement calling itself *Fascist* could never succeed in Britain. Second, he could not support the anti-Semitism that was creeping into the movement. Third, he disagreed with the whole idea of a dictatorship. Finally, he objected to the final end of the BUF goals—the replacement of parliamentary institutions by a corporate state.[36]

In changing his views, Rothermere was in all probability merely reacting to the feelings of his reading public. Opinion had become increasingly anxious about the developments in Germany. Rothermere had been quite generous in his enthusiasm for Continental fascism, but after the "night of the long knives" on 30 June 1934, when Hitler murdered a number of his own lieutenants without trial or without publication of their names, the worst fears about the nature of fascism seemed to be confirmed. It would have been difficult for any responsible newspaper to have supported the BUF after the events of 7 June and 30 June. Mosley insisted, however, that Rothermere was pressed into dropping his support by Jewish financial interests; in his autobiography, he wrote that Rothermere was "quite frank in explaining that he pulled out on account of his advertisers, and the firms in question were under Jewish influence."[37]

Meanwhile, the National Government was taking steps toward fulfilling the promise to meet with Opposition leaders. On 23 July, Gilmour met with Labour leaders and hinted that a consultation with the Liberals would follow. The discussion, which lasted about an hour and a half, was purely tentative.[38]

The Government did take definite action in some areas, however. On 26 July, the Air Ministry refused permission for groups of BUF members to train for flying in air clubs and aerodromes subsidized by public money. Furthermore, in a number of areas, special constables who were also members of the BUF were ordered to give up their posts in the Special Constabulary.[39]

On 31 July, Gilmour reported to the Cabinet the results of his discussions with four groups of Opposition leaders on the public-order proposals under consideration. This conference had not resulted in much, as Gilmour freely admitted, but it was significant that there had been no violent reaction to the suggestion that the police be permitted to enter meetings on the decision of the chief constable. The Opposition Liberals, he said, had been somewhat nervous about the proposals, and Sir Herbert Samuel had suggested that those relating to private armies could not be applied in practice. The Labour party had been hesitant about the meetings proposals but had welcomed proposals dealing with private armies. Lloyd George had sent a message to the effect that the Government was "making rather too much of private armies which would in due course die a natural death." At the conclusion of Gilmour's report to the Cabinet, Baldwin said that the conversations were so inconclusive that the Government would have to make up its own mind on the matter.[40] This was, in fact, the last time that the question of political uniforms and public order was fully discussed in the Cabinet until another two years had passed.

In August 1934, however, as the date of the Hyde Park rally came nearer, the Home Office again sought advice from the Opposition concerning the feasibility of a ban on political uniforms. According to James Maxton's account in the *New Leader,* the voice of the ILP, the Government put five questions to the Opposition leaders. The first related to the extension of police powers at public meetings; the second asked whether the Government should allow huge gatherings of people to parade to a central meeting when such a meeting could threaten the public order; the third question suggested that power be given to ban meetings that threatened "to interfere with the transaction of public business" or cause clashes between different sections of the population; the fourth proposal asked whether constables should be given power to control parade routes; and the fifth and most important suggestion was that organizations of military character that practiced drilling and the wearing of political uniforms be prohibited. The proposals implied in these questions were ostensibly aimed at the Blackshirts, but Maxton and the ILP warned that such provisions could be used against their own party.

A prohibition of large meetings, for instance, could have been used against the Hunger Marchers of the previous spring. The National Council of the ILP instructed its parliamentary members to oppose any legislation that would limit agitation, organization, and demonstration of the workers.[41] Whether such legislation would be introduced seemed to depend on the outcome of the massive Hyde Park rally.

The Hyde Park Rally

A movement such as the British Union of Fascists could not long survive without publicity. Especially after the *Daily Mail*'s support was dropped, therefore, it was imperative that the BUF stage another large, attention-getting rally. It was set for 9 September at Hyde Park.

Near the end of August, a newly formed group called the Coordinating Committee for Anti-Fascist Activities sent out a circular calling upon all London "working class organizations" to join in a counterdemonstration at Hyde Park. The circular was signed by John Strachey, D. N. Pritt, James Maxton, Lord Morley, the chief Opposition whip in the House of Lords, and Ellen Wilkinson, the suffragette and organizer for the National Union of Distributive Workers, who was at the time out of Parliament but would return in 1935 to represent the economically depressed district of Jarrow. The committee was not affiliated with the CPGB, but several of its members were sympathetic to the party.[42] The committee warned that an unorganized rally of anti-Fascists would probably be attacked by the Fascists with "calculated brutality." The *Daily Worker* printed an article, called "Deliver the Death Blow to Fascism in England," saying that the anti-Fascists could "deliver the death blow to British Fascism and set the country ablaze with the determination to prevent a repetition in this country of the happenings in Germany and Austria."[43] Six days later the *Worker* urged anti-Fascists to "strike a hammer-blow against Mosley's gangsters" and to "organise themselves as shock brigades."[44]

The Labour party regulars, however, followed a policy of shunning the whole affair. The National Council instructed all affiliated organizations of the Greater London area to refrain from taking part in the anti-Fascist demonstration. Apparently it was the opinion of the Labour leadership that such demonstrations would only advertise fascism, thus defeating the whole purpose of their actions.[45] Such a demonstration, furthermore, would also give recognition to the Communists.

The confrontation was threatening to turn into a first-class row. The Metropolitan and City Police canceled all leaves. The *Fascist Review* warned, "If the Reds carry out their intention of turning a peaceful political rally into a dog fight, it is sincerely hoped that the 'beating up' they will get will cool their ardour once and for all." Hundreds of leaflets calling for the anti-Fascist demonstration were dumped from a rooftop into Oxford Street. Someone strung an anti-Fascist slogan from the scaffolds in front of the Law Courts, and someone else shouted anti-Fascist slogans into the microphone during a BBC broadcast of a promenade concert.[46]

The CPGB was working harder than it had in preparation for the Olympia counterdemonstration. The *Daily Worker* warned, "This time it will not be a question of thirty Blackshirt thugs swarming on single anti-fascists and beating them up as was done at Olympia. They will have to deal with thousands of the best and most determined London Workers."[47] John Strachey and Harry Pollitt addressed a large anti-Fascist crowd in London during the week before the demonstration. Strachey stressed that if fascism could be "drowned in a sea of workingmen, Mosley and his men will be dealt the most deadly blow that has been aimed at them." Pollitt added, "Only slaves will agree to stay at home on Sunday. . . . We can put up a force and power such as no body in this country can wipe away."[48]

The TUC opposed a large counterdemonstration, but it did pass a resolution denouncing fascism and demanding that the Government make an unequivocal declaration that the drilling and arming of civilians should be suppressed. Walter M. Citrine's report to the TUC proclaimed:

> If the Fascists had their way there would be in Great Britain the same brutality and violence, the same suppression of Trade Unionism and the Socialist Movement, the same denial of free speech and free religion, the same resort to the bullying methods of dictatorship, that have signalized the triumph of Fascism abroad.[49]

Citrine also said that the National Council focused all its attention on the extreme Right, since communism had ceased to be a threat to the labor movement.[50]

The CPGB, however, was far from a negligible force; it was the single most important element in organizing the Hyde Park counter-demonstration. Mosley had announced:

> This organised Red violence has been met and defeated by the Blackshirts of the Fascist Defence Force all over the country. If Britain owed nothing else to Fascism, it already owes gratitude for this sharp check to the Red bully of the streets. . . . So far from promoting disorder, it has produced order in areas where an orderly public meeting was practically unknown.[51]

In answer to this proclamation, the *Daily Worker* promised, "The workers will not rest until they have closed down the party which exists for such work as was done at Olympia. . . . On Sunday their opinions will become engulfed in a sea of working class indignation and anger against the supporters of the bloody regimes in Germany."[52]

The invective against the BUF became so vitriolic that William Joyce, the propaganda director of the BUF, insisted in a court of law that the attacks in the *Daily Worker* were incitements to breaking of the peace. (The magistrate dismissed the charges.)[53] In the face of these Communist attacks, the *Blackshirt* proclaimed that the Hyde Park rally would see

> . . . the greatest and most loyal demonstration any political leader has ever been accorded in Britain. . . . Blackshirts will converge to the heart of our Empire; Blackshirts of every age and class, from every town and city in Britain, and from the cities across the seas.[54]

Behind the scenes, the Metropolitan Police Force was making contingency plans. Two days before the rally, Mosley wrote to Sir Trevor Bigham, a barrister-at-law, deputy commissioner of police, and twenty-five-year veteran of Scotland Yard, asking for special police protection from the anti-Fascists. Mosley, as usual extremely polite to the police, thanked Bigham for the courtesy of the officers involved in previous meetings.[55] Between six thousand and seven thousand police were made available for the Hyde Park meetings, and Police Commissioner Trenchard interrupted his vacation in Scotland to be in London for the rally.[56]

Behind-the-scenes activity also continued at the BUF and CPGB headquarters. From the BUF Deputy Chiefs of Staff's Office, a confidential memo went out to all Blackshirts.

> This rally must be considered and understood to be an exemplary parade of disciplined men and women, and the great propaganda value which it

> should have depends on members' behaviour by whose restraint in the face of insults, etc., will prove the strength of our Creed and Faith in our Leader, and the Movement.[57]

In a memo marked "IMPORTANT—MEMORIZE AND DESTROY," the CPGB Committee for Anti-Fascist Activities instructed their Shock Brigade unit leaders to disband their processions if ordered to do so by the police. When dispersed, the Communist demonstrators were then to make their way independently in groups of two or three and reassemble inside the park.[58] Publicly, Harry Pollitt claimed that the anti-Fascist demonstration would witness the culmination "of the greatest political campaign against Fascism that has yet been organized in this country."[59] The threats of the CPGB had their effect on the BUF. Neil Francis-Hawkins wrote to Scotland Yard asking protection from a suspected plot on the part of one hundred Communists who planned to dress up like Blackshirts and "beat Mosley up."[60]

On Sunday, 9 September 1934, the largest crowd ever gathered in Hyde Park assembled to hear Mosley or the anti-Mosleyites. The demonstrations were held within a few yards of each other. But there was no serious disorder; there were only minor incidents, with eighteen arrests and a few minor accidental injuries. Perhaps a large part of the crowd was too busy watching an autogyro that hovered two thousand feet above the meetings, keeping in radio contact with the police officers on the ground. It was the first such experiment with airborne crowd and riot control, and Lord Trenchard termed it "quite successful."[61]

The plan of the Metropolitan Police had been to keep the two demonstrations apart, but the size of the crowd meant an almost constant melding together. The anti-Fascists overwhelmed the three thousand Blackshirts by a large margin; some estimates put the crowd at over one hundred thousand people. While the anti-Fascists marched with their banners, bands, and songs, the Fascists waved Union Jacks and BUF banners. John Strachey's call to the workers had clearly been answered. Anti-Fascist banners proclaimed Workers Unite: Remember Vienna and Fascism Must Be Smashed, and two small boys were carried high under a banner proclaiming Youth Must Not Be Sacrificed.[62]

The anti-Fascists had come early, and their colorful procession had been turned into a long series of inflammatory speeches by the time the BUF arrived. A *Guardian* correspondent described the scene:

> A portion of the crowd, realising that at last the Fascists were coming, set off to meet their procession. Led by policemen and escorted by a smaller contingent of policemen that had kept watch over the anti-fascists, the procession came along the railed path. There may have been cheers, but they were drowned out by the booing and execrations of loud voiced individuals or small groups. There were shouts of "Mickey Mouse!" "Where's the Old School Tie?" "You look like Kippers side-ways!"—an unkind remark hit at the thin ones—and rude remarks were made to the ladies as they tailed along. Some of the Fascists held their head up and laughed, but most of them looked dejected and weary, as if exhausted by their long waiting to set out on a long journey to a possible ordeal. They made no reply to their enemies. They trudged on, twelve contingents of them, numbering perhaps 3,000.[63]

Others in the crowd that rushed to meet Mosley chanted, "1, 2, 3-4-5—We want Mosley, Dead or Alive." As the Mosleyites greeted each other with the Fascist salute, the anti-Fascist crowd responded with raised clenched fists and a few choruses of the "International." As each succeeding Blackshirt rose to address the crowd, the boos became louder, and the anti-Fascists began to chant "sit down, sit down" to the tune of Westminster chimes. The entire crowd, it was said, was largely made up of middle- and lower-class men with their wives and children all dressed in Sunday clothes—the type of people one would expect to find in Hyde Park on any Sunday afternoon.

At last Mosley himself took the rostrum. Bowing and smiling and saluting, he was forced to wait until the booing had calmed before he could begin his address. Ignoring his pleas for free speech, anti-Fascists drowned out his words for all but the closest listeners. Mosley, of course, considered such opposition to be the greatest tribute to Blackshirt strength and claimed that within two years the BUF had become the "most vital force in British politics." He ended his harangue by asking his followers to sing the "Fascist Hymn" in such a way that "all Britain would remember that [they] had stopped in Hyde Park on [their] road to power in England."[64]

When the Fascist meeting ended at the stroke of seven o'clock, mounted policemen were waiting to lead the Fascists out of the park. They went by different routes toward the Serpentine, along its banks and across the bridge, remaining in semimilitary formation. Chanting "We want Mosley," they gave their Fascist salute in unison to people along the route. The *Guardian* correspondent described them as "heroes returning from a battle that had not taken place."[65]

Naturally each side had its own version of its relative success at the rally. Mosley said that the opposition was "much weaker" than he had expected and that it was "definitely a Fascist crowd, that is, quite apart from our own members." Mosley praised the action of the police and observed that the small amount of organized violence had been directed not against the BUF but against the police. Regretting that the late arrival of some trains had kept some Blackshirt contingents from joining the rally, Mosley summed up that it was a "fine turnout of Blackshirts and a splendid reception from the vast crowd."[66]

The first issue of the *Blackshirt* following the demonstration said:

> The Blackshirt demonstration in Hyde Park last Sunday was a stupendous triumph for the British Union of Fascists. The opposition press, following their usual tactics, have endeavoured to belittle it. With lies that do credit only to their imagination, they have invented every conceivable kind of fabrication to attempt to minimize its importance. . . . The Blackshirts, however, have good reason to be proud of their leader and of themselves.[67]

John Strachey, secretary for the Committee for Cooperation and Anti-Fascist Activities, had a different view. "The Fascist demonstration was swamped by those members of the workers who went to the park. . . . All the objectives proposed by those who called for a counter-demonstration have been achieved." He considered the mass mobilization of anti-Fascists was what "prevented a repetition of such Fascist attacks on the workers as occurred at Olympia."[68] Strachey's evaluation became the official CPGB line. Emile Burns, a leader in the party, later wrote, "A hundred thousand London Workers had taken action with us against the Mosley rally in Hyde Park, undoubtedly dealing a heavy blow, from which [Mosley's] prestige never recovered."[69]

The opposing forces in Hyde Park each professed to be satisfied with the result, but perhaps neither was as pleased as the National Government and the Metropolitan Police. The official police summary estimated the crowd to be about sixty thousand, with about three thousand Blackshirt marchers and about fifty-six thousand anti-Fascist marchers. The Fascists had produced eighteen speakers from five platforms, while the anti-Fascists had twenty speakers on four platforms. The eighteen arrests were on charges of insulting behavior and obstructing or assaulting the police. Only six casualties were reported.[70] The day after the demonstration, Commissioner Trenchard sent a memo to all ranks of the Metropolitan Police Force expressing his satisfaction at the way in which the "task of preserving law and order under difficult circumstances was so admirably carried out." He attributed the success to the "good temper and tact displayed by all concerned."[71] The Home Office was pleased, of course, that the events of Olympia had not been repeated. And, while Trenchard did report that the meeting had "involved a very heavy drain on police resources,"[72] it was significant that order had been maintained in a volatile situation without recourse to additional legislation.

Opinion that such legislation would and should be forthcoming, however, remained widespread. The *Guardian,* on the day following the Hyde Park rally, observed that Thomas Inskip would "ignore the Fascist political theories and concentrate on stopping private military formations and the wearing of uniforms."[73]

Fascism and Labour

The Labour movement had come out strongly against the British Union of Fascists at the 66th TUC Congress, despite the adoption of the stay-at-home policy for the Hyde Park rally. At the annual meeting, Walter M. Citrine, general secretary of the TUC, presented the supplementary statement on fascism. In his address, he reiterated the general position of all British anti-Fascists.

> We are between two fires, as it were. On the one side, if we give too much publicity, we shall exaggerate its importance and perhaps help the movement in some measure. On the other side, if we underestimate or ignore it we are running a very considerable risk. But whatever the strength of the Fascist movement may be in this country, it is clearly apparent now to the public mind that the model of Fascism which is being pursued in this country is identical in method and operation with that pursued abroad. There is the same emphasis on military organisation, the same dressing up in uniform, the same parading about in armoured cars from meeting to meeting, the same ambulance section, the same transport section, the same uniformed and civilian Defence Forces. . . . Consequently we are right in demanding the resolution which I am moving that the drilling and arming of civilian sections of the community must end. If drilling and

> arming is to be regarded as a constitutional and inherent right of the subject in Great Britain, then Governments must realize that they cannot confine that right to one section.[74]

Citrine's long resolution emphasized the dangers of fascism and demanded "that the Government should make an unequivocal declaration that the drilling and arming of civilian sections of the community should be condemned as illegal and be suppressed without regard to those who may be responsible."[75]

There was virtually unanimous support for the resolution. Speaking in support of it, Charles Dukes, of the General and Municipal Workers and a former Labour M.P. for Warrington, asked, "If the Government is sincere in the preservation of democratic rights, why do they tolerate these developments?" He also questioned what the attitude of the Government would be if the Labour movement should suddenly put a quarter-of-a-million men in uniform.[76]

The suspicion that the Government secretly favored the Blackshirts at the expense of labor was widespread at the conference. TUC leaders charged that the whole ruling class of the country was behind the power of Mosley and would not hesitate to drop bombs on the workers when it became necessary for the maintenance of its rule.[77]

But such suspicions, which might logically lead to the belief that new laws would be useless, did not extinguish the demand for them. In the chairman's address to the 34th Annual Conference of the Labour party, Walter Smith said:

> In judging the intentions and promises of British Fascism, we are more impressed by what Hitler and Mussolini have done than by what Mosley has said. There is no place in the British national life for any semi-militarized political movement. . . . We say emphatically that it is far better for democratic government to put an end to the evil in the beginning than to wait until the evil is able to put an end to democratic government.[78]

Clearly, then, the Opposition leadership would support the Government in any reasonable legislation designed to regulate political uniforms and preserve public order. No such legislation was introduced, however. Instead, the Home Office was focusing its attention on the next large-scale rally, set for 29 September at Belle Vue Park in Manchester.

Belle Vue Park and the Relaxation of Tensions

The BUF scheduled a meeting for their northern members for three weeks after the Hyde Park rally. Three days before the Belle Vue meeting, John Maxwell, the chief constable of Manchester, wrote to M. T. Wilson, secretary of the Manchester Anti-Fascist Campaign Committee, that "under no circumstances will any procession be permitted." Although Maxwell assured Wilson that the same prohibition would apply to the Fascists, the anti-Fascists were adamant in their denunciation of the chief constable's actions. John Strachey called it an "interference with the rights of the subject" and "one of the expressions of bit by bit fascism."[79]

The National Council for Civil Liberties immediately got in touch with prominent politicians and well-known public citizens, including George Lansbury and H. G. Wells. The Council obtained permission to send, over their names, a strong protest to Maxwell and the lord mayor of Manchester. This was immediately followed by a letter pointing out that the ban established a dangerous precedent and that there was no legal justification for the banning of processions in advance. The communications received much publicity in the press, and a deputation was eventually sent to the Home Office.[80]

The protests apparently had some effect. Maxwell, although never officially withdrawing the ban, did allow an orderly anti-Fascist procession and demonstration to take place without police interference. The police, in fact, were scarcely to be seen. Three anti-Fascist groups marched through a steady drizzle to the park, while the Blackshirts were peaceably contained behind a "stout wooden barrier" bolstered by the police. A riot squad of firemen used their hoses to separate the two sections of the crowd,[81] but the whole affair "passed off with much noise but an entire absence of violence."[82]

There was no violence, but there were plenty of interruptions from the anti-Fascist forces. Mosley again climbed upon the free-speech horse. Defending his move to form a Fascist defense corps, Mosley said that in every city in which he had spoken there had been "organized attempts to prevent free speech by alien Jewish mobs. . . . If this was an indoor meeting with Blackshirt stewards," he warned, "these hooligans would be outside to yell in the streets."[83]

Mosley was already drifting to his full-scale attack on the Jews, which would take place during his Albert Hall speech of 28 October 1934. As several hundred anti-Fascists broke into a chorus of "The Red Flag," Mosley lost his temper.

> The mention of the Empire makes the mob yell louder than ever! Let them destroy it if they can, those Jewish rascals! The Red mob howls that we shall put them down. They are right. We shall put them down, but we shall put the nation up.[84]

The reaction of the press to the Belle Vue rally was comparatively mild. Perhaps the media were becoming accustomed to Fascist–anti-Fascist confrontations. In any event, instead of a renewed call for more legislation to prevent such occurrences, there were only a few mild condemnations. The *Guardian,* for insance, merely published a leader on the virtues of free speech. With a tongue-in-cheek appraisal of Mosley's speech, the leader writer commented, "If [Mosley's speech] represents also Sir Oswald Mosley's appeal to the intelligence of the public, the public ought to be given every chance of hearing about it."[85]

In the last three months of 1934 there were several other BUF demonstrations and anti-Fascist counterdemonstrations. None were of the size of Hyde Park or Belle Vue, and none contained the violence of Olympia. On the eve of a Fascist demonstration in a Liverpool stadium, the chief constable of that city issued a ban on any anti-Fascist processions for the night of the rally. The NCCL immediately protested, citing the example of the Manchester meeting three weeks before. The NCCL resolution stated firmly that there was "no justification in law for such a ban."[86] In spite of such pleas, the constable's ban was not lifted. Ignoring it, about five thousand anti-Fascists marched to the stadium to break up the Fascist meeting. This time the police did intervene, and during the course of the evening several people sustained minor injuries.[87]

Minor disturbances also took place in Worthing on 9 October and Plymouth on 11 October.[88] On 18 November, a scuffle took place at Woolwich.[89] In all cases, injuries and arrests were few, and none of the meetings ever got out of hand. On the occasion of Mosley's large rally at the Albert Hall on 28 October, one arrest resulted when police broke up a poster parade of only forty to fifty people.[90] When the comparison was made between the number of participants at the Albert Hall and Hyde Park rallies, disorders clearly appeared to be diminishing.

Perhaps the coming of colder temperatures affected the size of these rallies, or perhaps people were just losing interest. In any event, the police of the various cities affected, using existing laws, were easily able to maintain order. Only in one case, at Manchester on 26 November, did significant disorder take place. It began at the end of a Fascist rally and continued into the next morning. It was noisy, but there was little fighting. Eleven people were arrested during the demonstration, however, and six who had interrupted Mosley's speech were summoned under the Public Meetings Act.[91] The six were subsequently found guilty and were fined.[92]

1935—The Interlude

In a short history of the British Union of Fascists, Neil Francis-Hawkins, its director of organization, noted only one important meeting in 1935. This was in Manchester, in September, when Mosley launched his Mind Britain's Business campaign.[93] There were several other meetings, of course, but none, including the Manchester meeting, gained much attention from the press. Britain was hardly prosperous, but it was emerging from the depression. The National Government was occupied with the Cabinet changes that made Baldwin the Prime Minister, with the Abyssinian question, and, preeminently, with the General Election. The CPGB was busily pursuing a common front; the BUF was having troubles of its own.

The general public was becoming increasingly hostile to the BUF because it endangered the existing order in two ways. The first danger was the violence and lawlessness that accompanied the movement. In the months after Olympia, this danger seemed to subside. The second danger was the force it represented; fascism was a danger whether there was violence or not. Throughout the decade, as the fortunes of Continental fascism grew, Mosley was adversely affected. The invasion of Ethiopia evoked a violent hostility throughout Britain to all forms of fascism. Public opinion firmly supported the League of Nations and, through the "peace ballot," pressed the Government to do the same. In the midst of all the cries for support of Ethiopia, Mosley's Mind Britain's Business campaign was a mockery. Mussolini's callous disregard of the League severely hurt the BUF, for although independent of Italy, Mosley was clearly on his side.

The Ethiopian crisis began the transformation of roles that was completed during the course of the Spanish Civil War. By the time that the Government had backed off from its earlier pledges and the Hoare-Laval Pact became public in December 1935, anti-Fascist opinion was extremely strong. The Labour party, earlier filled with pacifists, began to move toward a policy of strong action against the dictators. The Conservatives, in seeking to defend their policy of nonintervention and neutrality, began to move to the policy of appeasement. In this almost revolutionary shuffle, the BUF had nowhere to go.

In January 1935, Mosley split the movement into two parts. There would still be Blackshirts, of course, but henceforth the wearing of this official uniform would be reserved for those who performed "conspicuous services." For those who had not the "dedicated Blackshirt spirit" but had "the political mind," a looser type of attachment was to be permitted. The *Guardian* commented that such a step was to "allow for the more prosaic mass who are ordinary people and not moved by any 'spiritual passion' for the 'brotherhood of Fascism.' " The newspaper saw Mosley as "taking a step towards reentering the Conservative fold."[94]

The action was generally taken as a sign of weakness. Reports at the TUC Congress of that year called it an attempt to "conceal the falling off in membership which otherwise would have been visible to the general public."[95] Shortly after the split, the *Fascist Week,* which had been sold on the streets in large quantities in 1934, was replaced by the *Fascist Quarterly*. Throughout the year, the BUF seemed to lose momentum.[96]

One of the long-range goals had been to increase activity and membership roles in the depressed areas, where Mosley thought Fascist propaganda would be particularly effective. It was a miscalculation. On 15 April, he addressed a meeting in Leicester. A short distance away, about 150 Communists were stopped by the local police. A short scuffle ensued, but although there were a few bruises, no serious injuries were reported.[97] This was one of the few times that the Fascists even attracted the attention of anyone outside London. In general, the BUF efforts were increasingly ignored or passively tolerated, and Mosley could point to few Fascist converts.

There seemed to be an attempt to forget about Mosley in 1935, one that might even suggest a planned oblivion. Herbert Samuel wrote, "Sir Oswald Mosley has faded away, the Rothermere press has forgotten about him. No one troubles any more about 'private armies.' "[98] At the TUC Annual Congress, it was reported that there was "quite definite evidence of a decline of the Fascist Movement. . . . So far as the British Union of Fascists is concerned . . . there is unquestionable evidence of a decline in membership. . . . There has been far less evidence of the Blackshirts at public meetings than there was formerly."[99]

The Manchester meeting that was judged by Francis-Hawkins to have been significant was more important to the BUF itself than to the public generally. The Mind Britain's Business campaign, of which it was a part, was intended as another escalation of anti-Semitic and pro-German propaganda. The meeting was not well attended and no violence took place. Mosley attacked the League of Nations and maintained that peace would only emerge from international fascism.[100] In moving into such general attacks on foreign policy, Mosley was sacrificing much of the domestic appeal of his movement.

The General Election of November 1935 posed a special problem for the BUF. From the beginning, it had promised to come to power through an election, and its vast claims of electoral power would eventually have to be tested. Mosley claimed that if Britain had Germany's system, he "could be certain of between 100 and 200 seats in Parliament even at this election."[101] But it was a bad time for the BUF to have to contest an election. The organization was still under the stigma of the Olympia violence and was short of both money and candidates. Mosley knew that he could not afford another loss such as he had suffered as the leader of the New Party.[102]

Mosley therefore decided on a stand that would keep the movement alive with the least amount of risk and expenditure. He said, "Blackshirts watch this futile farce and say 'Fascism Next Time.' " Governed by "long term principles," they decided to put no candidates into the field but to continue the steady work of perfecting their electoral structure before "challenging the Old Gang on their own favourable ground."[103]

By the end of 1935, then, Mosley was still trying to consolidate what little strength he had. He wrote in the *Fascist Quarterly:*

> Thus as the year 1935 closes, we can reflect upon equal success in propaganda and organisation. If we can never be happy until our task is

> complete, we can all be proud of every hour's work that we have done, every little sacrifice that we have made for the cause which is to save our people by unifying all that is noble in Nationalism and all that is successful in Socialism.[104]

Trying to inject optimism into his dwindling and discredited party, Mosley continued, "If the Blackshirts survived, not only intact, but with reinforced strength, the massed attack of the old order beginning at the Olympia meeting and ranging through all the steps of the sanctions racket, thus they can survive anything, and their victory is certain."[105] But in December 1935, it was obvious that the National Government had been the real victor, not only in the General Election, but also in the ongoing struggle to determine who would maintain internal order. In the next year, however, the BUF would challenge the Government's authority one more time.

Chapter 8

The Renewal of Political Violence

In 1936, King George V died, Germany remilitarized the Rhineland, Italy conquered Ethiopia, the Spanish civil war began, and Edward VIII gave up his throne to marry the woman he loved. In the year of three kings it would have been hard to keep a minority political movement such as the Blackshirts before the public eye. That Mosley was once again able to gain headlines in 1936 was not an indication of the growth of his movement, but of the renewed intensity of anti-Fascist activity. The Communist Party of Great Britain incited much of the activity; its ability to build upon events abroad made antifascism a popular sentiment. In late 1935, many people had believed Britain to be close to war with Italy. By autumn 1936, the passions aroused by the Spanish civil war were increasingly directed against the British Union of Fascists.

At the beginning of the year, the parties on both ends of the political spectrum voiced their goals and opinions. Equating Jewry and Communism, the January edition of the *Fascist Quarterly* proclaimed:

> A new year of Fascist strength lies before us. The Movement which has been bold enough to laugh, to scorn the concerted forces of the Jewish International Finance and the propaganda resources which it commands; the Movement which has successfully defied "Vested Power, Red Front, and Massed Ranks of Reaction," can be content with the defensive no longer. Having overcome the mighty obstacles placed in our way, we have now to work for our own victory.[1]

Meanwhile, the Marston Printing Company, the printer of all CPGB tracts, was turning out numerous pamphlets attacking fascism. In *Spotlight on Fascism,* John L. Douglas, tying communism to socialism in accordance with the popular-front objectives, wrote:

> Fascism is the enemy of Britain, all its talk of "Britain First" means the Bankers and Landlords first. It means first in the race to start the new

> world war of Imperialism. . . . Mosley (and Baldwin) are trying to tie the British people to Hitler's war plans. Who are the enemies of the countries? Not the communists and socialists, but the fascists.[2]

Other Communist tracts even used English history as a rallying point against the Fascists. In a pamphlet called *The March of English History,* the Communists declared that fascism "installs against the inquisition . . . , idealises and enthrones violence, brutality, terror, . . . the Divine Right of Kings, the use of torture, government by secret police, the Star Chamber, conscription, the press gang, all of this foulness which our fathers drove from English life."[3]

Such invective was commonplace and generally passed unnoticed by the great majority of Britishers. But a new problem was beginning to appear in London's East End. There had always been some anti-Semitism in this region, and in October 1935 the Home Office had directed the new commissioner of police of the metropolis, Sir Philip Game, "to take steps to make it clear such assaults [upon Jews] are regarded seriously by authorities."[4] By early 1936, these assaults had increased at an alarming rate. On 13 February, during oral answers, Sir John Simon was asked whether he was aware that Jewish shopkeepers in Shoreditch were being subjected to Fascist intimidation. Simon answered that he had been in touch with Sir Philip, who had informed him that the whole matter was "receiving the close attention of the police." Special steps were being taken, he said, to keep order in the district, and the police would "take action in any case which comes to their notice and in which sufficient evidence to justify proceedings [could] be obtained." Game, who had retired from the military in 1929, had served in the Boer War and World War I and commanded the Royal Air Force in India. For the last five years he had served as governor of New South Wales, where, curiously enough, his biggest headache had been the New Guard, the local Fascist organization. While some may have questioned his knowledge of day-to-day problems in keeping the peace in London, he claimed to know his men and denied that breaches of the law by Fascists were being "looked upon indulgently" by the police.[5]

Two weeks later, Simon was asked if he were aware of Fascist "annoyances and persecutions" of Jewish shopkeepers in Bethnal Green. He again assured the members that the police would "take every possible step to prevent such activities."[6] On 5 March, shortly before the full House debate on the subject, Simon was asked whether his attention had been drawn to the Jew baiting in Tottenham. He referred to his earlier answer and promised a full discussion.[7]

While none of the surrounding boroughs were free from Blackshirt activity, the boroughs of Stepney, Bethnal Green, and Shoreditch were the main centers of conflict in the East End. These areas underwent rapid industrialization in the nineteenth century and became heavily overpopulated. As late as 1930, in fact, Shoreditch, Bethnal Green, and Stepney were ranked second, third, and fourth among the London boroughs in terms of the number of people per acre. Furthermore, 18 percent of the population in Shoreditch, 17.8 percent in Bethnal Green, and 15.5 percent in Stepney were in poverty. This placed them second, third, and fifth poorest of the London boroughs.[8]

Among these three East London boroughs, there was a great variation as to the percentage of Jewish and foreign-born residents. Stepney had the largest number of foreign-born residents of any borough in England, while the foreign-born population of nearby Shoreditch was almost nonexistent. Likewise, 43 percent of all London Jewish families lived in Stepney, 15 percent in Bethnal Green, and only 6 percent in Shoreditch.[9] The heavy concentration of Jews in the East End made every proposed Fascist activity there a potential source of disorder. It is not clear to what extent the BUF preyed upon the latent anti-Semitism that was already in existence or to what extent the BUF created its own anti-Semitism, but the campaign to establish Fascist control in the center of anti-Fascist strength depended to a large extent on the prejudices of the non-Jewish population. To organize this element, therefore, Mosley's attention in 1936 was almost exclusively centered on the East End.

There were other anti-Semitic movements at work there. The BUF propaganda, it may be noted, was usually mild compared to that of Arnold Leese's Imperial Fascist League. The IFL circulated pamphlets charging that the real Jewish population of Britain was not the three hundred thousand figure that had been reported by Government sources, but was instead three million, "roughly the same number as there are unemployed Englishmen." The conclusion was that were it not for the Jews, there would be no unemployment. The pamphlet ended, "Britons awake, Boycott Jewish shops, Perish Judah."[10]

On 5 March 1936, Herbert Morrison brought the subject of anti-Semitism in the East End before the House for a full debate. Morrison, who represented South Hackney, was a former errand boy, shop assistant, and telephone operator who served as secretary of the London Labour party from 1915 until 1947 and would be Home Secretary from 1940 to 1945. In the debate, he cited several incidents of Jew baiting that included verbal and physical abuses, especially in his own district, and asked the Home Secretary for reassurances that he would "take such energetic steps as are within his power and are appropriate."[11]

Simon said that he welcomed the question because it especially concerned the Home Office, which was "charged with the duty of keeping public order and . . . preserving civil liberty." He considered it a subject on which "decent people" would not have two opinions. He called it a disquieting movement that "was potentially very dangerous" and said, "In this country we are not prepared to tolerate any form of Jew baiting." But as far as the Home Office was concerned, Simon said, they had "nothing to do with people's political philosophies," but had "merely to see that every citizen has a fair opportunity for living his life in peace and exercising the rights which we claim for ourselves."[12]

Simon reported that he had been consulting Sir Philip Game "with a view to seeing whether more effective measures can be devised to deal with the situation." As a result, it had been decided to detail additional police for duty in the East End, especially charged with "keeping a special lookout for provocative conduct calculated to lead to a breach of the peace or to injury. . . ." The Home Secretary also hoped that the ordinary citizen would aid the police in this matter.[13]

The debate brought another call for the prohibition of uniforms. F. C. Watkins, Labour member for Central Hackney, said that he could "not help wondering whether it wouldn't be a very great advantage to this country to prohibit the wearing of uniforms for political purposes." To Watkins, who as president of the Railway Clerks Association had no doubt seen his share of uniforms, if a man dressed himself in a uniform that differentiated him from most people, there was "produced in his mind a kind of psychological feeling which leads to very bad results."[14]

The Thurloe Square Incident

The incidents of Jew baiting increased dramatically, but they usually involved the actions of a handful of Blackshirts against an even smaller number of Jews. By March 1936, over eighteen months had passed since the huge Hyde Park rally and almost two years since the Olympia violence. The legislation considered in 1934 had been gathering dust. However, the Thurloe Square incident in march 1936 shocked the Government into considering anew the old question of public order and public meetings. When the Battle of Cable Street took place in October, forcing the Home Department to take immediate action, the Government was prepared to submit legislation within five weeks after the disorder. Thus, the Thurloe Square incident served as an instructive preface to large-scale disorder.

In February, Mosley announced that the BUF would hold a large rally in the Albert Hall on 22 March 1936. John Strachey, under the auspices of the Coordinating Committee for Anti-Fascist Activities and with the blessing of the CPGB, called upon all opponents of fascism to demonstrate outside the hall. The *Daily Worker* published several appeals for a large anti-Fascist demonstration.[15]

The Albert Hall Commission submitted the date and object of the meeting to the police, who took action under the Metropolitan Police Act of 1839. The police attempted to seal off the meeting from the public, prohibited any demonstrations within one-half mile of the Albert Hall, prohibited traffic within the area while the meeting was in progress, and allowed pedestrians into the area only after proper identification. When the police precautions were announced, George Hall, a Manchester councillor, observed that authorities "were slowly waking up to the fact that the Blackshirts had no other reason for existence than to provoke law abiding citizens."[16]

On Sunday evening, 22 March, while Mosley was addressing Blackshirts in the Albert Hall, his former friend John Strachey was standing on the roof of a van in Thurloe Square denouncing fascism in general and the refusal of the authorities to rent the Albert Hall to anti-Fascists in particular. Earlier, Percy Lamme, the assistant commissioner of police, had warned Strachey "that the Commissioner of Police of the Metropolis has given directions to the police that no formal processions will be permitted to within half a mile of the Albert Hall, and that no meeting will be permitted within that area."[17] Strachey apparently thought Thurloe Square was not in the prohibited area.

About half a mile away, the Albert Hall was draped in Union Jacks and Fascist insignia. Blackshirt buglers and drummers were flanked by boys wearing gray shirts and black ties—the uniform of the youth movement. Mosley came in under the glow of several blue spotlights and the sounds of a roll of drums and, according to the *Guardian* correspondent, the blare of "out of tune trumpets." Mosley dramatically marched to the rostrum under a cordon of outstretched Blackshirt arms. From the upper galleries, a woman, no doubt soon to be ejected, yelled, "Here comes the Emperor."[18]

Strachey had arrived at Exhibition Road, originally set as the site of the demonstration, and then led the anti-Fascists into Thurloe Square, which adjoins it. The anti-Fascist meeting began about the same time as the BUF rally. For about fifty minutes, while large detachments of mounted police and police on foot or in covered lorries patrolled the area around the Albert Hall, Strachey led a peaceful meeting.[19] The crowd, estimated at between one and two thousand, heard speeches by R. Willis of the Labour League of Youth, Bob McLennan of the National Unemployed Workers Movement, and the Rev. Leonard Schiff. Repeatedly there were requests by the speakers for moderation and order. According to witnesses from the NCCL, the only noises coming from the crowd were occasional bursts of applause.[20] According to Mrs. Geraldine Young, at the meeting as an observer for the NCCL, a police inspector arrived at Thurloe Square and spoke to the constables in attendance, asking one of them, "What is this place?" After the constable told him, the inspector asked the nature of the meeting, to which the constable replied, "Mainly communist." "Where is the nearest telephone?" the inspector immediately asked. A few minutes later, twenty mounted police and a van of foot constables arrived at the scene.[21]

The events that followed were the subject of a great deal of controversy. According to an official report prepared by the NCCL, when the police arrived there was a short conversation between the officer in charge and one of the demonstrators, with apparently no effort made to establish contact with the chairman. Sir John Simon said later in Parliament that a full ten minutes elapsed between the conversation and the baton charge that followed. An NCCL inquiry set the time at under two minutes. In any event, without further warning, the police advanced into the crowd, drawing their batons as they moved forward.[22]

In the House of Commons, Sir John Simon was questioned by seven different members concerning the Albert Hall meeting and the events at Thurloe Square. According to Simon's version, a body of about twenty mounted police and sixty foot police had gone to the square. Before their arrival, there were a number of disturbances, and members of the crowd were stopping traffic. A bottle was thrown at a police officer, but missed and broke a shop window. To prevent the approach of the police, a number of demonstrators had linked arms and appealed to the police to stand fast. The officer in charge told the demonstrators that they were in a prohibited area and were causing an illegal obstruction, whereupon the crowd began to throw stones and dirt. The officer then instructed the mounted police to disperse the crowd. They moved forward, and when the demonstrators tried to unseat the riders, truncheons were drawn. The crowd was dispersed in ten minutes and order was restored.[23]

Oblivious to the violence a half mile away, the Albert Hall meeting was proceeding peacefully. Advocating "the closest possible friendship with Germany, a nation with a blood brotherhood," Mosley was subjected to numerous catcalls from the audience. In most cases, the interrupters were ejected in accordance with Mosley's requests for a minimum of force. "We have made full arrangements," he said, "that outside the hall they shall be handed over to the police with a view to a summons being taken out against them." Nevertheless, there were several minor scuffles, and six people were treated at a nearby hospital.[24]

The BUF professed itself to be highly satisfied with the Albert Hall meeting. The *Fascist Quarterly* proclaimed, "No greater meeting has ever been held in the country than that which was addressed at Albert Hall on March 22nd by the Fascist leader Sir Oswald Mosley." The meeting, according to Fascists, showed that "the English people can express their feelings no less powerfully, no less spontaneously, than those continental peoples who have gained the reputation for being warm hearted and quick of temper."[25]

The Fascists claimed that the violence on the night of their meeting had not been their fault. The *Blackshirt* maintained that the police had been present only to protect the anti-Fascists. In its typical bombastic style, the Fascist organ proclaimed, "There were some five thousand Fascists, in and out of uniform, at the Albert Hall or near it and had they been attacked by this rabble, the only strain anywhere would have been on the hospitals and the legs of the survivors of the Ghetto Army."[26]

The CPGB saw the meeting in a different light. The secretariat of the London District Committee issued a statement saying, "Yesterday the people of London scored a further victory in the fight against Fascism. Mosley was revealed as a political bankrupt compelled to resort to an appeal to the lowest passion of his audience by an hysterical and violent attack on the Jews."[27]

Captain A. O. Hope, Conservative M.P. for Ashton, Strachey's opponent in the 1931 General Election and currently Lord of the Treasury, was an eyewitness to the Thurloe Square incident. Testifying before the House of Commons, Hope supported Simon's version, saying that the crowd was in an "ugly" mood. He said his own car had been pushed across the street, and when he went to retrieve it, he heard the crowd make threats to slash the tires and set it on fire.[28]

In response to a question from Dingle Foot, Simon said that of twenty-four persons arrested at the counterdemonstration, none had complained of mistreatment by the police. On the other hand, he reported that two police officers had received severe kicks and one officer was still suffering from an assault.[29]

At the request of the National Council for Civil Liberties, a meeting of M.P.s of all parties was held in a committee room in the House of Commons. Although pressed by several members to hold a public inquiry into the circumstances attending the Thurloe Square baton charge, the Home Secretary refused. The NCCL then invited certain persons of "independent standing" to form a commission to investigate the numerous allegations of police violence.[30]

On the day that Thurloe Square was discussed in the House, several members, including D. N. Pritt and Dingle Foot, reported that they had received several accounts of police misconduct.[31] The NCCL commission eventually called together as many witnesses as it could find. In all, 112 witnesses agreed virtually unanimously that the meeting was at all times peaceful and that the police charge was unwarranted. John Strachey testified:

> No warning was sent to me as Chairman of the meeting, nor to any of the speakers, by the police. There would have been no difficulty in sending a police officer to us to inform us that in their view we were causing an

obstruction or doing something which they considered was likely to lead to a breach of the peace. But no such warning was sent.[32]

Concerning the unnecessary violence on the part of the police, Philip Harding, a journalist, testified, "Eight or ten mounted police came along Alfred Place and charged the meeting with batons drawn, striking right and left." Another witness testified that an attempt had been made by the police to "break up the meeting with as much violence and damage as possible." A clergyman present at the meeting, the Rev. Stanley Evans, testified, "It is my considered opinion that the action of the police was completely unprovoked, that the use of violence was quite unnecessary, and that the brutality shown by the police was of such a nature to incite a hitherto peaceful crowd to a serious breach of the peace."[33] The NCCL inquiry also found that, measured as the crow flies, the distance from the center of the Albert Hall to the parked van was about ten yards inside the half-mile limit. Measured by the nearest route along a public thoroughfare, however, it was clearly outside the half-mile limit.[34] It seemed obvious that Strachey had made an effort to be, and thought himself to be, outside the half-mile radius.

The NCCL commission eventually issued a report based, so it claimed, only on evidence that would be admissible in a court of law. As expected, the report came out in favor of the anti-Fascists. The commission did admit, however, that breaches of the peace had occurred before, during, and after the Thurloe Square meeting, although this action had no direct connection with the meeting itself. Furthermore, the commission found a certain amount of obstruction. In the preface to the report, Harold Laski listed several conclusions of the commission and pointed out several contradictions in the version that Simon had given in Parliament. In contrast to Simon's assertions, Laski wrote that, from the NCCL evidence, the Thurloe Square meeting had been entirely peaceful, that attempts to rescue arrested men from the police were unrelated to the meeting, that the meeting was not within a prohibited area by a practical definition, that the police were never denied access to the meeting, and that police witnesses were unreliable or at least partially mistaken. Laski concluded, "There is no use denying that there is an ugly body of suspicion abroad about police behaviour in dealing with problems created by the fascist movement."[35]

Although Simon refused to make a public inquiry, he did ask for a confidential inquiry to be undertaken by the commissioner. On 17

September, almost six months after the event, Sir Philip Game submitted his report to the Home Secretary. Game reached far different conclusions from those of the NCCL inquiry. He stressed that the commission had concerned itself only with what took place at Thurloe Square, an approach which he found totally inaccurate. He also said that he could find no "overwhelming evidence" that the crowd remained perfectly peaceful throughout and that, in any event, the speakers on the van could not be aware of what was occurring in the outskirts of the meeting. Game also protested that the commission had ignored most of Captain Hope's report and pointed out that the NCCL commission did admit that some obstruction did occur. Regarding the public inquiry demanded by the NCCL, Game said his reluctance to grant the inquiry arose from no anxiety concerning its outcome, for he could not "conceive that any unprejudiced tribunal could come to any other conclusion than that the commission's report is a completely one-sided account of only part of the occurrences of the evening of March 22 completely divorced from what led up to it." His main arguments against a public inquiry were (1) what would it find six months after the event?; (2) there was no great public interest apart from the NCCL; (3) the grant of an inquiry would adversely affect police morale; (4) an inquiry would take up time and energy of the force when it was needed elsewhere; (5) D. N. Pritt's inquiry in the House of Commons was sufficient; (6) no press support for the council's demand existed; and (7) the NCCL was a

> . . . self contained body with no authority or statutory powers, whose principal activity is to criticize and attack the police on every opportunity they can find or make, and which has arrogated to itself the right to set up commissions to inquire into the actions of constitutional authorities in exercise of their responsibility. If they are accorded an inquiry, it would give them some status and encourage their troublesome activities.[36]

The "troublesome" nature of the NCCL served to make the Home Office and the Metropolitan Police more aware of the problems of impartially maintaining public order. It was, however, a huge job. Simon reported that thirty police had been stationed inside the Albert Hall, with another hundred just outside. The presence of police inside the building no doubt helped to prevent the Albert Hall meeting from turning into another Olympia. The officers received from the Blackshirt stewards those persons who were to be ejected and escorted them out of the building. The total number of police employed in connection with the Fascist meeting and the anti-Fascist counterdemonstration was about twenty-five hundred, with another four hundred kept in reserve. Simon estimated that the total extra expenditure for the evening was about three hundred pounds.[37] In such a massive undertaking, complete impartiality was hard to guarantee, but a week after the NCCL first began protesting the Thurloe Square action, Norman Kendal, the assistant commissioner of the Metropolitan Police, issued a secret memorandum to members of the force. He told all police officers, "It is to be particularly noted that action is to be taken in all appropriate cases, *irrespective of the Political party or Organisation to which the offender belongs.*"[38]

The Communist Response to Increased Violence

Shortly after the Thurloe Square incident, elements within the Communist Party of Great Britain began advocating the formation of uniformed Communist defense forces. That the workers as a class would smash fascism and capitalism had always been a maxim of the party, but this future ideal did little to help the individual who was assaulted by the Blackshirts. If the CPGB followed BUF tactics and donned red shirts, Britain would be in the uncomfortable position of having two uniformed paramilitary organizations opposing each other in a state of perpetual agitation.

The idea of a Red Defense Force was frequently discussed in such organs as the *Daily Worker* and *Discussion*. In the April edition of *Discussion,* an article written by "Young Worker" called for the formation of Workers Defense Groups for two reasons: First, it would vastly improve party discipline, which had been lacking in the CPGB for several years; and second, the successful action of such groups in staving off Fascist attacks would convince many socialist workers of the strength of unity.[39]

E. Burgess, in the same issue, further underlined these points by maintaining that a defense force was necessary for four reasons: (1) it would give substance and dignity to the Labour movement and appeal to "millions of youths"; (2) the experience of the Popular Front in France revealed the necessity of such a force; (3) it would activate large numbers of organized workers who did not see the value of trade unionism or political parties but would see the practical value of such a defense force; and (4) under the Emergency Powers Act and other "oppressive acts," the National Government, together with the Fascists, would "use the almost unlimited powers that they have in order to crush the worker's organisations." To form such a body, the party would have to issue a manifesto, and prominent men and women in the Labour movement would have to sign it to give it substance. This call would go forth at Labour meetings, trade union mass meetings, and congresses.[40] The emphasis on a common front was clearly reflected. An article in the *Daily Worker* claimed that the formation of Workers Defense Groups would show that all anti-Fascists, in spite of theoretical differences, could effectively work together to check Fascist violence.[41]

Opinion on this matter, however, was by no means unanimous. John Gollan, a leading member of the CPGB, dissented. He also used the new party approach to a common front to show that if the party could get mass agitation developed in a borough against Fascist brutality, could get the trades councils and local Labour party leaders, co-op guilds, and Labour Youth to go on record for "clearing out the fascists," and could get the issues raised in borough councils, it would be far more successful in fighting fascism. To Gollan, the way to develop the campaign against fascism was in the town meeting hall, the churches, and the councilmen's offices—not in the streets. "Defence forces or groups," wrote Gollan, "would only short circuit this struggle." Gollan concluded:

> I think it is time the Council of [*sic*] Civil Liberties were doing more to rouse people to this unity which seems to exist between the police and the B.U.F. which is the whole toleration of the Fascists by the National Government. However, in my opinion, one of the main ways of doing this is by developing a mass united struggle in the localities which could bring pressure on local M.P.s and the Government.[42]

Gollan's position was far more harmonious with the new image of the CPGB, and although support for the formation of defense groups continued, it never had official blessing. Without the defense force, the CPGB could choose when it wished to become involved in Fascist activities. If the leagues were formed, they would give the initiative to Mosley, for they would be almost obliged to react to every Fascist provocation. Furthermore, Gollan's program would gain all the propaganda benefits and spare the risk and expense of a defense force.

The question of defense forces and uniforms was especially important to the Young Communist League. At a meeting at Walthamstow on 15 May 1936, a brief discussion took place on the question, "Should we wear uniforms?" The general uniform proposed was a khaki shirt and a red tie. The overwhelming majority at the meeting strongly opposed the adoption of any uniform, with the major objection being that the wearing of uniforms might make the organization more sectarian. If a united front were to be achieved, they argued, such uniforms might serve as an obstacle. Furthermore, open identification with such a group was not always desirable, and it was feared that such a display would discourage new members. Finally, they wanted to dissociate themselves in every way from the actions of the Blackshirts, to avoid the charge that "one is as bad as the other." It was the opinion of the Young Communist League that only the weaker and hence less desirable mentalities would be attracted by the wearing of uniforms. The absence of any material uniform, they decided, would in itself constitute an excellent uniform to distinguish them from the Blackshirts.[43]

The CPGB was well aware that communism and fascism were often equated in the popular mind. Later in 1936, Harry Pollitt wrote:

> Let me say a few words on the question of Fascism and Communism. The attempt to make Fascism and Communism two sides of the same medal, whoever supports it, can only succeed in strengthening those forces that are working for the triumph of Fascism in Britain. Mosley had been given practically a free hand all the summer in his anti-Jewish propaganda in certain parts of East London. The results are to be seen in the present situation in East London, where it is no use disguising the fact that . . . prominent Jewish leaders in their conversation say it "begins to remind them of the eve of progrom [*sic*] atmosphere in Czarist Russia and Poland."[44]

Before the violence of October 1936, the CPGB took credit for protecting the Jews from Mosley's "progrom." The party insisted that if the leaders of the Labour party of London, trades councils, and Jewish organizations had formed the united front for which they had called, the Blackshirts would have been crushed earlier. Pollitt, among others in the CPGB, charged that the London police were politically biased, noting that three thousand uniformed policemen had protected Fascist demonstrations. If the Communist party would have caused such a mobilization, they argued, it would have been suppressed. The CPGB demanded "the dissolution of Mosley's Fascist organization, its barracks, uniforms, and processions, because the object of Fascism is the suppression of everything associated with democracy and freedom.''[45]

The British Blackshirts were viewed by many as the domestic version of the forces of Mussolini, which were completing their conquest of Ethiopia. Others saw them as representatives of the Nazi regime that had smashed the German trade unions, introduced laws against the Jews, and broken the treaty of Versailles by their remilitarization of the Rhineland. In July 1936, Mosley also came to represent Franco in the East End, perhaps the most pro-Republican section in London.

The National Government took its customary noncommittal position. Critics on the Left suspected that the Government was going to reach an accord with Hitler to allow him to turn his attention to an anti-Communist crusade. Independent and liberal opinion, already extremely suspicious of the Government over its domestic policies, joined with the Left in seeing sinister motives behind British foreign policy. The allegedly pro-German attitude of the ''Cliveden set'' and the refusal to take firm action against Mosley seemed to confirm their suspicions.

Following the turmoil of the Thurloe Square disturbance, the BUF had been comparatively mild in its public attacks on Jews, but individual assaults were still common. Throughout the summer of 1936, when the actions of the Continental Fascists gained even more publicity, tension grew in the East End.

In a letter to the editor of the *New Statesman,* an eyewitness to a Fascist meeting stated that he had heard a Blackshirt speaker refer to the Jews as ''venereal ridden vagrants who spread disease to every corner of the earth.'' When a number of people in the audience loudly protested this vilification, the police ordered them to be quiet under threat of being arrested for insulting behavior. The writer charged that the police acted as Fascist stewards and encouraged the Blackshirts in their provocative behavior.[46]

In May 1936, Mosley announced that the BUF had gone as far in three years as the Labour party had gone in forty and that they were now gearing up their election machine.[47] It was increasingly apparent that the machine would run on the fuel of anti-Semitism, and many thought it was time for the National Government to take action against the BUF.

On 25 May, following a Fascist-Communist encounter in Edinburgh, the question of introducing legislation prohibiting the wearing of political uniforms was again raised. But official reactions were antipathetic. The under secretary of state for Scotland had simply said it was "a matter of indifference to the crown authorities what colour of shirt a breaker of the law wears."[48] A day later, Sir G. Collins, Secretary of State for Scotland and one of the few Liberals remaining in the National Government, said that while he deplored any action by any section of the community that produced disorder, he was advised that "further powers seem to be unnecessary."[49] A short time later, on 28 May, in answer to a question concerning Fascist violence in Liverpool, Simon indicated that the local police were able to handle the incident.[50]

Sir John Simon was probably correct in his assurances. But the situation was deteriorating rapidly, and no one knew how long the police would be able to maintain order. The Jewish population was losing faith in the Metropolitan Police and the National Government as the anti-Semitic attacks continued. The CPGB was the only organization to fill the vacuum, and its East End membership grew rapidly.

The BUF, however, charged that the National Government was in the hands of Jewish press and cinema interests that monopolized the mass communications of the country. The *Fascist Quarterly* charged that the National Government rested on

> a House of Commons equally committed to and responsible for all its blunders; and on the continuing discredit of a Labour movement, itself lacking in all vital impulses and permeated and controlled by such Jewish-capitalist interests as those typified in the publishers and distributors of the *Daily Herald*.[51]

The first significant East End rally of the BUF took place on 7 June in celebration of the second anniversary of the Olympia rally. It was held in Victoria Park, at the end of the borough of Bethnal Green. The estimates of the London newspapers varied from a crowd of three thousand to a crowd of fifty thousand. The police estimated five thousand, of which there were only five hundred uniformed Blackshirts, a significant drop from the total of the Hyde Park rally. (The *Blackshirt* estimated the crowd to have been over one hundred thousand, with two thousand Blackshirts in uniform.)[52]

Some five hundred foot police and sixty mounted police patrolled Victoria Park. The crowd grew hostile and had to be dispersed by the police, and hand-to-hand fighting eventually broke out.[53] (The *Blackshirt* also reported that no violence "of any major proportion" had broken out.)

Through June the attacks on and provocations of Jews continued. On 16 June, after reports of Jew baiting in Stepney, George Lansbury asked Geoffrey Lloyd, the under secretary of state for the Home Office, if he were aware that "if a tithe of the energy which was forthcoming in dealing with Communists a few years ago were applied by the Department to preventing these insulting statements, and sometimes assaults, an end would be put to the present state of affairs." Lloyd only reiterated Simon's earlier assurances and promised that he would give further attention to the matter.[54] The next day, F. C. Watkins asked if Lloyd were aware of Fascist assaults in Hackney. Again Lloyd repeated Simon's promises.[55]

On 21 June 1936, another demonstration was held at Finsbury Park in northeast London. Simon said in the House that 573 foot police and 59 mounted police were on the grounds to prevent disorder. The precautions, he said, "were both necessary and adequate," and no disorder except for minor scuffles occurred, and these only on the edges of the Blackshirt meeting. He concluded that in light of the recent successes which the police had had in securing order, he was "not satisfied there is sufficient ground for proposing far reaching change in the law."[56]

Simon's assurances did little to help the Jewish shopkeeper keep Fascist bricks out of his window. The temporary lull in violence at meetings was frequently interrupted, such as by the Hulme Town Hall meeting in Manchester on 28 June, which resulted in several injuries and eight arrests.[57] But there was never a long interruption in the systematic Jew baiting conducted by individual Blackshirts in the East End. The Metropolitan Police stood as the only legal safeguard. The *New Statesman* said, "The only safeguard we have against the growth of political hooliganism is the popular faith in the police who have had in the past an excellent reputation for impartiality which they are in danger of losing."[58]

The impatience of those who wanted to see an end to the Jew baiting was shown by a debate in Commons on 10 July. D. N. Pritt raised the question of police partisanship and was joined by several M.P.s who related various incidents of Fascist name-calling and assault.[59] The Home Secretary was in an extremely difficult position, facing a problem new to British politics. Under existing laws, the police were probably doing their best. To the charges of police partiality, Simon answered that they were acting impartially and admitted that the Fascists were indeed a terrible nuisance to the police.[60] The long session did not, however, significantly improve relations between the police and the anti-Fascists.

The day after the long police debate, the *Guardian* insisted, "Difficult as it may be to use the machine of the law to prevent the abuse of free speech and public meetings, it cannot be impossible to find means of doing it, and Sir John must try again. Sir John's position is not to be envied. No man is more sincere in his desire to preserve liberty of speech and public meeting."[61]

Simon was taking steps to alleviate the tension. In a memo to Sir Philip Game, dated 16 July, Simon directed the commissioner to (1) concentrate police in the Jewish district; (2) make every individual police officer aware that grossly abusive language against the Jew was a serious offense; (3) take shorthand notes at all Fascist meetings in Jewish districts; (4) give definite instructions to all police officers that if unreasonable force was used by Fascist stewards for the purpose of ejecting interrupters it was the duty of the police to intervene promptly; (5) follow up the complaints of assault even if the individual assaulted could not identify his assailant; (6) report to the Home Office Communist and anti-Fascist organizations that planned to stage counterdemonstrations designed to prevent through violence a Fascist meeting from being held, with a view to the question of whether a magistrate should bind the organizers over to keep the peace; (7) keep a careful watch over Fascist publications; and (8) submit monthly reports to the Home Office giving an overview of the situation in the Jewish districts.[62]

The BUF rallies went on as before. In mid-July a Mosley rally at Corporation Field in Hull was dispersed only by a heavy thunderstorm.[63] It was at this rally that a would-be assassin's bullet penetrated Mosley's windshield, barely missing him.[64] That same day, a procession of anti-Fascists was formed in Victoria Park and marched through Bethnal Green. As they passed the local BUF headquarters, they were greeted with cries of "Hail Mosley" and several bags full of flour and soot, followed by a barrage of eggs. Herbert Morrison called these actions "deliberately calculated to produce a riot."[65]

Attention next centered on Manchester, where the Watch Committee gave the BUF permission to hold a procession on the condition that they did not wear uniforms. Furthermore, the route was to be laid out by the chief constable. After receiving the conditions, the Northern Headquarters of the BUF wrote to the chief constable:

> It is stated in the press that the denial to our organisation of the right of procession to a meeting is based on the fact that we wear uniforms. In order to test whether the Watch Committee is animated by a genuine objection to political uniforms or by political prejudice against Fascism, I now make application for permission for a march of our members to the meeting in everyday clothes. They will, of course, be accompanied by bands and banners, which have also been used by socialist processions through Manchester and other cities.[66]

Meanwhile, Neil Francis-Hawkins, the director-general of the BUF, said, "The British Union has decided to call the bluff of the Watch Committee. If they ban the march in plain clothes they are refusing the fascists exactly the same rights that they have accorded to the Socialists, and thereby will clearly be convicted of political prejudice."[67] To a certain extent, the rally was a test, but it was not a test of the Watch Committee's impartiality; it was a test of the practicality of legislation for prohibiting political uniforms and for regulating public processions.

The march proceeded peacefully. Most people, it seemed, were not even aware of the Blackshirts' identity. At Albert Croft Park, however, about two thousand anti-Fascists were already assembled with their own loudspeakers in place. Mosley's speech was uneventful and contained the usual attacks on the Jews as an "alien mob." Near the end of his speech, a number of scuffles broke out, and stones were thrown at Mosley. Mosley later criticized the Manchester police for allowing this to happen and pledged that BUF photographs would show Red violence in the midst of police protection. A few more stones were thrown as the Blackshirts left the park, but a heavy rainstorm helped the police prevent further disturbances. In all, eight men were reported arrested.[68]

The night after the meeting, Mosley issued a statement saying that the meeting had proved that the BUF could carry on their propaganda and that the Communist opposition would be the same whether or not they wore uniforms. He insisted that the Red opposition created more of a disturbance than had the recent Victoria Park rally when "the Blackshirts were in uniform and 100,000 people assembled."

These Reds, Mosley maintained, had also caused more disorder than the recent rally at Finsbury Park, where there had been uniformed Blackshirts and a crowd of 50,000. "In fact," wrote Mosley,

> . . . the experiences show that the attempt of our opponents, Conservatives and Socialists alike, to excuse Red violence by our wearing of the Blackshirt uniform, is sheer hypocrisy. Today's experience also shows that even if they deprive us of the propaganda value of the black shirt in their effort to arrest our progress, we can carry on exactly the same and still draw great audiences to hear our case.[69]

Not everyone agreed that the test had failed. On 27 July, Commander Locker-Lampson asked the Home Secretary if he were aware that the Manchester Town Council, in refusing Fascists the right to march in uniform, had been able to decide the meaning of *uniform*. He asked Simon if he would take steps to prevent the use of uniforms as defined by that decision. Simon answered that no real attempt had been made to define what constituted a uniform, but indicated that the Government was still looking into the matter.[70]

While the Government procrastinated over the question of political uniforms, events in Spain rapidly divided the British public into two distinct camps. Within weeks of the beginning of the war, it became obvious that Italy and Germany were aiding Franco. When the Republican side attempted to buy arms from Britain and France, however, they were blocked by the policy of nonintervention. With the growth of the Spanish Communist party, the Soviet Union began to supply arms for the Republican cause. In Britain, the CPGB did their best to project the struggle as one between fascism and the rest of the world. Some elements saw Franco as a patriot defending law, order, and Christianity from the evils of communism, but a much larger section saw him as a representative of Hitler and Mussolini. Public-opinion polls showed that support for Franco ranged between 7 and 14 percent, while support for the Republicans ranged from 57 to 72 percent.[71] Clearly it was not only the radical Left who made up this majority, but a vast collection of working class, middle class, and professional people. The Labour party and the Liberal party strongly backed the Republicans, but so did a significant number of Conservatives. To these people, the National Government, by taking a nonintervention stand, was clearly aiding the Fascists.

The passions aroused over the Republican cause resulted in a tremendous outpouring of sympathy and relief. Food, money, medical supplies, and soap were collected all over Britain. New heroes began to emerge, such as Potato Jones, who ran a Franco blockade with food for Republican Spain. Funds were set up in amost every community, and two thousand British volunteers went to fight against fascism.[72] The war in Ethiopia and the remilitarization of the Rhineland in March 1936 had caused deep mistrust of Mussolini and Hitler, but it was the Spanish civil war that heated the passions of the nation. In its reaction to this event more than any other, the National Government seemed to inculpate themselves of the CPGB charges of profascism. Spain provided the kindling in the East End; Mosley provided the spark.

The international events of the summer of 1936 also affected attitudes concerning public order and political uniforms. Harry Pollitt declared tht the National Government and the BUF were "fellow travelers on the road to Fascism." He argued that the Government would not consider the disbanding of Mosley's organization but would restrict the right of public meeting and demonstration. "In short," he said, "it proposes to follow up toleration of Fascist provocation by introducing Fascist legislation."[73]

From the Government's standpoint, the banning of fascism might have international repercussions. At a 29 July meeting of the Cabinet, Sir John Simon and Foreign Secretary Anthony Eden presented a joint memorandum proposing that "informal and friendly suggestions" should be made to the German and Italian governments through their London embassies that they should take steps to secure the closing down of branches of the National Socialist and Fascist parties in Britain, the presence of which was considered "unusual and undesirable here." But the rest of the Cabinet felt that at a time when the Government was trying to establish contacts with these governments, such action was inopportune. Furthermore, the question was raised whether the banning or Fascist fronts would not also lead to a clamor for the banning of the CPGB. In fact, some were even ready to do this. Ramsay MacDonald, now Lord President of the Council, called for a "close study" of the Communist situation. In the end, Baldwin instructed Simon and Eden to bring up the question at a more opportune time.[74] Eden's and Simon's proposed action would not directly have affected the BUF, which was, of course, independent of Italy and Germany. It showed, however, that there was growing sentiment in the Cabinet to do something about the whole problem of fascism in Britain.

The next day, a question in the House concerning the intimidation of Jewish shopkeepers brought forth another call for the banning of political uniforms. This time Simon was content to say that the commissioner of the Metropolitan Police had informed him that "the police are paying special attention to this matter."[75]

Game was not offering empty assurances. On 3 August, Sir Philip issued a long confidential memorandum on the East End situation to members of the force. It explicitly followed the recommendations sent by the Home Secretary the previous month. The first seven points recommended by Simon were especially dealt with, together with an appeal that

> . . . while it is not possible to lay down specifically at what stage the police should intervene if a speaker begins to indulge in offensive remarks, the Commissioner wishes all Police Officers to err on the side of action rather than inaction. . . . The Commissioner looks to all ranks of the Metropolitan Police to give him their utmost assistance in this matter and to use every endeavour to suppress the growing mischief of assaulting or abusing a particular section of the community and to prevent any tendency for it to develop into serious trouble.[76]

Point eight of Simon's recommendations was a monthly report to the Home Office. The first such report was sent 9 September. Game reported that the number of arrests arising from quarrels between Fascists and anti-Fascists during the month of August totaled eighteen Fascists and thirty-five anti-Fascists, compared to twenty Fascists and nine anti-Fascists in July. The average number of arrests per month from 1 January to 30 June 1936 was six Fascists and ten anti-Fascists. The rise in the total of arrests among anti-Fascists, however, gave warning of the increased tension in the East End. Game reported to Simon that information had been received that one influential section of the BUF was opposed to Mosley's efforts to tone down Jew baiting as a retreat detrimental to party prestige, morale, and discipline. "In the absence of Sir Oswald Mosley," wrote Game, "this section has evolved a plan for deliberately courting prosecution by the delivery of a carefully prepared anti-semitic speech by one of the party leaders at a large rally, possibly that to be held on October 4th."[77]

A week later, F. A. Newson of the Home Office sent a memorandum to Game saying that Simon had called his report "an admirable report for which I am most grateful to Sir Philip Game. There is no doubt that the latest police arrangements are having a very good effect."[78]

The police arrangements only had a good effect as long as there was little challenge to them. The anticipated split in the BUF was delayed a few months as something like a state of civil war came near to breaking out in the East End. Previous police contingency plans were inadequate to this challenge. At last, the events of 4 October 1936 jarred the Government into proposing strong legislation on public order.

Chapter 9

4 October 1936—Catalyst for Legislative Action

East End disturbances were becoming ever more frequent and violent in early autumn 1936. It seemed doubtful, however, that the National Government would take definite legislative action without a major public disturbance on a scale at least as great as the Olympia Hall demonstration of 1934. Until the upheaval of 4 October, the National Government and the Metropolitan Police firmly believed that they could control the forces building in the East End. The Battle of Cable Street drew public attention to those forces and to the inadequacy of existing legislation for controlling them. The product was the Public Order Act.

The commissioner's report to the Home Secretary for September showed an increase over August of eighty-two Fascist and anti-Fascist meetings in London, sixty-five of them in the East End. The total number of arrests was down slightly, to only thirty-two, of which ten were Fascist, ten were Communist, eight were anti-Fascist, and four were "other." Game also reported that there had been organized opposition at 33 percent of the Fascist meetings, and on three occasions it was necessary for the police to close the meetings. According to Game, timely intervention by the police prevented disorder in several other cases. Less than 5 percent of the anti-Fascist meetings encountered opposition from the Fascists.[1] The report did not actually reach Simon until after the 4 October disturbance, but the Home Department was no doubt aware of this increased activity.

A week before the march through the East End, Mosley held a big rally in Leeds that was a prophetic preface to Cable Street. The Leeds Watch Committee had been urged to take the same steps that the Manchester Watch Committee had taken in July. The Leeds Committee refused to ban uniforms, but in deference to the police it did order the Fascists to change their route to avoid the Jewish sections. The meeting attracted a crowd of about twenty-five thousand. The procession to it was relatively uneventful, but when the Blackshirts turned to march away they were hit by a volley of stones. Mosley, who had been hit several times and had had to duck repeatedly during his speech, charged that "catapults" had been used.[2] In all, about twenty Blackshirts were injured, one requiring hospitalization. Three anti-Fascists were charged with disorderly conduct.[3]

In London, news of the impending Blackshirt invasion brought a wave of protest and indignation from the East End. The Jewish People's Council prepared a petition, which with almost one hundred thousand signatures was sent to the Home Secretary. The petition read:

> We the undersigned citizens of London view with grave concern the proposed march of the British Union of Fascists upon East London. The avowed object of the Fascist movement is incitement to malice and hatred against sections of the population. It aims to destroy the friendship and goodwill which has existed for centuries among the East London population, irrespective of race and belief. . . . We therefore make an earnest appeal to His Majesty's Secretary of State to prohibit this march and thus retain peaceful and amicable relations between all sections of East London's population.[4]

Deputations were also sent to the mayors of Bethnal Green, Shoreditch, Stepney, and Poplar—the sites of the proposed Fascist meetings—asking them to use their influence to prevent the rallies from being held.[5] On Thursday, 1 October, a deputation of mayors from these boroughs visited the Home Office to urge that the Fascist march be banned completely or, at the very least, that the route be diverted. Headed by the mayor of Stepney, the delegation was received by the deputy under secretary, Alexander Maxwell, a career bureaucrat who had been at the Home Office for thirty years. After an interview of more than an hour, the mayors reported that the matter "was under consideration" by the Home Office. Maxwell advised the deputation not to do anything on their own.[6]

As usual, the Communist party of Great Britain took the lead in organizing a counterdemonstration against the Blackshirts. The concerted drive for a popular front had still not resulted in any formal associations, but the ILP did join the CPGB in the call for resistance to the BUF march. The Labour party and the TUC still advocated a hands-off policy. The Labour party had earlier in the year rejected yet another CPGB application for membership. In the opinion of the National Executive Committee, the victories of fascism on the Continent were in part facilitated by campaigns for "Communist dictatorships" that preceded them. Fearing that the CPGB would use the Labour party as a base for its own advantage, the committee said that such affiliation would "inevitably assist the forces of reaction, would endanger existing liberties, and would retard the achievement of socialism."[7] At the TUC Congress, Walter Citrine denounced the CPGB attempt at a common front by saying:

> After years of derision of it, after pouring out gallons of ink in denunciation of its leaders, after abuse of its leaders as pillars of capitalism, and after denouncing its attempts to capture Parliament, . . . we have the incongruous spectacle of the Communist's organisation wanting to come into our midst and be part of our Movement.[8]

It was obvious that bygones would not be bygones simply because of Mosley.

George Lansbury, while advising all anti-Fascists to stay away from the demonstration, did write a note to Simon asking that the march be diverted. This was the only official Labour action on the matter. Meanwhile, the CPGB ws turning out thousands of pamphlets to incite opposition to the Fascists. In one such pamphlet, the party borrowed a slogan from Spain and Verdun: "Fascism seeks to ban the people's way. Fascism must not pass. With your help, THEY SHALL NOT PASS."[9]

The *Daily Worker* charged that Mosley was promoting civil war in the East End and called for a protest "in scores of thousands." Conjuring up the Spanish civil war, the CPGB newspaper said:

> Remember the massacre at Badajoz and Irun, remember Olympia. Remember that Fascism means the destruction of free speech, of Trade Union, Labour, and Cooperative organisations. It means concentration camps and torture chambers. Londoners want no Hitler tortures or Franco butcheries here. Assert your rights and end Fascist hooliganism in East London.[10]

The active defense of the CPGB naturally had its effect on the Jewish citizens. Basil Henriques, a warden of an East End settlement, summed up the Jewish position:

> No self-respecting Englishman of the Jewish religion can listen to the speeches without bursting with indignation. Few realize the foulness of

> the mud being flung at us at our own doorstep. The Jew feels he must do something in self defense. The only party which is militantly attacking Fascism is the Communist. Thus, contrary to the political view of the vast majority of them, they are being so terrorized as to be forced into the ranks of Communism, thereby only intensifying anti-Semitism.[11]

Not all Jews were "forced" to become members of the Communist party, of course, but Henriques was partly correct. By joining the CPGB, Jews were playing into the hands of the BUF. It was important to fascism that the Jews be identified with communism; therefore it was important that the CPGB show itself strong in East London. Without the presence of a real or at least imagined Communist threat, the BUF could not hope to exploit it.

On the Friday night before the Blackshirt invasion, the all-night cafes of Whitechapel were filled with Communists, ex-servicemen, Greenshirts of the Social Credit party, and Jewish champions discussing plans for Mosley's arrival. Shopkeepers in the main roads were boarding up their windows. The London correspondent for the *Guardian* reported, "Tension is increasing."[12]

The Battle of Cable Street

The BUF planned to assemble in Royal Mint Street, near Tower Bridge, and march in four columns to meetings in Shoreditch, Stepney, Bethnal Green, and Limehouse. On the day of the march, red flags fluttered from buildings throughout the East End. They Shall Not Pass was chalked everywhere. Communists, the Ex-Servicemen's Movement Against Fascism, and the Jewish People's Council passed out handbills and broadsheets. The National Unemployed Workers Movement called for a human barricade. CPGB vans with loudspeakers drove throughout the district. By noon the streets were filled with crowds estimated as high as one hundred thousand.[13]

Many side streets were cordoned off by the Metropolitan Police long before the march was due to start. No one was allowed to pass unless he could satisfy the cordon officer that he had legitimate business, but somehow the streets were soon filled.[14] Councillor H. Roberts, the mayor of Stepney, said that she had never seen the crowds so thoroughly aroused and angry. "I cannot help but think," she said later, "that all this could have been avoided had the Home

Office and the Commissioner of Police done before the march what they were compelled to do during the march."[15]

Police tried to keep the mob moving. Frequently, raised truncheons were used to push back the crowd, and eventually a barricade was formed between the demonstrators and the route of the Blackshirts. Before the march began, Fenner Brockway of the ILP telephoned the Home Office in a last-minute attempt to get the authorities to intervene. "I told the Home Office," Brockway said, "that if they did not stop or at least divert the procession, this would be their responsibility. It may be serious."[16] Unknown to Brockway, the police had already decided to stop it.

In Cable Street, a crowd seized material from a builder's yard and began to throw up a barricade of their own. They overturned a lorry across the street and used corrugated iron, barrels, coal, broken glass, and upturned paving stones. The police who rushed the barricade were met with a shower of rocks and of marbles, which were thrown beneath the hooves of the horses. Reinforcements were called, and a baton charge was finally ordered. The police and the crowd clashed, with several injuries to both sides.[17]

Unaware of the street war raging in Cable Street, Mosley arrived at Royal Mint Street to the cheers of twenty-five hundred to three thousand Blackshirts. The leader wore a black military jacket, gray riding breeches, jackboots, a black peaked military hat, and red arm bands. Almost immediately after arriving, he met with Sir Philip Game and other high police officials. After a few minutes, Mosley returned to consult with his senior officers. Without much protest, the Fascists abandoned their plans for the meetings and proceeded to march westward along the Embankment.

A very dangerous situation had been avoided. But news that the march had been abandoned did not reach many parts of the East End for some time afterward, and crowds continued to battle police in Cable Street and in Aldgate. When anti-Fascists eventually heard of Mosley's retreat, they greeted the news as a great victory and marched around crying, "They did not pass." It was many hours before the police succeeded in dispersing the crowd, restoring order, and treating the injured.[18]

In a statement issued to the press the night of the confrontation, the CPGB said:

> East London workers, supported by all London in united action, have barred the road to Mosley. Gentile and Jew, Catholic and Protestant,

> Labour and Communist, men, women, and children determined that Fascism shall not pass here, have given Mosley the most humiliating defeat ever suffered by any figure in English politics. . . . Mass action of the working people have exposed the pro-Fascist attitude of the Home Office, which sought till the last possible moment to enable Mosley to march and is responsible for the baton charges and arrests made today. Fascism did not pass, Fascism shall never pass. No confidence in the National Government, but confidence in United Labour's power to act, is the great message from East London. Forward now to the United Front all over Britain.[19]

Blackshirt opinions were quite different. The official BUF statement reported how well the Blackshirts had obeyed the police, but went on to charge that this was "the first occasion on which the British Government has surrendered to Red terror." The statement concluded:

> On this occasion, Socialists, Communists, and Jews openly organised not only to attack the meetings, but to close the streets of London by violence to members of the public proceeding to their legitimate meetings.
>
> The Government has taken no action against the organisers of this violence and illegality. On the contrary, they have banned the march and meetings of the British Union. Under the present Government, therefore, free speech can be prevented by anyone who can organise violence against it, in defiance of the law but with impunity from the Government. The corruption and decadence of government could not be more clearly demonstrated. The necessity for Fascism could not be more clearly proven. When government cannot govern, the nation soon sends for those who can. We look forward with confidence to the verdict of the people.[20]

The Battle of Cable Street provided the subject for much of the folklore of both the Communists and Fascists. A BUF pamphlet was soon circulated with vivid descriptions of how the Communists had attacked the police.[21] The next issue of the *Blackshirt* claimed, "The Union Jack was officially handed over to Whitechapel by the Government of Great Britain. And Simon, poor Simple Simon, has proved once and for all that the Government is too weak to govern."[22] The BUF also blamed the police, but asserted that they had "no doubt been circumscribed and hampered by such instructions as they received from higher authorities."[23] They also blamed the violence on the "Socialist, Communist and Jewish elements, who did not scruple to import into peaceful East London thousands, if not tens of thousands, of the dregs of the industrial cities."[24]

On the night of the disturbance, Scotland Yard issued the following official statement:

> A fascist assembly was held in the East End today, and largely owing to one of the finest days of the year, many people were attracted to it including a large number of women and children.
>
> Prior to the arrival of Sir Oswald Mosley, a disorder broke out among those who had collected to oppose the fascist marchers and resulted in a number of arrests.
>
> In view of the very large crowds, the Commissioner of Police for the Metropolis decided that the procession through the East End should not be permitted owing to the great likelihood of further breaches of the peace.
>
> The fascist procession, therefore, was escorted by the police along the Embankment to the Temple station, where it was dispersed. A portion of it reformed and caused minor disorders in Trafalgar Square and the Strand.[25]

According to a report in the *Times*, Sir Philip's decision to stop the procession had the full backing of the Home Office. The Home Office had decided to give Game the entire responsibility for making such a decision after the deputation of mayors had met with Sir Alexander Maxwell.[26] In his annual report, Game stated that there was "little doubt that serious rioting and bloodshed would have occurred had the march been allowed to take place."[27]

The Aftermath of 4 October

If the Battle of Cable Street had occurred within a few weeks of Olympia, there would have been a greater sense of alarm. The violence had been real to the participants in the disorder, but others tended to scoff at the incidents. In both the editorial and the report from its London correspondent, the *Guardian* refused to take the matter seriously. The leader, referring to Mosley's charge that the "British Government had openly surrendered to Red terror," said, "Whatever our Fascists borrow from abroad, they have not lost the British sense of humour."[28] To the police, who were forced to detail hundreds of additional men into the East End, there was nothing humorous about it. Furthermore, there was evidence that the disorder would continue.

A police memorandum, working up from a junior inspector to Division H Inspector Lloyd Williams, reported on the actions of the

Jewish Ex-Servicemen's Movement. At each stop on its way up the police chain of command, the memorandum was changed to recommend more police to hold in check the "victory march" of the anti-Fascists.[29] A later memorandum indicated that the BUF strength had not been broken either. The Special Branch reported to Sir Philip Game on 1 November, "Efforts of the Communist Party to consolidate the 'tremendous victory over Fascism' met with very poor response, and in general anti-fascist meetings have been attended by smaller audiences than in previous months, while the speaker's utterances thereat have on several occasions been received with apathy and even derision." On the other hand, the Special Branch reported, "There is abundant evidence that the Fascist movement has been steadily gaining ground in many parts of East London and has strong support in such districts as Stepney, Shoreditch, Bethnal Green, Hackney, and Bow."[30]

The Special Branch estimated the 4 October crowd at about one hundred thousand, "undoubtedly the largest anti-Fascist demonstration yet seen in London." The BUF had asserted that the protesters were imported, but the official report stated that of the eighty-three arrested, only one had given an address outside London. The report noted the treatment of seventy persons for injuries and acknowledged considerable damage to property.[31]

In a letter to Geoffrey Lloyd of the Home Office, Sir Philip Game said that apart from the special arrangements on 4 October and again on 11 October, the average number of police supplied daily from other divisions to the East End had been 291. The cost of transportation in getting the police there and back was listed as over five hundred pounds. On 4 October, over thirty-five hundred additional police were drafted into the East End at a transportation cost of 150 pounds, and on 11 October, two thousand police were drafted at a cost of 135 pounds. "All the time, of course," wrote Game, "the major portion of the man power of the local division has been employed in connection with 'Jew baiting.' "[32]

Three days after Cable Street, the Manchester City Council gave permission to the BUF to hold a demonstration at St. George's Park in Hulme, but only after deciding that no uniforms could be worn. Alderman S. Woolham said, "If people would just keep away, the Fascists would cease to exist in six months."[33] This was perhaps wishful thinking, though. In London the people were not keeping away. On 9 October, a BUF meeting at the Hammersmith Town

Hall was interrupted several times by protesters, while a large ILP and Communist anti-Fascist meeting was held a short distance away. Several hundred people blocked the streets, and mounted police were called in to restore order.[34]

On the Sunday following the Battle of Cable Street, a crowd of ten thousand marchers joined a CPGB procession out of Victoria Park. At one point, about one hundred police charged the crowd in Whitechapel, where a fight had broken out. Nine arrests were made. While this was going on, about one hundred fifty youths raided several Jewish shops in Mile End Road.

Mosley, meanwhile, was in Liverpool, where hostile crowds filled the streets as the Blackshirts marched to their meeting. There were demonstrations along the whole route of the procession, but serious disturbances were avoided except at two points where the police made truncheon charges. A dozen arrests were made and three people were treated for injuries. The three hundred Blackshirts who marched were led by forty to fifty policemen who "cleared the way with quick rushes."[35] The arrests were mainly for disorderly conduct, but one man was arrested for wielding a sword; he said he was there to fight Mosley because "this man is trying to make my town and city another Hitler and Spain."[36]

Elsewhere in Britain that Sunday, a Fascist speaker at Bedford was knocked off his stand three times and police had to disperse the crowd. At the Mound in Edinburgh, ten thousand people attended an open-air Fascist rally, but few heard the speaker because of constant interruption from demonstrators. Several scuffles broke out in Tunbridge Wells in Kent as several thousand protesters blocked a Fascist march. Fascist attempts at making speeches were met with a shower of rotten eggs, rotten tomatoes, and various wilted vegetables.[37]

By now the public was no longer laughing. The *Guardian,* for instance, wrote that there "was being created a highly dangerous atmosphere of terrorism and violence that can only lead to counter-violence." The paper advocated using existing legal means "if the Government is determined enough. The Fascists can be rendered harmless if we keep our heads and are not afraid to curb their un-English manifestations."[38]

On 14 October, Mosley returned to the East End in force. He addressed two separate crowds, each numbering about four thousand. This time there was no disorder, thanks to hundreds of police who kept the Fascist meeting from being overrun by a Communist meeting a short distance away. In his speech, Mosley was as outspoken as ever about the Jews. According to the report in the *Guardian,* one of the most noteworthy things was "the evidence of more East End support for Fascism than one had expected."[39]

The Special Branch also reported that Mosley's meetings grew in size and were orderly. A report to the commissioner concluded, "Briefly, a definite pro-Fascist feeling had manifested itself throughout the districts mentioned since the events of October 4th and the alleged Fascist defeat is really a Fascist advance. It is reliably reported that the London membership has increased by over 2,000."[40] On 17 October, the BBC reported, "Sir Oswald Mosley expressed his satisfaction with the progress of Fascism in Great Britain, and stated that the Fascists have reached the culminating point of the first stage of the development of the movement in this country."[41]

The commissioner's report to the Home Secretary for the month of October was not very sanguine. Game informed Simon that 151 arrests had been made during the month. Of these, 16 were Fascist, 90 anti-Fascist, 11 Communist, 10 Jews, and 24 "others." A total of 83 of the anti-Fascists and 5 of the Fascists had been arrested on 4 October. Of the 151 total, 111 arrests had been made at Fascist meetings, while 22 arrests were made at anti-Fascist meetings. The remaining arrests occurred on an individual basis.[42]

The potential for violence in the East End was certainly not dispersed when Game stopped the 4 October march. The atmosphere remained tense and explosive when Parliament reassembled to hear the King's speech on 3 November. According to official Metropolitan Police records, 7,440 special constabulary had been added to the regular force in the period from 11 October to 3 November.[43] Although the M.P.s who gathered at Westminster in November differed as to the best form for the proposed public order bill, few differed as to its need.

Chapter 10

The Public Order Act

When the public order bill was presented in the House of Commons for its second reading, Sir Percy Harris, M.P. for Bethnal Green and the chief whip of the Liberal party, said, "No one can say that in the action we are taking here we are showing undue haste. We have been slow to take action and we have done so only when the necessity was proved."[1] The necessity had been proved at Cable Street. Almost two-and-a-half years after the violence at Olympia had shown the threat to the order of the realm, the National Government took legislative action.

Instead of asserting leadership, the Government had allowed the situation to develop to the point where disturbances like those of 4 October were not only possible but probable. Thus, the Government was forced to follow a public demand for action. Two days after the events in the East End, the *Guardian* reported that there was general agreement among both critics and defenders of Sir John Simon that the time had come for the Government to deal with the anti-Semitic activities of the British Union of Fascists.[2]

The BUF also knew that its activities would soon be curtailed. In the *Fascist Quarterly*'s leader for October, the Fascists proclaimed, "The struggle of British freedom is arising. The question is whether Englishmen shall be allowed to plead their country's cause on their own streets, or whether they are to be silenced by an oriental army of occupation."[3]

Preparations for the Public Order Act

Parliament was in recess, and no official action was likely until after Parliament met. While the Cabinet secretly discussed the bill, a number of persons publicly called for action. Particularly vocal were those in the Labour party. Joseph Toole, lord mayor–elect of Manchester, criticized the Government's lack of action, saying that if Mosley had been a poor man, a trade unionist, or a Communist, instead of a "wealthy titled aristocrat," the disorders would not have arisen because his semimilitary organization would have been suppressed long before. He warned, "Sir John Simon and the Government ought to realize that if a second army is tolerated in this country there is no reason whatever why a third army should not exist." Toole reflected on the wisdom shown by the Manchester Watch Committee in allowing a Blackshirt procession without uniforms. "The effect upon the political education of the citizens of Manchester was electric," he said, "and this, combined with the fact that we carefully planned a route which avoided the largest Jewish community in our city, did, I think, go a long way towards securing the obvious results that all democrats are anxious to obtain."[4]

The annual congress of the Labour party opened the day after the disturbances in the East End. This provided it with a unique political opportunity, and the most was made of it. Herbert Morrison, representing the National Executive, moved a resolution:

> This Conference views with grave concern the tragic and deplorable events of yesterday in the East End of London; condemns the Government's unwillingness to ban the Fascist march, in spite of the obvious danger of a breach of the public peace; condemns the provocative tactics of the Fascists; and records its view that whilst freedom of speech must be preserved, the encouragement of civil disorder, racial strife, and parade of force and militarized politics, and the use of political uniforms should be forbidden.[5]

In moving the resolution, Morrison said that he had no more sympathy with the Communists or the ILP, which sponsored the counterdemonstration, than he had with the Fascists. "It will be a bad thing for East London," he continued, "and a bad thing for the country, if that interesting part of the world becomes a cockpit of organized battle between Fascists on the one hand and Communists on the other." Joseph Toole seconded the motion, citing the Fascist disturbances in Manchester. The National Executive strongly criticized Simon's failure to act earlier, a failure that Morrison called "weak and cowardly."[6]

Addressing his constituents at Cleckheaton, Simon answered

some of the charges made by the Labour party. He said that the Home Office had specifically warned Mosley that, if circumstances called for it, they would require the meeting to be held elsewhere or abandoned. The Home Secretary protested that he had no power under law to ban any meeting in advance. He also pointed out that the right to hold political meetings was a fundamental part of the liberty of the subject, warning that if this right were denied, "there would be an end of free speech and no unpopular cause would ever gain a hearing."[7]

The Labour party spokesmen were not soothed by Simon's assurances. Herbert Morrison said he feared that the East End would become the battleground of organized fascism and communism and appealed to Simon to "get the situation in hand before it is too late."[8]

In the highest councils of the National Government, Ramsay MacDonald advocated measures to prevent "deliberate planning to create disorder under the cloak of freedom of speech." He considered matters to be reaching a "serious condition" when "a crowd of uniformed people thought it a splendid thing to insult the Jews."[9] Meanwhile, Baldwin was receiving scores of letters and telegrams, including one from Mrs. H. Roberts, the mayor of Stepney, who demanded, "What do you propose to do to prevent a repetition of . . . last Sunday's disorder?"[10]

By 14 October, as the Cabinet met for the first time since July, there were renewed cries for increased protection in the East End. In Stepney, there was sentiment for a special brigade of volunteers enrolled as special constables to help the police keep order. The BUF, meanwhile, insisted that it meant to continue its East End campaign for the London County Council elections, scheduled for March 1937. In the aftermath of the disorders, however, a number of their meetings had been canceled, frequently because their lease had been rescinded on the meeting hall.[11]

In the Cabinet meeting, the Home Secretary submitted a report he had compiled two days earlier. He asked that the Cabinet give prompt consideration to the problems presented by the events of 4 October. It was his opinion that some sort of legislation was needed and that it would be very difficult to meet the substantial demand for it by standing pat. The Home Secretary added, "There cannot be the slightest doubt that the Fascist campaign . . . is stimulating the Communist movement so that the danger of a serious clash is growing. I have information from Government supporters in East London that the Jewish element is tending to throw itself into the arms of the opposition and the strain on the Metropolitan Police (large numbers of whom Sunday after Sunday have to dispense with their customary leave) is deplorable." He said that the police maintained their "invariable steadiness and impartiality" and pointed to the fact that a large Jewish delegation had voluntarily reported that allegations of bias made against the Metropolitan Police were unfounded.[12]

Simon's proposals for legislation were presented with the understanding that no new powers should be conferred upon the Home Secretary. He pointed out that express statutory powers placed in the hands of the Home Secretary might induce Parliamentary challenge on every occasion and, furthermore, "if a Government of the strong party complexion came into office hereafter, such powers might be used in partisan fashion." He also suggested that any new legislation should not be directed against a particular organization but should apply generally wherever the conditions named in the legislation were found.

Simon thought, therefore, that if laws were to be passed regulating political uniforms, it would also be necessary to consider some action regulating processions. "Otherwise," he said, "the proposals might have the aim of being directed against the Fascists only, while the rowdyism and disorder created by the political opponents of Fascism remain untouched."[13] It was obvious from the start, then, that the National Government meant to use the violence in the East End as an excuse to act against the extreme Left as well as the Fascists. The tradition of repression of leftist elements that had continued through the Incitement to Disaffection Act was about to be extended.

Simon placed his memorandum before the Cabinet to demonstrate the desirability of strengthening existing laws "in order to insure the preservation of public order." The memorandum expressly stated that the necessity arose from the East End disturbances as well as Fascist incidents in Leeds, Manchester, Liverpool, and other provincial cities. It proposed that a small ministerial committee consider whether any legislative proposal should be put forward by the Government and that any such legislation be announced in the Speech from the Throne.

The Cabinet supported Simon's suggestions, expressing the view that if the Government were to make it clear that they would not allow minorities to be attacked or public order disturbed, the bill would be supported by a large part of the population. The Cabinet also recognized that "the usual criticisms would be encountered as to the danger of interfering with the liberties of the people," but argued that it was necessary because "some sections of the population insisted on abusing their liberties." A ten-member committee was directed to meet at once to consider Simon's proposals.[14]

After the meeting, two ministers, Thomas Inskip, now Minister for the Co-ordination of Defense, and Duff Cooper, Minister for War, hinted to the press that proposals for legislation to assure public order were to be forthcoming. Inskip said, "I hope that we shall find measures—if measures be necessary—to curb these disturbances without in any way restricting the liberties which you and I cherish." Cooper said, "Steps must be taken to see that order—the greatest gift a Government can give—is observed in England."[15]

Two days later, Herbert Morrison, on behalf of a special Labour party conference, urged the Home Secretary to deal with the prohibition of uniforms, the control of street processions, and the better recording of speeches at Fascist meetings. Morrison concluded, "We feel bound to warn the Government that unless rapid and decisive action is taken a situation may evolve which will make futile every desire to promote harmony in the social and economic life of East London."[16]

Simon met with a special Labour party deputation on 20 October at the Home Office. The deputation urged on the Government the gravity of the situation in the East End and the risks of its becoming worse unless immediate action were taken. Simon offered assurances that the Government was giving "immediate and careful consideration to the problems involved," but reminded the group that he was not in a position "to anticipate the announcement to Parliament of the Government's intention." The Labour leaders said they were "satisfied."[17]

At the next Cabinet meeting, on 21 October 1936, Simon asked the members to add the public order bill to their list of priority bills for the new session. He said that although the bill was not yet drafted, all within the committee agreed that legislation would be necessary with respect to the "difficult matter of uniforms, military organisation for political purposes, and the control of processions."[18]

Five days later, the Committee on the Preservation of Public

Order presented its report to the Cabinet. The committee had gone through several drafts of proposed clauses and reached a provisional agreement about what these clauses should contain. There had been general acceptance of most of the provisions, but the one involving processions was more difficult. The majority, however, felt it necessary to include a clause on this subject, believing that amendments for dealing with processions were sure to be pressed from various quarters in the House of Commons.[19]

On 3 November, the day of the King's speech to Parliament, the proposals for a public order act were further considered by a Cabinet subcommittee, and the draft bill was prepared for approval by the Cabinet. The report of the subcommittee called clause 2, which dealt with private armies, the "kernel of the Bill." Simon hoped that this clause, which would cause great anxiety among civil libertarians, would be

> . . . universally accepted, since everyone dislikes the introduction of foreign methods into the politics of this country, and since the formation of one private army invariably leads to the formation of other forces. Indeed, evidence is not lacking that the existence of the quasi-military Fascist organization is already causing certain of the political opponents of Fascism to band themselves into an organisation for the purpose of countering Fascism by force.[20]

Simon concluded his report by saying that the object of the committee had been to propose only such changes in the law "as might appear to be called for by the present situation without any unnecessary interference with the liberties of the subject." In his opinion, the bill held the balance "as evenly as possible between the rival factions of Fascism and Communism," and according to his interviews with the Opposition, he was convinced that the bill would be "openly supported" by the other side of the House.[21]

The next day he presented the draft bill to the Cabinet and reported that his inquiries as to the attitudes of the parliamentary Opposition had produced a "highly satisfactory result." The Cabinet agreed to approve the bill in principle and to authorize the Home Secretary to proceed with it as soon as possible.[22]

On the last day of the old parliamentary session, Vyvyan Adams, a Conservative barrister and author, chairman of the British Commonwealth Peace Society, and an M.P. for West Leeds, asked Geoffrey Lloyd about the progress made in the "stamping down of anti-Jewish manifestations" and if his department would take legislative authority to ban all uniforms. Lloyd replied that according to the commissioner of police there had been a reduction of "the grosser forms" of anti-Semitism in the East End, but that the Fascists were continuing their policy of Jew baiting through "innuendo and veiled abuse." Regarding the second part of the question, Lloyd said he could not "anticipate the statement of the legislative programme."[23]

Introduction of the Public Order Bill

The publication of the public order bill was received with wide public approval. The same people who had so vociferously attacked the incitement to disaffection bill now acclaimed the public order bill. Several parts would come under attack in committee and before the second and third readings, but there was initially a reserved acceptance of it in Parliament.

In the Speech from the Throne on 3 November, six days before the bill was published, King Edward said:

> My ministers have come to the conclusion that the existing law requires amendment in order to deal more effectively with persons or organisations who provoke or cause disturbances of the public peace. A bill for strengthening the law without interfering with legitimate freedom of speech or assembly will be submitted to you.[24]

During discussion of the King's speech, Stanley Baldwin said, "If ever there was a Bill which in my view it is the duty of the whole House to attempt to shape, it is [the public order bill], because its substance touches every one of us whatever our political views may be." He regarded it as a "matter of great importance and urgency."[25] Later in the discussion, Hugh Dalton expressed the hope that the Government would stamp out the Fascist movement in Britain. Dalton had helped lead the fight for the 1935 Labour party resolution calling for sanctions against Italy, and his efforts in getting the Labour party to abandon pacifism would earn him a position as Secretary of Economic Warfare in Churchill's War Cabinet. Referring to Mosley, Dalton said, "It is time that the Government put its thumb not on all the petty little followers, the people who march around in their black shirts, but the Government should put their thumb on the Fuhrer, the Duce, himself." He called for the Government to tell the members where Mosley got his money.[26] A few days later, Simon, while not giving specific figures, said, "Both in the case of Fascist and Communist organizations, their funds have been supplemented from abroad."[27]

Willie Gallacher, the Communist M.P., was still interested in the events of 4 October. He asked Baldwin whether he would allot a day for discussing Simon's refusal to ban the Fascist march in advance and whether the Government would order "immediate disbanding" of the BUF. Baldwin replied simply, "No, Sir."[28]

At this time, no one outside the Cabinet had yet seen the actual text of the bill. Both Fascists and anti-Fascists were actively speculating on its contents. The Jewish People's Council was organizing to promote two legislative items: the first would have made it an offense to say or write "any words calculated to bring any racial community into public hatred or contempt"; the second dealt with the wearing of political uniforms. J. W. Bently, chairman of the council, said that although there was already sufficient legislation to prevent occurrences such as the Battle of Cable Street, "the Government is not working with strong enough determination to see that these disorders are brought to an end, and in order to avoid any possible misunderstanding, we are proposing these acts."[29]

The BUF was not idly waiting for the law that threatened to cripple it. On 1 November, Mosley addressed three thousand Blackshirts at Blackburn and announced plans to contest the next general election. He said that the first one hundred candidates would be revealed shortly. In regard to the imminent legislation on uniforms, Mosley countered that it was not the clothes "that made the cause—it was the spirit of the movement which created it."[30]

At a meeting in Manchester's Free Trade Hall, Mosley charged that the National Government could have stopped Communist disorders by existing laws. He said the reason that the National Government did not use them, but instead sought fresh powers to use against the BUF, was that "the Conservative and National Government today has sunk so low that it is ready to use even Socialist and Communist violence, and connive at it in order to check, if they can, the progress of a movement which they fear most as a challenge to their corruption."[31]

Shortly before the public order bill was introduced, the *Guardian* expressed the view of many:

> It would seem that the less drastic the Bill is, the better. The Fascist menace is not so bad that we need to make fundamental changes in the law, although we must certainly make it more quickly responsive.[32]

On 9 November 1936, the public order bill was introduced in Parliament. Presented by Sir John Simon, supported by Ramsay MacDonald, Minister of Health Sir Kingsley Wood, Attorney-General Somervell, and Under-Secretary Geoffrey Lloyd, it was designated as a bill to

> . . . prohibit the wearing of uniforms in connection with political objects and the maintenance by private persons of associations of military or similar character; and to make further provision for the preservation of public order on the occasion of public processions and meetings and in public places.[33]

There were three main objectives in the bill—the prohibition of uniforms, the prohibition of paramilitary organizations, and the control and regulation of public processions and assemblies. There were precedents for some of the proposals, but the bill strengthened existing laws and more closely defined offenses. Concerning political uniforms, the new bill said:

> Subject as hereafter provided, any person who in any public place or at any public meeting wears [a] uniform signifying association with any political organisation or with the promotion of any political object shall be guilty of an offence.[34]

This provision, frequently demanded during the preceding two-and-one-half years, met little opposition. But there were doubts in some quarters—the National Council for Civil Liberties among them—about a further provision, which allowed the chief of police to permit the wearing of such uniforms on "any ceremonial, anniversary, or other occasion [which would not] be likely to involve risk of public disorder." The NCCL held that on "all occasions the wearing of political uniforms is provocative" and considered the provisions to be leaving a "dangerous power of discrimination in the hands of the executive."[35]

This provision had its counterparts in the laws already passed in other countries of Europe, such as Norway, Finland, Denmark, Switzerland, Holland, and Sweden. The Swedish law read:

> His Majesty, the King, may, when it is thought necessary for the safeguarding of order and security, prohibit the wearing of uniforms and similar articles of clothing used to indicate the wearer's political opinions. Such prohibition shall also apply to any part of a uniform, armlets, or similar decorative marks.[36]

The British bill left all definitions of what constituted a political uniform to the courts on the general principle that while the courts might not be able to define a political uniform, they would know one when they saw one. Protection against unwarranted prosecution under this portion of the act was provided by a provision making prosecutions the responsibility of the Attorney-General.

The prohibition of paramilitary organizations was in clause 2. Persons were guilty of an offense if they were members or adherents of any organization

> . . . (a) organised or trained or equipped for the purpose of enabling them to be employed in usurping the functions of the police or of the armed forces of the Crown; or (b) organised and trained or organised and equipped either for the purpose of enabling them to be employed for the use or display of physical force in promoting any political object, or in such manner as to arouse reasonable apprehension that they are organised and either trained or equipped for that purpose.[37]

There were precedents. In the reign of Henry VII, Chief Justice Fineux had ruled on the legality of such a private army. He was quoted in the 1506 Yearbook:

> If one has been threatened that if he comes to such a market, or into such a place, he will be beaten there, in that case he may not make an assembly of men to assist him, to go there in safeguard of his person, because he needeth not to go there, and he may have remedy by surety of the peace.[38]

In 1819, soon after the "gagging bills" and the Peterloo Massacre, the Six Acts had prohibited unauthorized drilling. Parts of the acts had been repealed, but the prohibition of drilling remained on the statute book.[39]

In general, clause 2, section 1 was well received. There was, however, some objection to the second part of it, which defined quasi-military organizations. The NCCL, for instance, was concerned that the provision against organizations trained or equipped "for the use or display of physical force" could be used to prohibit a mass demonstration or peaceful picketing. Small amendments would have made this acceptable to the Opposition. The same was true of section 2, which required that all prosecution had to be instituted by the Attorney-General; of section 3, which concerned the dismantling of paramilitary organizations and the confiscation of their funds; and of section 5, which provided for a right of search similar to that in the Incitement to Disaffection Act.[40]

It was section 4 of clause 2 that caused the greatest amount of protest. This made acts or statements of any apparent adherent of an organization admissible in evidence for the prosecution of its leaders. It would enable the prosecution to give evidence taken from agents provocateurs who had no connection with the organization, thus reversing the old principle of English law that a man was only responsible for his own acts.

The third major objective of the bill was dealt with in clauses 3, 4, 5, and 6, which concerned the control of public meetings and processions. There were already a number of judicial decisions involving the restricting of assemblies. In 1695, a gathering of people and coaches around a new playhouse in Lincoln's Inn Fields was held to be a nuisance and was prohibited in *Betterton's Case*. In 1834, a Fleet Street bookseller, angry at the actions of church authorities insisting upon their rates, exhibited in his window an effigy of a bishop walking arm in arm with the devil. In *R.* v. *Carlisle,* his exhibition was prohibited for obstructing the thoroughfare by attracting an unseemly and disrespectful crowd. Regarding the holding of public meetings on highways, it had been ruled in 1795, in *Dovaston* v. *Payne,* that highways were not only dedicated to the public use, but that they had to be used primarily for passage.[41]

These decisions, however, affected only the control of meetings once they had started. Except when local regulations were involved, a meeting assembled for a lawful object could not be prohibited in advance. This was part of the fundamental principle of English law that a subject's liberty could not be infringed upon unless he had committed or was about to commit an illegal act. A meeting could not become unlawful until its participants had assembled, and even then, if turbulence was the cause of the complaint, the authorities had to consider the delicate question of whether the turbulence was directly caused by the meeting or by the independent wrongdoing of its opponents. It was not an easy question for the police to determine, especially since if they acted wrongly, they did so at the peril of legal action against themselves.

Meetings within London were governed by the Metropolitan Police Act of 1839, which gave the commissioner of police the power to make regulations, as the occasion required, for the route to be observed by all carts, carriages, horses, and persons. It also gave him power to prevent obstructions of the streets and thoroughfares within the metropolis.[42] It was this power that Sir Philip Game had used on 4 October 1936 to divert the Fascist march and prevent the BUF meetings.

A magistrate could bind over a person convicted of disorderly conduct under the 1839 act, but it was thought that the maximum penalty of forty shillings was now inadequate, particularly in the case of a person who had a vast organization behind him and who may have made speeches deliberately for the purpose of insulting a certain section of the population. Under the Public Order Act, clause 7, the penalty for conviction was raised to a maximum of three months imprisonment or a fifty-pound fine.[43] Other inadequacies in the 1839 act were that it did not apply to a public meeting held on private grounds and that it applied only to London. Under the Public Order Act, clause 5, the law was extended to the entire country, and any person in any public place or meeting who used threatening, abusive, or insulting words or behavior with intent to provoke a breach of the peace could be charged with an offense.[44]

Clause 4 of the public order bill was accepted without dissent. It stated, "Any person who, while present at any public meeting or on the occasion of any public procession, has with him any offensive weapon, otherwise than in pursuance of lawful authority, shall be guilty of an offence."[45]

Clause 3 and clause 6 caused the greatest concern on the Left. Clause 6 amended the Public Meetings Act of 1908 to give it enforcement machinery. The 1908 act stated:

> Any person who at a lawful meeting acts in a disorderly manner for the purpose of preventing the transaction of business for which the meeting is called together shall be guilty of an offence, and if the offence is committed at a political meeting held in any parliamentary constituency between the date of the issue of a writ for the return of a member of Parliament for such a constituency and the date at which a return to such writ is made; he shall be guilty of an illegal practice within the meaning of the Corrupt and Illegal Practices Prevention Act, 1883, and in any other case shall on summary conviction be liable to a fine not exceeding five pounds, or to imprisonment not exceeding one month. (2) Any person who incites others to commit an offence under this section shall be guilty of a like offence.[46]

A number of cases had been tried on this provision. In 1911, in *Burden* v. *Rigler,* it had been ruled, "The justices have no right to assume that, simply because the meeting was held on a highway, it could be interrupted notwithstanding the provisions of the Public Meeting Act of 1908." In 1913, in *M'ara* v. *Magistrates of Edinburgh,* Lord Dunedin said, "The streets are public, but they are public for passage . . . , and there is no such thing as a right of the public to hold meetings as such in the streets.'' In 1924, *Aldred* v. *Miller* likewise held, ''There is no such thing as a private right in any individual to make use of any public street for holding public meetings.''[47] In effect, the courts had ruled that public meetings might legally be prevented by political or religious opponents, simply by charging obstruction.

Clause 6 of the Public Order Act added two sections to the 1908 act. These enabled a constable to request the name and address of a person reasonably suspected of an offense under the act and to arrest that person if he refused to give his name or if the constable suspected him of giving a false one. After obtaining the names and addresses of the persons suspected of an offense, the constable was to give this information to the chairman of the meeting.[48]

To the NCCL this clause ''seemed highly undesirable.'' It appeared to its opponents that the object was to suppress political terrorism and that disclosing the names and addresses of members of one political party to their opponents would only invite reprisals. Enforcement would give the appearance of cooperation by the police with the political faction that organized the meeting. Most serious of all, opponents believed that giving the police the power of arrest without warrant of any person suspected of giving a false name or address would mean in practice that the police could justify any arrest on the grounds that they did not believe that person.[49]

But these clauses, together with three remaining clauses that concerned the implementation of the act, were all relatively acceptable to the Left. In clause 3, however, opponents of the National Government saw a real threat to their existence. Section 1 of clause 3 stated that if an officer of police believed that a procession could cause serious disorder, he could change the route and prohibit the procession from entering any specified street or public place. Section 2 said that if a chief officer of police was of the opinion that the powers conferred on him in section 1 were insufficient, he could apply to the appropriate borough or urban district council for an order prohibiting all processions through the area. Section 3 gave the commissioner of the City of London or the commissioner of the Metropolitan Police the right to make such an order with only the consent of the Home Secretary.[50]

The parliamentary Labour party was concerned about this clause, and wanted to amend it; but the ILP and the CPGB put forth the strongest opposition. To them, it was an attack on the Left; and it has been noted that, according to Cabinet minutes, this was indeed an important motive of the National Government. The Left opposed all of clause 3, remarking that the police already had the power to divert processions in most major towns. Furthermore, the validity of the procession could not be tested in a court of law since the right to ban processions was made to depend on the opinion of a police officer.[51] The right to organize processions without consent from the executive had always been one of the basic rights assumed to inhere in the British Constitution.

When the original text of the bill was released, D. N. Pritt said, "The provisions with regard to uniforms and quasi-military organizations are pretty good, but the section dealing with processions is simply infamous." He also objected to clause 6 because in his opinion it meant that "the police may arrest anyone."[52]

Later, in an article in the *New Statesman,* Pritt charged that the bill "put into the hands of the executive a weapon which may enable it, one day when the temptation arises, to cripple and even to annihilate ordinary political parties to which it is opposed. In this respect, parts of the Bill almost recall the Incitement to Disaffection Bill as originally introduced." He went on to complain that the bill gave a "clear impression that the mentality of the Government is reactionary, and indifferent to the 'rule of law' and indifferent to freedom."[53]

As might have been expected, the extreme Right and the extreme Left both condemned the bill. Even before the text of the bill was published, the CPGB was afraid of it. John Strachey, quoting the original title of the bill, believed that it would be "Madness" to allow the National Government to "make further provision for the preservation of public order on the occasion of public processions and meetings."[54] When the text was finally published, the *Daily Worker* said the bill "does not suppress Mosley's organisation. Through the legal mazes of its Bill, [the National Government] cunningly seeks to divert the attack into an attack on democracy and the working class movement." The *Worker* also protested that the bill gave the police the power to take the name and address of a heckler at a Blackshirt rally and turn this information over to a Fascist chairman and to arrest without warrant any heckler suspected of giving a false name or address. This was "a very elastic power of arrest."[55]

The Communists also objected to the bill's failure to strengthen the law against illegal drilling specifically by the Blackshirts; instead, it could be used against any association that could be accused of being "organised and trained" for "the use of physical force" in promoting any political object. To the Communists, it was not difficult to see how a "reactionary" judiciary could use this power against the Hunger Marchers or for suppression of the whole CPGB.[56]

As might be expected, the Fascists even more vehemently protested the public order bill. They claimed that not a single member of the BUF had ever been convicted for interfering with meetings of others, while over five hundred of their opponents had been convicted for such an offense; so, the *Blackshirt* complained, the public order bill discriminated in favor of their opponents. It said that the prohibition on uniforms would not greatly affect the organization, but admitted that it would deprive the Blackshirts of an effective method of propaganda.[57]

Like the CPGB, the BUF particularly objected to section 4 in clause 2, which seemed to impair the great principle that guilt must be proved by the prosecution while the accused did not need to prove innocence. The *Blackshirt* wrote:

> This Bill destroys many principles on which British law has been built for centuries in order to permit political corruption and police methods of a South American Republic to be introduced into British public life. We rely with confidence on British public opinion to combat the Parliamentary corruption which has gone far.[58]

The parts of the bill that dealt with "quasi-military organisations" did not affect them, the Fascists said, since the long-declared object of the BUF was to "win power by the capture of a majority at a General Election by constitutional methods." When the bill was introduced, they had already selected the first hundred constituencies to be contested.[59]

The Socialist League "viewed with the greatest concern" the terms of the bill, which constituted "in the hands of the capitalist Government a formidable menace to working class rights." There was criticism, too, from the Jewish People's Council, which perceived dangerous loopholes in the drafting; the bill was so loosely worded that it "might react in favour of the Fascists."[60] But moderate progressives, while cautious, on the whole approved. A *Guardian* leader pointed out several minor flaws in the bill but was confident that the "Home Secretary [would] show himself more anxious to get through a measure that will infringe as few liberties as possible rather than one which under cover of meeting an emergency will extend the already extensive powers of the executive and the police over the subject."[61]

The Public Order Bill in Parliament

Introducing the bill for its second reading, the Home Secretary said that he was not discussing whether it was Communists who made Fascists or vice-versa. "The point is," he said, "that we should do our best to act even handedly in the matter and base ourselves on general principles. Let us deal with it now, . . . not by giving power to the Administration to proceed by Orders in Council, but by laying down in statutory form . . . the rules which ought to apply, and by leaving breaches of the law to be dealt with by the Courts."[62]

Regarding the uniform clause, Simon told the M.P.s that it was the unanimous view of the chief officers of police in the areas principally affected that the wearing of political uniforms was a source of special provocation, and that this had also been the view of several deputations to the Home Office. He also reminded them that in Sweden, Norway, Denmark, Finland, Switzerland, and Holland the law had been changed to achieve this purpose. He explained that the Government had not attempted to define what constituted a uniform but would leave that to a court of law. He was "quite certain" that an attempt to incorporate a description of a uniform into the bill would not serve its intended purpose. Further, since no prosecution under this section could be undertaken without the authority of the Attorney-General, the danger of private interpretations of the term was eliminated.[63]

For the most part, Simon's explanations were devoted to assurances that the legislation either was clearly needed or merely clarified existing laws. His summary was well received. J. R. Clynes spoke for Labour, saying that, although the Opposition did not agree with all aspects of the bill, "there will be no wrecking amendment or needless obstruction, but there will be on our part an attempt to make good better and to delete from several parts of the Bill portions of it and phrases in it which we think may be harmful and certainly are unnecessary." These parts were, of course, the ones that dealt with increased police at meetings and increased interference with processions. In Clynes's opinion, the bill attempted "too much."[64]

The bill was approved in some quarters precisely because it seemed to be directed against the Communists as well as the Fascists. This was particularly true of the Conservatives, although some openly sympathetic to Mosley did express reservations during the committee stage. That was even true of some Labourites. J. J. Tinker, the Labour M.P. for Leigh who had served as private secretary at the War Office and at the Admiralty during the two Labour Governments and who claimed to have been harassed by the Communists during the London County Council elections, said that the House could not afford to look at only one side of the issue. He argued, "I am not going to be strangled by any action by any communist cancer that may be holding temporary power in any part of London."[65] Still, many of the non-Communist Left feared that the Government was taking power that could be used against the working class. Kingsley Griffith, Liberal member for West Middlesbrough and a barrister who had served as the parliamentary private secretary to Herbert Samuel during the early days of the National Government, spoke for many when he said, "I regret the Bill. In its nature it is an increase of the executive; in its nature it is a decrease in the liberty of the individual."[66] To the opposition parties, however, it was worth it if the Fascists could be controlled.

The international situation contributed to the bill's acceptance. R. H. Bernays, Liberal M.P. for North Bristol and a newspaperman who had served as a special correspondent in Germany during Hitler's first few months in power, said that in ordinary times he would approach the bill with "repugnance and distrust," but

> these are not ordinary times. We have in country after country witnessed democracy collapse under the hammer blows of force. Only in the relatively brief period of the Parliamentary Recess we have seen no fewer than three popular governments either perish or become so enfeebled that they are already ripe for the sickle. I refer to Greece, Rumania, and Spain. The downfall of every democracy since the war, I believe, can be traced to one root cause, failure of the government to realize the danger in time to take resolute and courageous action.[67]

After all suggested amendments were down on the order paper, it was clear that the Government already had its bill. It was now sent to its committee stage, which in this case was a committee of the whole House. Before the session, Simon announced that the Government would accept an amendment to section 4 of clause 2 to change the burden of proof to the prosecution. It was welcomed as an indication of the Government's willingness to meet criticism "in a generous way."[68]

On 23 November, the first day of committee, there were several amendments proposed that seemed to give the Left good reason for apprehension. Numerous M.P.s were openly sympathetic to Mosley and hostile to the Communists. Captain A. H. M. Ramsay, Conservative M.P. for Peebles and Southern, moved an amendment to insert the words "or carries a flag or banner bearing a provocative device or inscription." An extremely conservative military man who became president of the Right Club and was detained under defense regulations in May 1940, Ramsay freely admitted that it was aimed at the Red flag. Ramsay was joined in this position by Commander R. T. Bower, Conservative member for Cleveland, who said that he could see no reason why Mosley should be singled out and added, "Many of us on this side hope that the Government will see to it that if the Fascists are to be attacked in this particular way, that other nuisance of the like character will also be attacked." This amendment was refused, and another by M. Thurston, Conservative for Thirsk and Malton, seeking to confine the prohibition of uniforms to public places, was withdrawn. Dingle Foot voiced a common attitude when he interrupted, "Don't let us get into the position that it is going to be an offence to be provocative."[69]

Clause 2 was changed slightly in committee. Simon introduced a provision:

> Provided that in any proceedings against a person charged with the offence of taking part in the control or management of [a quasi-military organisation] it shall be a defence to that charge to prove that he neither consented nor connived at the organisation, training, or equipment of members or adherents of the association in contravention of the provisions of this section.[70]

The amendment was accepted. This was a needed safeguard to protect organizations from the irresponsible actions of an undirected minority.

Simon also suggested alterations to the by now notorious section 4 of clause 2. Some of the language was altered to take away the vagueness of an "adherent" to a political organization. The words *persons appearing to be* and *unless it is proved that those persons were not members or adherents thereof* were dropped on the Lord Advocate's suggestion.[71]

There was also some objection to the search provision found in section 5 of clause 2. Several members wanted to omit it, but Herbert Morrison and other influential members of the Opposition supported the Government's position, and the amendment to delete was voted down. (There was inserted, however, the customary gallant provision that women should always be searched by women.)[72]

Discontent with clause 3, the one allowing prohibition of processions, remained. George Buchanan, Independent Labour member for Gorbals, a former patternmaker who became vice-chairman of the Glasgow Trades Council, charged that the clause might well be used "against the legitimate aspirations of very poor people." Sir Stafford Cripps, Aneurin Bevan, Dingle Foot, and Herbert Morrison all expressed reservations about this part of the bill. Willie Gallacher claimed that the bill was "doing the job that Mosley is concerned with doing. It is not a question of advertising Mosley, but of doing his job. This is directed against the working class." Nevertheless, Morrison, speaking for the Labour party, said that subject to amendments that they might make, they would support the clause, since the general principle had been endorsed at the Edinburgh Conference. The next day the committee divided 247 to 13 to accept clause 3.[73]

The rest of the bill required little discussion in the committee stage. After a scant two days the bill was reported, as amended. Before the third reading, George Lansbury said, "I should think that no Bill has ever been passed, as this will be passed, without a vote against it, which was so intensely disliked. The reason why we are going to allow this Bill to go through is solely because of the circumstances in which we find outselves."[74] The circumstances surrounding the passage of the Public Order Act could hardly be stated more clearly: it might be an invasion of civil liberties, but it seemed necessary to stop extremism and restore order.[75]

On 8 December, the bill was read for the first time in the House of Lords. Five days later it passed its third reading and returned to the Commons with only a few minor amendments.[76]

Some citizens opposed it. On 6 December over two hundred and fifty delegates at a conference organized by the NCCL protested the bill. Harold Laski and W. H. Thompson of the NCCL were the principal speakers. Laski dealt with the political aspects of the bill, saying it could only be understood "in relation to the post war declining phase of democratic liberty which, in turn, is the reflection of the declining economic system. . . . It is one in a series of measures of which each has got its appointed place, and whose cumulative effect is very serious in regard to restrictions upon democratic rights and liberties." He spoke of the powers already granted under the Emergency Powers Act, the Trades Disputes Act, and the Incitement to Disaffection Act, and of "the working into the fabric of our Constitution the methods of the police states of the continent."[77]

But public attention was deflected from Laski's concerns by what H. L. Mencken called "the greatest news story since the resurrection": King Edward announced that he would abdicate his throne to marry Mrs. Wallis Simpson. The public immersed itself in the affairs of royalty (while the BUF supported the King and the CPGB heaped contempt on the whole show). Little attention was paid when the public order bill was returned to the floor of Commons. The Lord's amendments, dealing only with the language, were accepted without opposition. The next day George VI gave his assent to the Public Order Act.[78]

Reception of the Public Order Act

The Public Order Act was disliked by nearly everyone, but nearly everyone had wanted it. Amost at once, however, certain elements on the Left began to attack the inherent threats they found in it. A person charged with wearing a political uniform could be detained for up to eight days, pending the Attorney-General's decision; a Fabian tract warned that it would be easy for the police to use this as a pretext for temporary detention of any person whose political activities were causing embarrassment to the executive.[79]

The NCCL criticized the amendments as doing little to modify the "dangerously wide powers" that the act put in the hands of the executive. The organization thought it "unfortunate" that the bill had been accepted "for what it is not, an attempt to deal with the menace of Fascist methods." It claimed that the clauses affecting processions and insulting words and behavior were "closely parallel to the emergency decrees which in Germany restricted the rights of the working class and peace organisations and precipitated the coming into power of the National Socialists."[80]

It is significant that the NCCL compared the act to German laws instead of the laws passed in Scandinavia, Switzerland, and the Low Countries. Mistrust of the National Government was so widespread on the Left that its every action was seen as having Fascist rather than democratic motives. This suspicion was found not only among organizations such as the CPGB, the ILP, and the NCCL, but was also common among all parts of the Labour party and large parts of the Liberal party. The suspicions arose from the way in which the Government had come into power and its domestic treatment of unemployment and the dole. By 1936, this distrust was heightened by the National Government's unclear and often ambivalent foreign policy. Because of its acquiescence in Mussolini's Ethiopian aggression and Hitler's moves in Europe, and because of its policy of nonintervention in Spain, it frequently gave the impression that it was willing to join hands with the dictators. The Left determinedly opposed this policy on all sides, so it is not surprising that any action taken by the National Government was met with suspicion.

The Communists joined the Fabians and the NCCL in their warnings. R. Palme Dutt, a journalist with a passion for economics and India who was now using his talents for the CPGB, claimed that the National Government was "restricting civil liberties, giving open protection to Mosley's Fascist organisation, and utilizing the public indignation against Mosley in order to carry through the Public Order Bill and direct the attack against the working class and democratic rights of organisation and propaganda."[81] The *Daily Worker* also fretted.

But much of the Left apparently accepted the argument that it was intended to constrain the Fascists. The BUF also believed this. Sir Philip Game's November report to Simon said that the public order bill was a major topic of conversation at Blackshirt rallies. According to notes taken by police, the Fascists charged that the National Government, "realising the growing strength of the British Union of Fascists, introduced this new legislation as a means of crushing the organisation."[82] The official BUF position on the Public Order Act was summed up in the *British Union Quarterly*. The act was described as

> . . . a desperate and frantic curtailment of free expression at a moment when free expression becomes increasingly menacing to the corrupt financial democracy which tyrannizes over the people. The British Union, accustomed to obeying the law, to receiving no favours, to suffering the most odious discrimination, can not only bear this new imposition

> but can triumphantly rise superior to it. The National Socialist is influenced more by inner reality than outer signs and symbols.[83]

In his memoirs, Sir John Simon said he was satisfied with his work on the Public Order Act. "What was in jeopardy," Simon wrote,

> . . . was the toleration which had so long been a grand characteristic of British political life, for the freedom we stand for essentially involves a willingness to let others express opinions which we abominate. . . . The solution was found in the Public Order Bill, which prohibited, under penalty, the wearing of political uniforms in public. To those who wanted "uniforms" defined and put queries on borderline cases, I replied that it would be for the magistrate to decide. In fact, there was little the courts could do, once the act was passed, for it operated like a charm.[84]

Chapter 11

Public Order and Civil Liberties, 1937–1939

The Public Order Act went into effect on 1 January 1937, more than two years after similar laws had been passed in other countries and the BUF had reached its peak. The purpose was not so much to meet a threat to the government as to control the disturbances that had rocked the East End. The act was fairly successful in this purpose, but its critics were right; the Fascists could be controlled, but so could everyone else. In appraising Britain's defense against extraparliamentary movements, more must be considered than the effect on fascism.

First, to what extent was public order restored and maintained? The legislation directed against extremists was partly successful in restoring peace in the East End, but not sufficient to prevent a small-scale repetition of the Battle of Cable Street. There were no fewer political meetings in London in the two years following the passage of the Public Order Act, although the number seems to have declined in other parts of the kingdom. Sporadic Jew baiting continued in the East End. So far as maintaining public order went, the act was not an unqualified success.

Second, to what extent did this legislation affect the civil liberties of groups that did not seek by improper means to take over the state? Harmless groups, such as the Social Credit party's Greenshirts, were affected by the prohibition of political uniforms. The provision providing for the prohibition of processions in an entire area worked against groups that had never thrown any stones. Furthermore, the Public Order Act, like the Incitement to Disaffection Act, may have discouraged political activity merely by the threat of legal action. The effects, since they were inhibitive rather than repressive, are impossible to assess. They may have been considerable.

Third, to what extent did the legislative effort to defend democracy against those who advocated its destruction work as planned? Proof that it did might be found in the fact that democratic government survived in Britain, but it is questionable whether it was ever in danger. Britain was not, at the time, fertile ground for planting fascism or communism; in all likelihood, neither movement would have threatened the state. Demoralization and disarray, even if partial, were more immediate dangers, and the laws may have helped prevent them.

The effect of the National Government's policies in these areas cannot be easily determined, but it is worth examining each area in greater detail.

Public Order, 1937–1939

After Simon's directives to Sir Philip Game calling for monthly reports on extremist political activity, the Home Office was regularly informed on Fascist and anti-Fascist meetings. The reports provide a barometer of extremist activity in London between September 1936 and March 1937. After the latter date, the reports continued but were less informative. The report for November 1936 showed a sharp decrease in the amount of extremist activity compared to September and October. According to Game's figures, Fascist activity after the Battle of Cable Street dropped considerably, and anti-Fascist activity declined even more. The Fascists held fewer meetings each month. Thirteen Fascist meetings and only eight anti-Fascist meetings had led to disorder and unrest in October.[1] The November figures showed seven disorderly Fascist meetings compared to two disorderly anti-Fascist meetings. Of the fifteen arrests made in November, eleven were made at Fascist meetings and four at anti-Fascist meetings.[2] Game made no comment on the connection of these figures, but it can probably be assumed that most anti-Fascist arrests came at Fascist meetings.

The table below shows a marked decline in the political activity of both Fascists and anti-Fascists during the months of November and December 1936 and January 1937. This was due to three factors. First, after the violence of October, there was a tendency to reduce some of the more ostentatious political activities. While the public order bill was being discussed in Parliament, the BUF did not wish to encourage the M.P.s by staging a repetition of 4 October. Second, it was during this period that the abdication of King Edward diverted attention from everything else. Finally, seasonal fluctuations were normal. The BUF prided itself on "keeping Christmas," and the colder weather made outdoor rallies less comfortable.

In this table, compiled from Sir Philip Game's confidential reports to Sir John Simon, two sets of figures stand out. The average number of people at both Fascist and anti-Fascist meetings was drastically down from the September and October figures. More arrests of Fascists were made in September and October than were made during the next four months together; the number of anti-Fascist arrests made from November 1936 through February 1937 was only 15.9 percent of the total of September and October 1936.

The increase in political activity in February resulted from the BUF campaign in the London County Council (LCC) elections of early March. The March figures show a drop of 56.8 percent in the number of Fascist meetings in that month.

Attendance and Arrests at Fascist and Anti-Fascist Meetings

	Month								
	July 1936	Aug. 1936	Sept. 1936	Oct. 1936	Nov. 1936	Dec. 1936	Jan. 1937	Feb. 1937	Mar. 1937
Fascist meetings			180	172	131	61	103	22	96
Anti-Fascist* meetings			241	201	172	70	141	184	157
Average attendance: Fascist			244	520	120	106	135	n.d.	n.d.
Average attendance: anti-Fascist*			312	240	130	100	170	n.d.	n.d.
Arrests: Fascist	20	18	10	16	4	11	7	3	n.d.
Arrests: anti-Fascist*	9	35	22	135	11	2	6	6	n.d.

*includes "Communist," "Jews," and "others"

The Public Order Act had been in effect for only a month when Game reported to Simon, "On the whole, little public interest has been shown [in Fascist meetings], and several meetings were abandoned after abortive efforts to attract an audience." Likewise, Game reported in regard to anti-Fascist meetings, "The general public displayed no particular interest," and he noted that the Spanish civil war had overshadowed the usual anti-Fascist activity and that Franco, Mussolini, and Hitler had been getting more attention than the BUF.[3]

With the exception of an altercation at the Hornsey Town Hall in late January, at which Mosley appeared in a plain dress black shirt, there were no significant clashes between Fascists and anti-Fascists during the LCC elections. Trouble had been expected, however. Lord Jessel, president of the London Municipal Society, wrote a message to Sir Philip Game warning him that trouble was anticipated at Shoreditch, Limehouse, and Whitechapel.[4]

The LCC elections passed peacefully, with the BUF failing to win any seats. A week after the polling, Game wrote to Simon:

> The Public Order Act of 1936 seems to have killed the wearing of political uniforms without any need for prosecution. Sir Oswald Mosley wears a semi-fascist uniform but has instructed his followers not to do so, and a black shirt is now seldom seen. . . . May I suggest that unless and until Jew baiting shows signs of becoming troublesome once more, the special monthly report might now be discontinued.[5]

Simon did not agree with Game's suggestion that the reports be discontinued, for he believed that conditions like those that prevailed in October 1936 might recur.[6] The reports therefore continued, but much less attention seems to have been given to them.

On 1 May 1937, which had been designated by Mosley as National Socialist Day, the Blackshirts paraded from Limehouse to Bethnal Green. This time the parade passed without creating a ripple, probably because of a bus strike that kept many people away.[7]

By the summer of 1937, however, tension in the East End was rising again. In early June, four Fascists appeared before a Thames police court and were charged with insulting behavior under the Public Order Act. The magistrate, John Harris, told the defendants to keep out of meetings that did not concern them and told them not to support their principles with their fists. The charges against two of the defendants were dropped while the other two paid only a 40s fine.[8] The leniency of the magistrate heightened the frustration already felt in the East End. When Mosley applied for permission for a BUF march through the area on 4 July, a general outcry arose in the district. The Fascists had applied for permission to meet in Limehouse and march in procession by one of two routes to Trafalgar Square. Both passed through the main streets of Jewish sections, as any route from Limehouse to Trafalgar Square would.

In reply to a question in the House by F. C. Watkins, Sir Samuel Hoare, who had succeeded Simon at the Home Office in June 1937, said that action would be taken under the Public Order Act, clause 3, section 3, to close a large part of the East End to all processions for a six-week period. The area involved included the metropolitan boroughs of Stepney, Bethnal Green, Poplar, Bow and Bromley, Shoreditch, and parts of Finsbury, Hackney, and Islington. Hoare said, "In the particular circumstances obtaining at present in the East End, and in view of the risk of serious conflict between the Fascists and their opponents, there is no alternative to the making of an order in pursuance of the powers conferred."[9]

Fascists and Communists alike criticized Hoare's action. The BUF declared, "The decision amounts to a public statement that whenever Socialists and Communists decide to organise a riot in order to prevent their opponent's propaganda they will receive the assistance of the Government to achieve their purpose." Conversely, the secretary of the London District Committee of the CPGB said the action constituted "a suppression of the democratic rights of the London Labour, Trade Unions, and Co-operative Movement."[10]

Two days later, Hoare reported to the Cabinet that he had conferred with the leaders of the Opposition and with their consent had published a notice prohibiting processions in the designated areas. He reported that as a result of his action, Mosley had changed his plans and was now planning to march through Kentish Town, an area with few Jews but many Communists. There was no ban this time, although the police would attempt to confine the march as far as possible to certain streets. The Cabinet approved the decision of the Home Secretary.[11]

Hoare said he could not regard "a mere threat of opposition to a proposed political demonstration" as sufficient grounds for prohibiting it. He continued, "Every political creed, however much one may differ from it, has equal rights, interference with which can be justified only in the most exceptional circumstances such as those which obtain in the East End of London."[12]

On 4 July, the procession passed peacefully from Kentish Town down Tottenham Court Road to Trafalgar Square. Mosley's

"Triumphal March" was supposed to have been a gigantic demonstration with supporters from all over Europe. The organ of the NCCL, *Civil Liberty,* noted that they had made a "very careful count" and that the exact number of marching Fascists was only 1,985.[13] The *Times* estimated that there were six thousand marchers, all without uniforms, but that this number was dwarfed by onlookers and protesters, who often drowned out Mosley's words as he tried to speak. There was no attempt to rush the police lines, however, and although nineteen persons were arrested, mainly for insulting words and behavior, order was easily kept.[14] To keep the peace on this summer Sunday, 2,383 police were employed with an approximate expenditure of one hundred fifty pounds.[15]

The ban on political processions in the East End was renewed for another six-week period in August, and afterward every three months until the BUF was disbanded in 1940.[16] In late summer 1937, the BUF announced plans for a march on 3 October to celebrate the fifth anniversary of the formation of the BUF and the first anniversary of the Battle of Cable Street. With East London under the ban, Mosley chose a new route through Bermondsey and South London. The Jewish population there was not large, but a considerable protest against the march arose nonetheless. On 20 September, a deputation from Bermondsey visited Sir Alexander Maxwell at the Home Office, trying to draw attention to the dangers of disorder if the Fascist march were allowed. The deputation uged that adequate steps be taken by authorities to preserve order.[17] The CPGB was not content to rely on the Government, however, and called for a counterdemonstration.

The Bermondsey affair had the bloodiness of the Battle of Cable Street, but little of the significance. A year earlier, each side felt as though it had faced its foe on the field of battle and had won a victory. Bermondsey was little more than a noisy street riot. A total of 106 arrests were made, while 28 people, including 2 policemen, were injured. The procession was divided into about twenty contingents with a few brass bands and several banners, but there were no black shirts on the backs of the twenty-five hundred Fascists. To the tune of "Tipperary" they marched behind thirty mounted police and in front of several police vans. Mosley marched in the center of the first row, saluting to the left and to the right. Repeatedly the police changed the route as some of the streets became so clogged with protesters that the procession could not pass.[18] Only after a number of delays did the Fascists arrive at the meeting place. The BUF could brag that they did pass, but it was a rather empty boast.

The meeting was delayed when protesters threw fireworks at the Fascists and at the police. Several of the fireworks throwers were arrested, and in answer the crowd turned its attention on the police. Booing and jeering turned into physical attacks, batons were drawn, and the police were forced to advance on the protesters. Mosley was eventually able to speak for about an hour with relatively few interruptions. At the same time, a Communist meeting was held a few hundred yards away. According to the report in the *Times,* both speeches were moderate. Mosley later described himself and the British Union as "satisfied." The ILP, which had joined the CPGB demonstration, issued a statement that said, "With regard to the events of the day, it may be regarded as a victory for the working class inasmuch as Mosley did not get through certain areas where he said he was determined to march."[19]

In general, the reaction to the Bermondsey violence was apathetic. It caused little stir in Commons and only tired comment in the press. The leader in the *Times* said that the Bermondsey disorder "should not . . . lead to any nervous demand for strengthening the law so recently amended." It judged the police preparations to be as good as possible, saw the spirit of the Administration in dealing with such disorders as adequate, and thought the Home Secretary was guided by regard for "that toleration of all political views which is the essence of true political liberty, and his decision [to allow the meeting] is certainly not open to censure."[20]

In sentencing to six weeks imprisonment one of the men arrested for inciting the mob at Bermondsey, the magistrate, Bernard Campion, said, "I am thankful that the newer provisions of the Public Order Act enable me to inflict greater punishment when language is used by the leader of a mob which puts the police in such an ugly situation as they were in this case."[21]

The violence at Bermondsey was an exception to the generally peaceful gatherings held by the Fascists and anti-Fascists in the years just before World War II. The British Union held only one more massive meeting, at Earls Court Exhibition Hall on 16 July 1939. The new hall, the largest in Britain at the time, was the first of its kind that the British Union had been able to hire for over a year. The size of the gathering was impressive; the *Guardian* estimated a crowd of twenty thousand people.[22] The uniforms were gone, but in their stead the new British Union insignia adorned tapestry throughout the hall. The new emblem was a thunderbolt within a circle—the thunderbolt representing action and the circle representing unity.[23] Critics dubbed it "a flash in the pan."

The meetings now were much more peaceful, but they were still numerous. The peace campaign of the British Union attracted a sizable following. According to the Reports of the Commissioner for the years 1937 and 1938, their number actually rose after the Public Order Act. In 1937, the Metropolitan Police had to supervise 11,804 meetings, of which over 7,000 were Fascist or anti-Fascist.[24] In 1938, the total number of meetings supervised by the police rose to 12,483.[25] In both cases this was an increase over 1936.

By January 1939, the monthly Special Branch reports on extremist political activity, which had often numbered over ten pages two years earlier, were being neatly condensed into two pages. The number of Fascist meetings covered by or reported to the Special Branch for November 1938 was 71; there were 114 anti-Fascist meetings. For the month of December, the figures were 32 and 60 respectively. The special reports on meetings were discontinued at this time.[26] The declining intensity of extremist activity since the passage of the Public Order Act suggested that it had been at least partially responsible for restoring order.

Public Order and Civil Liberties, 1937–1939

At the time of the passage of the Public Order Act, many people of the Left had voiced serious reservations about some of the dangers to civil liberties that they believed to be inherent in the language of the bill. Under the auspices of the National Council for Civil Liberties, a Conference on Fascism and Anti-Semitism was held on 25 April 1937. Alfred M. Wall, secretary of the London Trades Council, in his address to the delegates charged that the Public Order Act was not being enforced against the Fascists. He cited three different occasions on which the police had been requested to arrest Fascist speakers who vilified Jews and had refused to act. Surely, descriptions of the Jews as "hook-nosed, yellow skinned, dirty Jewish swine" and "venereal ridden vagrants" constituted an offense. During the LCC elections, the Fascists had marched through Jewish areas chanting, "The Yids, the Yids, We Gotta Get Rid of the Yids!"; "Roll on the Pogrom"; and "We Want Jewry's Blood."[27] To these offensive sounds, however, the police were alleged to have often turned a deaf ear.

A notable clash came during the LCC elections at Hornsey Town Hall on 25 January 1937. A week before the meeting, Mosley wrote a polite letter to the superintendent of the Hornsey police pledging to "co-operate in every way with the police and to afford them every facility in the maintenance of order." "If . . . you do not desire the police to be inside the hall," he continued, "our stewards will be instructed to eject any person creating a disturbance with the minimum of force necessary to secure their removal from the meeting."[28]

The night of the meeting, Mosley appeared in a double-breasted grey lounge suit, a black flannel shirt with an attached black collar, and a black tie. He demanded that the Government take action against him personally and make a test case to establish whether or not a black shirt could be defined as a uniform. He charged that the Public Order Act subjected the BUF to "legalized Blackmail" and that it was instituted to check the Fascists.[29] All of this was the usual bill of fare at such meetings. When interruptions occurred, BUF stewards forcibly ejected the interrupters. Persons ejected charged unnecessary brutality, and two members of the audience, acting individually, each sought out a constable in order to identify their assailants. In both cases, the police ignored them and refused to take action.

Observers for the NCCL were at the meeting. Through several members of Parliament, they demanded that Sir John Simon undertake a public inquiry. Compared to Olympia, however, the Hornsey meeting was minor. When Simon did make a private inquiry, Sir Philip Game reported that only three complaints had been made and that in one case the Fascist stewards had evicted a man for making derogatory remarks about Mosley's wife. Game's report was strongly in support of his men and concluded on a note of exasperation with the continued excessive vigilance of the NCCL:

> To sum up, I think there is little doubt that the Fascist stewards were somewhat out of hand and over-violent at the meeting. We have indications that this was the view at the meeting. We have indications that this was the view at Fascist headquarters. As against this, it is difficult to

> have very much sympathy with, for instance, a man who goes to a professedly loyalist meeting and insists, in spite of protests, in remaining seated during the national anthem.
>
> The Council of [*sic*] Civil Liberties has, as always, done their best to exploit the disorder, primarily caused by their own supporters, in order to attack the police. I should most strongly deprecate giving a fictitious importance to this self-constituted body by acceding to their demand for a public inquiry.[30]

Simon accordingly refused a public inquiry. In a letter to Fred Messer, a dedicated pacifist, an ardent supporter of the No More War Movement, and a Labour M.P. who lived near Hornsey, Simon summed up a police report regarding the Fascist brutalities and police inaction at the Hornsey Town Hall: "I want to say quite categorically that I am satisfied that there is no foundation whatever for the suggestion that the police had 'received orders not to go into the hall and not to interfere with Fascist assaults on my account.' "[31] Simon did remind the officers of their duty, however, and in 1940 Ronald Kidd, secretary of the NCCL, was able to write that there had been no reported cases where the police had failed to intervene in an outdoor meeting after the Hornsey meeting.[32]

Reports of hooliganism during the polling for the LCC elections were numerous, but it was probably no worse than in many elections not involving the Fascists. There were complaints of electioneering at the polls and intimidation, but the failure of the BUF to win a single seat seemed to be the most important outcome. On 14 July 1937, police broke up a small Fascist meeting at Stepney Green. A meeting of the Ex-Servicemen's Movement held nearby was also dispersed. Arrests included that of a whistling man on his way home with the family's milk, and of another man who, while searching for his ten-year-old daughter, blew his nose in a manner that offended the police inspector. Both "offenders" were charged with insulting behavior under the Public Order Act. The magistrate later dismissed both cases, saying, "It would be a sad state of affairs if it were a criminal offence . . . to whistle."[33]

In many cases, anti-Fascists felt that the ban instituted by Sir Samuel Hoare was discriminatory. The Bethnal Green's Trade Council planned to hold a trade union recruitment march and demonstration on Sunday, 18 July, with Dan Chater, a Labour M.P. for Northeast Bethnal Green and a prominent worker in the cooperative movement, scheduled to speak. The police commissioner banned the march on the grounds that it was a political procession. Hoare backed Game's decision, saying that a demonstration "addressed by a Labour M.P. could not be non-political. . . . It was necessary to take all possible precautions to see that no public disorder occurred in the area."[34]

Some elements saw the continuation of sporadic Jew baiting as a sign that the police were partial to fascism. An article in *Civil Liberty* claimed that the Government was "looking ahead to a time when there may be serious disaffection in the rank and file of the police, and to a time when they might find it convenient to make use of the Fascists as a special constabulary." The article attempted to prove that this was the case by noting both the reluctance of the Government to initiate the Public Order Act and the continuation of Jew baiting.[35] The charge was unfounded and unsuccessful as propaganda; the police were respected by most of the population for success in dealing with a very difficult problem. It does show, however, that in their attempt to discredit the Government, certain elements of the Left were losing all sense of proportion. This was partly because of the Government's domestic actions, but by 1937, foreign developments were the predominant contributors to this attitude, which at times was close to paranoia.

Other sorts of dissatisfaction in the first year of the Public Order Act were voiced at the 37th Annual Labour Party Conference. Councillor H. Solomons charged that the parliamentary Labour party had placed "in the hands of the Government the power to suppress all working-class activities." He demanded that the parliamentary Labour party take the first opportunity to describe in the House of Commons the "various ways in which this act is being used to suppress working-class agitation in this country." H. Lubbock, in seconding the motion, described several incidents of Fascists receiving light treatment from the police, and said, "The liberty of the people in this country has been very seriously prejudiced by this Public Order Act."[36]

But Labour on the whole did not agree. Clement Attlee, speaking for the National Executive of the Labour party, answered these charges by saying that the banning of uniforms had had "an extremely useful effect." On the basis of information that came to him mainly from the trouble spots in East London, he believed that the act had on the whole been successful.[37]

In spite of the Government's actions to promote public order impartially, critics could point to numerous cases where those actions had not been sufficient to prevent disorder. They could suggest grounds for anxiety that the police were using the act for class purposes and in ways that infringed the proper rights of the subject. Still, the amount and intensity of public disorder did decline, and the threat of prosecution under the provisions of the Public Order Act was no doubt a major deterrent.

Chapter 12

Conclusion

In the months before the outbreak of World War II, the extremist threat to British society and public order had become negligible. With the disappearance of the black shirts went the most provocative reason for waving the red flag. The National Government, acting with deliberate caution and unhindered by inspired leadership, had muddled through and preserved the social order.

The Blackshirts of Britain had never really recovered from the stigma of Olympia. The BUF was a minor threat to the realm thereafter, but it did constitute a genuine threat to British Jews, and its presence was a constant irritant in the East End. The Public Order Act weakened the menace considerably, though.

The BUF could not long survive in a publicity vacuum. The black shirt had been a principal means of advertisement and identification. The provisions of the Public Order Act concerning processions meant that Fascist and Communist bands could no longer march with clashing symbols to draw attention to their own virtues and the other's dangers. Mosley nevertheless pledged to accept the new act. The day before it went into effect, he issued a public statement:

> The British Union of Fascists has taken counsel's opinion on the Public Order Act, which comes into force on January 1. In the opinion of counsel—1) the Blackshirt uniform is illegal, 2) an ordinary shirt of black colour with tie worn under an ordinary suit is legal, 3) our organisation is not otherwise affected. It is the consistent policy of the Movement to obey the law of the land. The Blackshirt uniform, therefore, will not be worn by members in any public place or at any public meeting.[1]

The Fascists accepted it, but they did not like it. The *British Union Quarterly* claimed that meetings in Manchester and Leeds, at which no black shirts were worn, produced greater disorder than meetings where black shirts had been worn. The reason, they argued, was that the Blackshirts had always distinguished themselves by their compliance with the police. At uniformless meetings, therefore, the distinction was obliterated and the task of the officer was much more difficult.[2]

Such arguments were intended to bolster the spirit of those whose enthusiasm for the BUF was declining. The LCC elections provided a test of strength, and the results were depressing. The BUF ambitions were modest enough. A total of six candidates stood for LCC seats from Bethnal Green Southwest, Shoreditch, and Poplar. Included in the list of candidates were Alexander Raven Thomson, a sort of professional Fascist, E. G. "Mick" Clarke, a furniture worker known as the "Julius Streicher of the BUF" and a "terrific mob orator," and William Joyce—destined for a dramatic future as Lord Haw Haw—who was the number two man in the organization and one of its best speakers.[3] Lesser-known candidates were Ann Brock Griggs, the chief woman's organizer, Charles Wegg-Posser, who later was involved in Labour party politics and became a bitter anti-Fascist, and J. A. Bailey. Mosley himself chose not to risk his position by the probable loss of yet another election.[4]

According to Mosley, the BUF decided to contest the LCC elections in the East End because "the enemy should be attacked where his 'corrupt power' was the strongest."[5] He led a vigorous campaign, and several of the more prominent members of the BUF were sent into the district to support the candidates. The campaign, although abusive, was generally peaceful.

The only thing that changed in the election was the BUF. The Labour party kept all six seats. Thomson and Clarke did finish ahead of their Liberal opponents, but the election was not a success for the BUF. The best showing was in Bethnal Green, where its candidates received 23.17 percent of the vote; its worst showing was in Shoreditch, where Joyce and Bailey polled only 14.8 percent of the vote. Almost eight thousand people voted for Fascist candidates; still, the result was generally accounted a disaster. All energies and funds had been concentrated on the area where they could expect the most support, but less than one-fourth of the people in a Fascist stronghold had voted for the party. It seemed obvious that the way to power in Britain would not be through the ballot.[6]

Mosley was not one to publicly admit defeat. He soon announced that according to his figures the BUF had won a greater victory than Hitler in his first election contest. Mosley argued that the Nazis in 1928 had polled only 2.7 percent of the vote, but that this gave them twelve members in the Reichstag. In 1930, 18 percent gave them 107 members. When compared to the 23.17 percent of the votes gained by Thomson and Clarke, Mosley was able to claim that the BUF had achieved better results in their first election than any other Fascist or National Socialist party. Mosley failed to mention that Hitler's elections had been national while his had been only in a small, carefully chosen section of a municipality.[7] The *British Union Quarterly* wrote, "To have expected victory, in the sense of the actual return of the six candidates, would have been a fantastic delusion for any accurately informed person." Despite gaining no seats, they considered their objectives to have been achieved.[8]

Two weeks after the election, Mosley met with his staff and announced that he was reducing the number of salaried persons from 143 to 30. The action was due to the party's financial condition in the wake of the LCC election, but the move had some elements of a purge. William Joyce and John Beckett, who had steadily fallen from favor since the minor split in January 1935, were now eased out. With John McNab, editor of the now defunct *Fascist Quarterly*, and Captain Vincent Collier, one of the leading National Propaganda officers, they formed the National Socialist League.[9]

The new organization attracted little attention. Shortly after it was formed, Sir Philip Game informed Simon, "Up to the present, very little public interest has been shown and at the six meetings held by the National Socialist League, the largest audience numbered less than a hundred persons."[10]

While the Fascists splintered, the CPGB made little headway in their quest for a common front. In early 1937, Sir Stafford Cripps of the Socialist League, James Maxton of the ILP, and Harry Pollitt issued a call for unity of the working-class movement. The unity campaign declared as its purpose opposition to fascism in all its forms, to the National Government "as the agent of British capitalism and Imperialism," to all restrictions on civil and trade union liberties, and to the mobilization of Britain.[11]

Even if all members of these three groups had been united, their force would still have been small. The Labour party remained aloof from all Communist unity pleas. Noting the attempt to form a common front against fascism, Game wrote to Simon on the eve of the LCC elections:

> The Communist Party has taken up the attitude that whether the Labour Party wants its support or not is immaterial. . . . In reality, it appears to

be simply a further example of the Communist Party's usual practice of making political capital out of any situation that can be utilized to this end.[12]

The CPGB had harsh words for the Labour party after the LCC elections, claiming that such success as Mosley had in penetrating the East End was "due to the stagnant, disunited and inactive character of the Labour Movement in East London boroughs."[13] These denunciations were mild compared to the vitriolic invective aimed at the National Government, which the CPGB claimed was "a threat to world peace and to democracy at home." It charged that the Government had passed "several acts of Parliament taking away hard won liberties and connived at Mosley's activities while suppressing, whenever possible, Communist demonstrations."[14]

At the 1937 Labour Party Conference held at Bournemouth, the annual report of the National Executive contained a firm statement against a united front. Sir Stafford Cripps and Harold Laski had both pleaded for such a front, Laski saying, "If I have to choose between appearing upon a platform in the pursuance of our common aim with Mr. Harry Pollitt or Mr. Winston Churchill, I have no doubt at all that my proper place is with Mr. Harry Pollitt."[15] Pollitt had promised that the CPGB was "ready to discuss with representatives of the Labour Party at any time they like, and under any circumstances they choose to name, what can be done to bring the Communist Party and the Labour Party together in united action."[16] But the delegates to the 37th Annual Conference did not even have an opportunity to vote on the united front. The Labour party felt that it did not need the Communists to fight fascism.

The CPGB continued to grow in membership before the war, but not enough to constitute a threat to the established parties. The BUF was unable to exploit a fear of communism, fascism's familiar path to power. Membership continued to dwindle. A slight increase in attendance at BUF meetings occurred after war had been declared, when Mosley continuously called for peace and asked his audiences to vote for or against war.[17] The Emergency Powers Regulations, which were passed in 1939, placed restriction on propaganda activities, and when Mosley and other leading members of the British Union were interned in 1940, the party was already for all practical purposes dead.

Mosley never caught the spirit or imagination of the British people. An excellent speaker and an original thinker, he was never able to inspire the trust that could have made him credible as a leader. Sir Herbert Samuel, the Liberal, seems accurately to have assessed Mosley's sort of personality when he wrote:

> Egoism unbalanced by altruism hurts the egoist himself, whether he be a person or a State. It decides his own moral character, and leads to actions which his conscience must condemn; with loss of self respect comes loss of effectiveness. And it is certain to provoke resentment in others . . . . An aggressive patriotism does not serve the ends of patriotism, and so is not patriotic at all.[18]

In 1938, Beverley Nichols, the author, wrote, "Mosley . . . is one of the three most dynamic personalities in the Empire today. And the men he has inspired are animated by something akin to a religious faith. Yet he receives less publicity in England than the colour of Miss Marlene Dietrich's fingernails."[19] This was partly because Marlene Dietrich was "news"—and Mosley was not. A potentially great parliamentarian manqué, his influence extended little beyond the door of the insignificant British Union headquarters.

In Birmingham there was only slight and insignificant Fascist activity in the two years before the Second World War. In Manchester there were still a few public meetings, but on the whole these too were insignificant. Only badly supported activity was reported in Sheffield. In Bristol and Yorkshire, political activity was back to the normal pre-BUF state.[20] In London, Simon said later, "Mosley's men looked and felt very different in ordinary clothes, and the police used their power of controlling processions with their usual good sense. So this nuisance, which had so seriously threatened public order, evaporated."[21]

The Blackshirts were reduced to the "status of a schoolboy secret society."[22] The Public Order Act had been introduced mainly to insure domestic tranquility, but it was also partly successful in keeping fascism on the other side of the English Channel. The parades and banners and clicking of heels seemed silly in light of the real danger that emanated from Berlin. To its credit, the British Union did not work to become a fifth column; but although Mosley ordered his followers to do nothing to impede the war effort, a large number of World War II traitors did come out of the Mosley movement.[23]

The Left continued to grow in spite of the Public Order Act. Mosley's strength diminished as the strength of the Continental

Fascists grew; but the Left grew with it. In the process British leftists learned the technique of provoking violence for propaganda purposes. In this, they were not unlike the antiwar activists in the United States during the sixties. Like their recent American imitators, the Left was able to win a part of the population to its views, and antifascism became dominant. The Communist Party of Great Britain, however, was never able to convert this sentiment into mass support. After all, the social structure had survived World War I and its aftermath and to a large extent had also survived the depression. In this tradition of stability, national complacency, and self-awareness, imported ideas were largely rejected. Extremism was simply unable to grow in British soil.

It is important to remember, however, that there was never an assurance that such would be the case. The National Government of Ramsay MacDonald and Stanley Baldwin has not been widely praised. Its foreign policy was unimaginative at its best. Its economic policy was hardly farsighted, and whatever success Britain had in escaping the grip of the depression is not directly attributable to the actions of the Government. On the domestic scene, it acted only when it had to and with a minimum of grace. Yet, it did not fail. While other democracies were withering or crashing down, the National Government preserved the existing order. The potential for vicious attacks on the civil liberties of the British subject may have existed, but only rarely were such liberties even questioned. As the world political situation deteriorated, Britain, more than any other European nation, possessed the internal strength to oppose fascism.

Domestic Fascists and Communists might still confront each other with rival newspapers and street corner speeches, but now "the contest seemed not so much between the Right and the Left as between Hitler and the Human Race." As Michael Wharton has noted, in the tense and emotional atmosphere of late 1939, "the extraparliamentary parties seemed to have less and less to say that was worth hearing."[24] The defense of Britain was no longer to be found in the Houses of Parliament or on street corners, but rather in the skill of the RAF and in the narrow expanse of the English Channel.

Notes

Notes to Chapter 1, Introduction

1. Karl Loewenstein, "Militant Democracy and Fundamental Rights," p. 424.
2. Herbert L. Samuel, *Belief and Action,* p. 135.
3. Great Britain, *Hansard Parliamentary Debates* (Commons), 5th ser., 290:2021.

Notes to Chapter 2, Legislation Affecting Civil Liberties

1. See Karl Loewenstein, "Legislative Control of Political Extremism in European Democracies," p. 770.
2. Arthur Marwick, *The Deluge,* p. 139.
3. Great Britain, *Parliamentary Papers* (1914), 1, "Defence of the Realm," p. 1.
4. Marwick, *The Deluge,* p. 139.
5. Charles Loch Mowat, *Britain Between the Wars, 1918–1940,* pp. 6–7.
6. Great Britain, *Hansard Parliamentary Debates* (Commons), 5th ser., 118:795.
7. Stuart Bowes, *The Police and Civil Liberties,* p. 22.
8. *Parliamentary Papers* (1920), 22, "Report of the Commissioner of Police of the Metropolis," p. 5.
9. Cecil Frederick Nevil Macready, *Annals of an Active Life,* 2 vols., 1:301–2. Macready went on to warn that this would provide an "opportunity which would not be neglected by those who were already making insidious efforts to undermine the discipline of the troops."
10. *Parliamentary Papers* (1920), 22, "Reports of His Majesty's Inspectors of Constabulary," pp. 2–3.
11. Ibid.
12. *Hansard* (Commons), 118:795–96.
13. Ibid., 819.
14. Ibid., 2459.
15. Ibid., 820.
16. Ibid., 796.
17. Ibid., 2458.
18. Ibid., 2446.
19. Ibid., 2453–54.
20. Ibid., 2458.
21. Ibid., 2475.
22. James Harvey and Katherine Hood, *The British State,* p. 140.
23. Victor L. Allen, *Trade Unions and the Government,* p. 158.
24. *Parliamentary Papers* (1920), 22, "Report of the Commissioner of Police of the Metropolis," p. 5.
25. Allen, *Trade Unions and the Government,* p. 158. This was the occasion of the first use of troops in a postwar strike. Its main impact was in Liverpool, Birkenhead, and Bootle, where more than half the police force joined the strike. A thousand troops were sent to Liverpool to maintain order and fought with fixed bayonets against looters and rioters, resulting in one fatality. Over five hundred troops patrolled Birkenhead. Bonar Law even ordered warships to move up the Mersey River as a precautionary measure (ibid., p. 124).
26. Bowes, *The Police and Civil Liberties,* pp. 22–23.
27. *Hansard* (Commons), 118:2446.

28. David Williams, *Keeping the Peace,* p. 193.
29. Bowes, *The Police and Civil Liberties,* p. 26.
30. Ibid.
31. This decision recognized as valid a search that resulted in the discovery of documents not in the possession of the person named in the warrant, but containing evidence of an offense committed by any person, even though the search and seizure were illegal in regard to other documents discovered on that occasion. See Emlyn Capel Stuart Wade and G. Godfrey Phillips, *Constitutional Law,* p. 175.
32. *Hansard* (Commons), 135:1537.
33. Ibid. 34. Ibid., 1542.
35. *Parliamentary Papers* (1920), 2, "An Act to Amend the Official Secrets Act," p. 2.
36. *Hansard* (Commons), 135:1543.
37. Ibid., 1560.
38. *Parliamentary Papers* (1920), 2, "An Act to Amend the Official Secrets Act," p. 3.
39. Ibid. 40. Ibid., p. 4. 41. Ibid., p. 6.
42. One of the members of the Government's majority was a young Conservative named Oswald Mosley, whose activities sixteen years later would provide the occasion for other legislation denounced as contrary to traditional and civil liberties; *Hansard* (Commons), 136:1582.
43. Ibid., 979.
44. David Williams, *Not in the Public Interest,* p. 104.
45. Ibid., p. 94. 46. Ibid., pp. 45–46.
47. It is interesting to note that the prosecution was directed against the son who had written the book rather than the father who had communicated the secret documents to his son. Perhaps the elder Lansbury, the leader of the Opposition in the House, would have relished the prosecution and court exposure more than Inskip would have liked; *Guardian,* 21 March 1934, p. 4.
48. Harry Street, *Freedom, the Individual, and the Law,* pp. 211–12.
49. Ronald Kidd, *British Liberty in Danger: An Introduction to the Study of Civil Rights,* p. 89.
50. According to his biographer, "Much frenzied government activity was needed to redeem the promise of Hewart the politician in 1920 and bypass the judgment of Hewart the judge in 1938." See Robert Jackson, *The Chief,* pp. 323–24.
51. National Council for Civil Liberties, *The Record of a Decade of Work for Democracy and Civil Liberty,* p. 6.
52. Ibid., *The Strange Case of Major Vernon,* p. 7.
53. Ibid., pp. 7–8.
54. *Times,* 3 September 1937, p. 13.
55. Denis Nowell Pritt, *From Right to Left,* pp. 155–56; *Times,* 28 October 1937, p. 10.
56. G. Lloyd George, *Freedom of the Press and the Challenge of the Official Secrets Acts,* p. 19.
57. National Union of Journalists, *The Official Secrets Acts and Individual Freedom,* p. 2.
58. Wade and Phillips, *Constitutional Law,* p. 506.
59. National Council for Civil Liberties, *The Record of a Decade of Work,* p. 7.
60. Kidd, *British Liberty in Danger,* p. 100.
61. Ibid., pp. 56–57.
62. National Council for Civil Liberties, *Notes for the International Conference of the International Judicial Association, 1937,* pp. 11–12.
63. Ibid., *The Record of a Decade of Work,* p. 4.

64. L. J. MacFarlane, *The British Communist Party*, p. 117.
65. Allen, *Trade Unions and the Government*, p. 124.
66. *Parliamentary Papers* (1920), 1, "Emergency Powers," p. 1.
67. Ibid., p. 2. 68. Ibid., p. 1. 69. Ibid., p. 2.
70. *Hansard* (Commons), 133:1888–90.
71. MacFarlane, *The British Communist Party*, pp. 117–18.
72. Allen, *Trade Unions and the Government*, pp. 188–89.
73. James Klugmann, *History of the Communist Party of Great Britain*, 2:259–60.
74. Harold Edford Priestly, *Voice of Protest: A History of Civil Unrest in Great Britain*, p. 297.
75. Allen, *Trade Unions and the Government*, p. 192.
76. Harvey and Hood, *The British State*, p. 182.
77. Allen, *Trade Unions and the Government*, p. 126.
78. *Hansard* (Commons), 207:2136–38.
79. Ibid., 2182.
80. *Parliamentary Papers* (1927), 3, "Trade Disputes and Trade Unions," p. 4.
81. Kidd, *British Liberty in Danger*, p. 54.
82. Harvey and Hood, *The British State*, pp. 200–201. After the entire act was repealed by the Labour Government in 1946, all of these organizations reaffiliated with the Trades Union Congress. Only the Union of Post Office Workers, however, reaffiliated with the Labour party immediately after repeal.
83. Mowat, *Britain Between the Wars*, p. 337.

Notes to Chapter 3, Communist Party of Great Britain

1. L. J. MacFarlane, *The British Communist Party*, pp. 28–29.
2. Henry Pelling, *The British Communist Party: A Historical Profile*, p. 3.
3. Ibid., p. 6. 4. Ibid.
5. Communist Party of Great Britain, *Official Report: Communist Unity Convention*, p. 4.
6. Ibid. 7. Ibid., p. 15. 8. Ibid., pp. 7–8.
9. Kenneth Newton, *The Sociology of British Communism*, p. 20.
10. Pelling, *The British Communist Party*, pp. 24–25.
11. Walter L. Arnstein, *Britain: Yesterday and Today*, p. 274.
12. John Ross Campbell, *What Is the Use of Parliament?*, p. 2.
13. David Williams, *Keeping the Peace*, p. 185.
14. *Times*, 7 August 1924, p. 9.
15. Williams, *Keeping the Peace*, p. 185.
16. MacFarlane, *The British Communist Party*, p. 137.
17. Ibid.
18. James Klugmann, *History of the Communist Party of Great Britain*, 2:74.
19. Ibid., p. 79.
20. MacFarlane, *The British Communist Party*, p. 138.
21. Great Britain, *Hansard Parliamentary Debates* (Commons), 5th ser., 188:2075.
22. Ibid., 2185–86.
23. *Times*, 2 December 1925, p. 15.
24. Pelling, *The British Communist Party*, p. 36.
25. MacFarlane, *The British Communist Party*, p. 302.
26. Pelling, *The British Communist Party*, p. 72.
27. Communist Party of Great Britain, *Class Against Class*, p. 29.

28. Pelling, *The British Communist Party,* pp. 51–53.
29. Harry Pollitt claimed to have visited Moscow twenty-seven times between 1921 and 1930.
30. Pelling, *The British Communist Party,* p. 65.
31. Rajani Palme Dutt, *The Workers' Answer to the Crisis,* p. 5.
32. Pelling, *The British Communist Party,* p. 67.
33. Ibid., p. 68.
34. Ibid.
35. A. J. P. Taylor, *English History, 1914–1945,* p. 349.
36. National Council for Civil Liberties, *The Record of a Decade of Work for Democracy and Civil Liberty,* pp. 3–4.
37. *Guardian,* 23 February 1934, p. 9.
38. Ibid., 24 February 1934, p. 13.
39. *Daily Worker,* 26 February 1934, p. 4.
40. Minutes of the Cabinet, 21 February 1934, CAB 23/78, 6/34/15, p. 26, Public Records Office (hereafter cited as PRO).
41. *Guardian,* 24 February 1934, p. 13.
42. Ibid., 26 February 1934, p. 9.
43. Ibid., 1 March 1934, p. 18.
44. Ibid.
45. Ibid., 11 April 1934, p. 7.
46. Ibid., 12 April 1934, p. 6.
47. Ibid., 5 July 1934, p. 8.
48. Communist Party of Great Britain, "To Fascism or Communism?" (pamphlet), pp. 22–23.
49. Ibid., *Communist Political Education: A Manual for Workers' Study Groups,* p. 94.
50. Ibid., p. 23.
51. Ibid.
52. Pelling, *The British Communist Party,* p. 76.
53. Trades Union Congress, *Report of Proceedings at the 65th Annual Trades Union Congress—Brighton, 1933,* ed. by Walter M. Citrine, p. 174.
54. Pelling, *The British Communist Party,* p. 77.
55. *Guardian,* 22 April 1935, p. 12.
56. Labour Party, *Report of the 34th Annual Conference—Southport, 1934,* p. 10.
57. Ibid.
58. Trades Union Congress, *Report of Proceedings at the 66th Annual Trades Union Congress—Bournemouth, 1934,* ed. by Walter M. Citrine, pp. 210–11.
59. Pelling, *The British Communist Party,* p. 74.
60. Ibid.
61. Klement Gottwald, *A People's Front,* p. 18.
62. Georgi Dimitrov, *What You Can Do Against Fascism and War,* p. 11.
63. Communist Party of Great Britain, "The Class Struggle in Local Affairs," p. 26.
64. Pelling, *The British Communist Party,* pp. 87–88.
65. Anthony Eden, *Facing the Dictators,* p. 571.
66. Newton, *Sociology of British Communism,* p. 159.
67. Ibid., pp. 20–21.
68. Ibid.
69. Pelling, *The British Communist Party,* p. 81.
70. Newton, *Sociology of British Communism,* p. 69.
71. Pelling, *The British Communist Party,* p. 80.
72. Michael Wharton, "A Few Lost Causes," p. 81.
73. A. J. P. Taylor, "Confusion of the Left," p. 76.

Notes to Chapter 4, British Union of Fascists

1. Robert Benewick, *Political Violence and Public Order,* p. 24.
2. William Joyce, "Obituary of Sir Edward Carson," p. 28.
3. E. D. Hart, "Early Fascists," pp. 277–88.
4. William Joyce, "Thomas Carlyle—National Socialist," p. 427.
5. Benewick, *Political Violence,* p. 26.
6. It was even rumored that Miss Lintorn-Orman wore a sword to all Fascisti rallies; Colin Cross, *The Fascists in Great Britain,* p. 57.
7. Benewick, *Political Violence,* pp. 27–28.
8. George E. G. Catlin, "Fascist Stirrings in Great Britain," p. 542.
9. George Thayer, *The British Political Fringe: A Profile,* p. 15.
10. Catlin, "Fascist Stirrings," p. 542.
11. Cross, *Fascists in Great Britain,* p. 64.
12. Benewick, *Political Violence,* p. 45.
13. Michael Wharton, "A Few Lost Causes," p. 86.
14. Catlin, "Fascist Stirrings," p. 542.
15. Walter A. Rudlin, *The Growth of Fascism in Great Britain,* p. 117.
16. Mosley's identification with England could, in fact, hardly have been more solid. His grandfather, the fourth baronet, was identified with the famous John Bull cartoon as the embodiment of true British characteristics. See Benewick, *Political Violence,* p. 52.
17. Ibid., p. 53.
18. Arthur Harold Booth, *British Hustings,* p. 159.
19. Benewick, *Political Violence,* pp. 54–55.
20. M. I. Cole, ed., *Beatrice Webb's Diaries, 1924–1932,* p. 243.
21. R. J. A. Skidelsky, "Great Britain," pp. 259–60.
22. For an interesting account of this period, contrast Oswald Mosley's *My Life,* pp. 229–63, with Gregory Blaxland, *J. H. Thomas: A Life for Unity,* pp. 234–38. See also Harold Nicolson's balanced account in his biography *King George V,* pp. 445–46.
23. Cross, *Fascists in Great Britain,* p. 38.
24. *Times,* 27 May 1930, p. 22.
25. Nicolson, *George V,* p. 446.
26. Cross, *Fascists in Great Britain,* p. 41.
27. Dean Eugene McHenry, *His Majesty's Opposition: Structure and Problems of the British Labour Party, 1931–1938,* p. 234.
28. For an almost day-to-day account of the rise and fall of the New Party, see Harold Nicolson's *Diaries and Letters,* vol. 1. Nicolson was the editor of the party's newspaper, *Action.*
29. Harold MacMillan, *Winds of Change,* p. 247.
30. C. E. M. Joad, *The Case for the New Party,* pp. 7–8.
31. Ibid., pp. 10–13.
32. Rebecca West, *The New Meaning of Treason,* p. 47.
33. Benewick, *Political Violence,* pp. 80–81.
34. J. R. Jones, "England," p. 63.
35. Skidelsky, "Great Britain," p. 259.
36. Ibid., p. 231.
37. Brigitte Granzow, *A Mirror of Nazism: British Public Opinion and the Emergence of Hitler, 1929–1932,* p. 150.
38. Mosley, *My Life,* pp. 303–4.
39. Benewick, *Political Violence,* p. 96.

40. Great Britain, *Hansard Parliamentary Debates* (Commons), 5th ser., 285:360–61.

41. Ibid., 290:1341. 42. Ibid., 1875–76.

43. *Daily Mail,* 15 January 1934, p. 12.

44. Kingsley Martin, "Fascism and the *Daily Mail,*" p. 274.

45. *Daily Mail,* 27 April 1934, p. 13.

46. Leo G. Rosten, "The Rise of Oswald Mosley," p. 493.

47. Benewick, *Political Violence,* p. 110. Contrast the trend in these figures with those figures on the Communist party membership cited on p. 44.

48. Ibid., pp. 134–35.

49. Oswald Mosley, *The Greater Britain.* See also The British Union of Fascists, *Miscellaneous Pamphlets and Letters,* British Library, London.

50. Or 4d if unemployed; British Union of Fascists, *Pamphlets and Letters,* British Library.

51. Mosley, *The Greater Britain,* p. 24.

52. Oswald Mosley, *Ten Points of Fascist Policy,* p. 8.

53. William Joyce, *Dictatorship,* p. 11.

54. Oswald Mosley, *Fascism in Britain,* p. 5.

55. Ibid., p. 7.

56. William Joyce, "Fascism and India" (pamphlet), p. 19.

57. Ibid., p. 2.

58. Benewick, *Political Violence,* pp. 142–48.

59. Mosley, *The Greater Britain,* p. 13.

60. Ibid., *Mosley's Message to British Union Members and Supporters,* p. 1.

61. Ibid., *Blackshirt Policy,* p. 8.

62. *British Union Quarterly* 1 (January 1937): 1.

63. *Fascist Quarterly* 2 (January 1936): 5.

64. Ibid., pp. 89–100.

65. Mosley, *My Life,* p. 336.

66. Benewick, *Political Violence,* pp. 151–52.

67. *Blackshirt,* 2 November 1934, p. 2.

68. See A. K. Chesterton, "What the Jews Did in the War" (pamphlet).

69. Alexander Raven Thomson, "Big Fish and Little Fish: Finance, Democracy, and the Shopkeeper" (pamphlet), p. 1.

70. Mosley, *Ten Points of Fascist Policy,* p. 5.

71. *Guardian,* 15 April 1935, p. 13.

72. *Blackshirt,* 17 May 1935, p. 5.

73. *Times,* 21 April 1933, p. 11.

74. *Hansard* (Commons), 318:1779.

Notes to Chapter 5, Incitement to Disaffection Act

1. J. R. Clynes, *Memoirs,* p. 197.

2. Michael Wharton, "A Few Lost Causes," p. 87.

3. G. M. Young, *Stanley Baldwin,* p. 167.

4. Robert Rhodes James, ed., *Memoirs of a Conservative: J. C. C. Davidson's Memoirs and Papers, 1910–1937,* p. 376.

5. Ibid.

6. Noreen Branson and Margot Heinemann, *Britain in the Nineteen Thirties,* p. 5.

7. Vindicator [pseud.], *A Strong Hand at the Helm,* p. 97.

8. *Guardian,* 6 October 1934, p. 16.

9. H. Montgomery Hyde, *United in Crime,* p. 57.

10. Arthur Harold Booth, *British Hustings,* p. 139.
11. Great Britain, *Hansard Parliamentary Debates* (Commons), 5th ser., 288:157.
12. Ibid. 13. Ibid., 740–42. 14. Ibid., 740. 15. Ibid., 749.
16. Not all of this seditious literature was spread by penniless and unsuspecting boys. Douglas Hyde reported that he and several other young Communists drew lots to drop copies of the *Soldier's Voice* over the barracks walls at Bristol. See Douglas Hyde, *I Believed,* p. 45.
17. David Williams, *Keeping the Peace,* p. 45.
18. Harry Street, *Freedom, the Individual, and the Law,* p. 202.
19. James E. MacColl and W. T. Wells, "The Incitement to Disaffection Bill, 1934," p. 354.
20. *Hansard* (Commons), 288:739–40.
21. Ibid., 775–76.
22. Williams, *Keeping the Peace,* p. 80.
23. *Hansard* (Commons), 288:751.
24. Great Britain, *Parliamentary Papers* (1933–1934), 2, "Incitement to Disaffection," p. 1.
25. Ibid.
26. *Hansard* (Commons), 288:746.
27. Ibid., 774. 28. Ibid., 750. 29. Ibid., 765.
30. *Parliamentary Papers* (1933–1934), 2, "Incitement to Disaffection," p. 2.
31. *Hansard* (Commons), 388:767.
32. Ibid., 847–48. 33. Ibid., 825–27.
34. *Parliamentary Papers* (1933–1934), 2, "Incitement to Disaffection," p. 2.
35. *Guardian,* 12 April 1934, p. 8.
36. *Hansard* (Commons), 288:242–44.
37. Michael Stewart, *The British Approach to Politics,* p. 191.
38. *Guardian,* 17 April 1934, p. 8.
39. Ibid., 12 April 1934, p. 9.
40. *Hansard* (Commons), 288:807–8.
41. *New Statesman and Nation,* 26 May 1934, p. 789.
42. William MacElwee, *Britain's Locust Years, 1918–1940,* p. 187.
43. *New Statesman,* 2 June 1934, p. 844.
44. W. H. Thompson, *Civil Liberties,* pp. 57–60.
45. Williams, *Keeping the Peace,* p. 199.
46. Emlyn Capel Stuart Wade and G. Godfrey Phillips, *Constitutional Law,* p. 175.
47. *Hansard* (Commons), 188:761.
48. *Daily Worker,* 12 April 1934, p. 1.
49. Conclusions of Cabinet, 9 October 1934, CAB 23/77, 52/33/4, pp. 11–12, PRO.
50. Ibid., 18 October 1933, CAB 23/77, 53/33/6, p. 13, PRO.
51. Ibid., 23 February 1934, CAB 24/247, no. 53, copy 36, PRO.
52. Ibid., 28 February 1934, CAB 23/78, 7/34/5, p. 9, PRO.
53. Ibid., 3 March 1934, CAB 24/247/62, copy 37, *Secret,* PRO.
54. Ibid., 7 March 1934, CAB 23/78, 8/34/6, pp. 10–11, PRO.
55. Ibid., 2 March 1934, CAB 23/78, 11/34/10, p. 15, PRO.
56. A. V. Dicey, *Introduction to the Study of the Law of the Constitution,* 9th ed., p. 188.
57. *Parliamentary Papers* (1933–1934), 6, "Report on the Incitement to Disaffection Bill with the Proceedings of the Committee," p. 2.
58. *Guardian,* 9 May 1934, p. 14.
59. Ibid., 8 May 1934, p. 2. 60. Ibid., 9 May 1934, p. 2.
61. *Times,* 31 May 1934, p. 9.
62. Ibid., 1 June 1934, p. 10.

63. *Guardian,* 1 June 1934, p. 6.
64. Ibid., 6 June 1934, p. 14.
65. Ibid., 13 June 1934, p. 5.
66. *Times,* 13 June 1934, p. 11.
67. *Guardian,* 20 June 1934, p. 11.
68. Ibid., 27 June 1934, p. 5.
69. *Parliamentary Papers* (1933–1934), 6, "Report on the Incitement to Disaffection Bill with the Proceedings of the Committee," pp. 20–21.
70. *Times,* 16 July 1934, p. 8.
71. *Parliamentary Papers* (1933–1934), 6, "Report on the Incitement to Disaffection Bill with the Proceedings of the Committee," pp. 20–21.
72. *Hansard* (Commons), 291:2073–75.
73. *Parliamentary Papers* (1933–1934), 6, "Report on the Incitement to Disaffection Bill with the Proceedings of the Committee," p. 27.
74. Walter Bagehot, *The English Constitution,* p. 149.
75. *New Statesman,* 3 November 1934, p. 609.
76. Ibid., 21 April 1934, pp. 590–91.
77. Ibid., 12 May 1934, p. 707.
78. National Council for Civil Liberties, *The Record of a Decade of Work for Democracy and Civil Liberty,* pp. 8–9.
79. *Guardian,* 7 May 1934, p. 2.
80. Ibid., 25 May 1934, p. 9.
81. Ibid., 10 May 1934, p. 11.
82. Ibid.
83. Ibid., 1 June 1934, p. 6.
84. *Free Speech and Assembly Bulletin,* no. 8 (June 1934), p. 4.
85. Trades Union Congress, *Report of Proceedings at the 66th Annual Trades Union Congress—Bournemouth, 1934,* ed. by Walter M. Citrine, p. 183.
86. Communist Party of Great Britain, "Sedition Bill Exposed" (pamphlet), p. 18.
87. Ibid., pp. 15–16.
88. *Daily Worker,* 12 April 1934, p. 2.
89. Ibid., 23 April 1934, p. 3.
90. *Guardian,* 31 May 1934, p. 6.
91. *Hansard* (Commons), 290:565.
92. *Guardian,* 9 May 1934, p. 4.
93. Ibid., 3 May 1934, p. 10.
94. Ibid., 5 May 1934, p. 17.
95. Ibid., 6 July 1934, p. 14.
96. Ibid., 23 April 1934, p. 11.
97. Ibid., 24 July 1934, p. 18.
98. Ibid., 28 April 1934, p. 13.
99. *Free Speech and Assembly Bulletin,* no. 8 (June 1934), p. 3.
100. Ibid., p. 6.
101. Ibid., p. 5.
102. Ibid., p. 7.
103. James, *Memoirs of a Conservative,* p. 410.
104. Thomas Inskip to Ronald Kidd and the National Council for Civil Liberties, 8 June 1934, file JC/585, Trades Union Congress Library (hereafter cited as TUC Library), London.
105. Ronald Kidd to Thomas Inskip, 10 June 1934, filing case 2, section 1, National Council for Civil Liberties Records (hereafter cited as NCCL Records), University of Hull Library.
106. Ronald Kidd to the editor of the *Spectator,* 6 July 1934, filing case 2, section 1, NCCL Records, University of Hull Library.
107. Denis Nowell Pritt to Ronald Kidd, 17 July 1934, filing case 2, section 1, NCCL Records, University of Hull Library.
108. Kidd to Inskip, 23 July 1934, filing case 2, section 1, NCCL Records, University of Hull Library.
109. E. M. Forster, "Notes of a Deputation Received by the Attorney-General at

the House of Commons on Monday, July 30, 1934, re. the Disaffection Bill," filing case 74, section 5, NCCL Records, University of Hull Library, p. 12.

110. Ibid., p. 35. 111. Ibid., p. 41.

112. Kidd to Inskip, 28 October 1934, filing case 2, section 1, NCCL Records, University of Hull Library.

113. Ronald Kidd to the Prime Minister's Secretary, 13 July 1934, filing case 2, section 1, NCCL Records, University of Hull Library.

114. *Hansard* (Commons), 292:2456.

115. Rosten, "The Rise of Oswald Mosley," p. 498.

116. *Guardian,* 19 October 1934, p. 3.

117. Ibid. 118. Ibid., 22 October 1934, p. 11. 119. Ibid.

120. Michael Foot, *Aneurin Bevan,* 1:199. See also Alan Bullock, *The Life and Times of Ernest Bevin,* p. 552.

121. *Labour* 2 (September 1934): 3.

122. *Guardian,* 29 October 1934, p. 12.

123. Ibid.

124. Williams, *Keeping the Peace,* p. 188.

125. National Council for Civil Liberties, "The Incitement to Disaffection Bill: How It Now Stands" (broadsheet).

126. *Guardian,* 23 October 1934, p. 12.

127. *Times,* 26 October 1934, p. 7.

128. *Guardian,* 31 October 1934, p. 9.

129. *Hansard* (Commons), 293:47–50.

130. *Guardian,* 1 November 1934, p. 9.

131. Conclusions of Cabinet, 31 October 1934, CAB 23/80, 38/34/8, p. 15, PRO.

132. *Hansard* (Commons), 293:113–17.

133. Ibid., 165–76. 134. Ibid., 271–74. 135. Ibid., 297–98.

136. Ibid., 582–83. 137. Ibid., 525–28. 138. Ibid., 608.

139. *Guardian,* 7 November 1934, p. 2.

140. *Times,* 7 November 1934, p. 7.

141. *Punch,* 21 November 1934, p. 577.

142. *Hansard* (Commons), 293:1771.

143. Ibid., 2305.

144. *Guardian,* 6 July 1934, p. 14.

145. Wade and Phillips, *Constitutional Law,* p. 365.

146. Williams, *Keeping the Peace,* p. 190.

147. Ronald Kidd, *British Liberty in Danger,* p. 67.

148. *Hansard* (Commons), 293:201–40.

149. Harry Street, *Freedom, the Individual, and the Law,* p. 205.

150. Kidd, *British Liberty in Danger,* p. 6.

151. Communist Party of Great Britain, *The Workers United Front and the I.L.P.*

152. Ishmael [pseud.], "That's Sedition—That Was" (pamphlet), p. 1.

153. *New Statesman,* 9 June 1934, p. 880.

154. Trades Union Congress, *66th Annual TUC,* p. 315.

155. Trades Union Congress, *Report of the Proceedings at the 67th Annual Trades Union Congress—Margate, 1935,* ed. by Walter M. Citrine, p. 397.

156. National Council for Civil Liberties, *Notes for the International Conference of the International Judicial Association, 1937,* p. 4.

Notes to Chapter 6, Olympia

1. Robert Benewick, *Political Violence and Public Order,* p. 169.
2. *Guardian,* 13 March 1933, p. 9.
3. Benewick, *Political Violence,* p. 90.
4. *Guardian,* 22 January 1934, p. 6.
5. Ibid., 19 February 1934, p. 13. 6. Ibid., 27 March 1934, p. 7.
7. *Daily Worker,* 24 April 1934, p. 1.
8. *Guardian,* 5 May 1934, p. 9.
9. *Daily Worker,* 4 June 1934, p. 1.
10. Ibid.
11. *Blackshirt,* 8 June 1934, p. 7.
12. *Fascist Week,* 18–24 May 1934, p. 1.
13. *Guardian,* 4 June 1934, p. 8.
14. *Daily Worker,* 2 June 1934, p. 3.
15. Ibid., 6 June 1934, p. 3. 16. Ibid., 7 June 1934, p. 1.
17. Benewick, *Political Violence,* p. 169.
18. *Guardian,* 8 June 1934, p. 6.
19. *Times,* 9 June 1934, p. 11.
20. Great Britain, *Hansard Parliamentary Debates* (Commons), 5th ser., 290:2003.
21. Quoted in Vindicator [pseud.], *Fascists at Olympia,* p. 15. This pamphlet was composed of statements in Commons and in the press concerning the Olympia violence.
22. F. Yeats-Brown to Robert Kidd, 20 June 1934, filing case 40, section 1, Inquiry of Olympia, NCCL Records, University of Hull Library.
23. Ronald Kidd to F. Yeats-Brown, 26 June 1934, filing case 40, section 1, Inquiry of Olympia, NCCL Records, University of Hull Library.
24. *Blackshirt,* 15 June 1934, p. 1.
25. *Guardian,* 4 June 1934, p. 13.
26. Ibid., 11 June 1934, p. 9.
27. *Daily Mail,* 14 June 1934, p. 18.
28. *Guardian,* 9 June 1934, p. 13.
29. *Daily Worker,* 9 June 1934, p. 2.
30. *Guardian,* 8 June 1934, p. 20.
31. *Hansard* (Commons), 290:1343.
32. *Guardian,* 12 June 1934, p. 10.
33. *Hansard* (Commons), 290:1343.
34. Ibid., 1344. 35. Ibid., 1345. 36. Ibid., 1692.
37. Benewick, *Political Violence,* p. 172.
38. Oswald Mosley, *My Life,* p. 297.
39. *Times,* 9 June 1934, p. 11.
40. *Hansard* (Commons), 290:1930.
41. Ibid., 1695–99. 42. Ibid., 1919. 43. Ibid., 1694.
44. Ibid., 1919–20. 45. Ibid., 1926. 46. Ibid., 1990.
47. Ibid., 1957. 48. Ibid., 1959. 49. Ibid., 1345–46.
50. Henry Pelling, *The British Communist Party: A Historical Profile,* p. 83.
51. *Daily Worker,* 13 June 1934, p. 2.
52. *Guardian,* 18 June 1934, p. 6.

Notes to Chapter 7, After Olympia

1. Andrew Boyle, *Trenchard,* p. 652.
2. *Guardian,* 21 February 1934, p. 8.
3. Ibid., 23 February 1934, p. 9.
4. Joseph Baker, letter to the editor, *Guardian,* 4 May 1934, p. 22. See also Baker's book, *The Law of Political Uniforms, Public Meetings, and Private Armies,* pp. 114–15.
5. Baker, letter to the editor, *Guardian,* 4 May 1934, p. 22.
6. C. E. Lewis, letter to the editor, *Guardian,* 19 May 1934, p. 5.
7. Oswald Mosley, *Fascism in Britain,* p. 10.
8. James Drennan [William Edward David Allen], *Oswald Mosley and British Fascism,* p. 244.
9. Baker, *The Law of Political Uniforms,* p. viii.
10. Trades Union Congress, *Report of the Proceedings at the 66th Annual Trades Union Congress—Weymouth, 1934,* ed. by Walter M. Citrine, p. 99.
11. Minutes of Cabinet, 23 May 1934, CAB 24/249/144, copy 35, *Secret,* PRO.
12. Ibid. 13. Ibid., 30 May 1934, CAB 79, 22/34/7, p. 11, PRO.
14. Ibid., p. 12.
15. Ibid., 13 June 1934, CAB 79, 24/34/1, pp. 1–2, PRO.
16. Ibid., p. 1.
17. Conclusions of Cabinet, 13 June 1934, CAB 79, 24/34/Appendix, p. i, PRO.
18. Ibid. 19. Ibid., pp. ii–iii. 20. Ibid., pp. iii–iv.
21. Minutes of Cabinet, 13 June 1934, CAB 79, 24/34/1, p. 2, PRO.
22. Great Britain, *Hansard Parliamentary Debates* (Commons), 5th ser., 290:1937–38.
23. Ibid., 1992.
24. Trades Union Congress, *66th Annual TUC,* p. 449.
25. Labour Party, *Report of the 34th Annual Conference—Southport, 1934,* p. 19.
26. Ibid.
27. Trades Union Congress, *66th Annual TUC,* p. 450.
28. Labour Party, *34th Annual Conference,* p. 19.
29. *Guardian,* 29 June 1934, p. 15.
30. Conclusions of Cabinet, 4 July 1934, CAB 79, 27/34/9, p. 15, PRO.
31. Cabinet Papers, 11 July 1934, CAB 24, 250/189, copy 38, PRO.
32. Minutes of Cabinet, 18 July 1934, CAB 79, 29/34/2, p. 2, PRO.
33. Ibid., p. 3. 34. Ibid., p. 5.
35. Robert Benewick, *Political Violence and Public Order,* p. 183.
36. *Daily Mail,* 19 July 1934, p. 12.
37. Oswald Mosley, *My Life,* p. 343.
38. *Guardian,* 14 July 1934, p. 8.
39. Trades Union Congress, *66th Annual TUC,* p. 450.
40. Minutes of Cabinet, 31 July 1934, CAB 79, 31/34/7, p. 16, PRO.
41. *Guardian,* 17 August 1934, p. 9.
42. Ibid., 25 August 1934, p. 9.
43. *Daily Worker,* 16 August 1934, p. 4.
44. Ibid., 22 August 1934, p. 2.
45. *Guardian,* 25 August 1934, p. 9.
46. Ibid., 5 September 1934, p. 9.
47. *Daily Worker,* 7 September 1934, p. 1.
48. *Guardian,* 5 September 1934, p. 9.
49. Trades Union Congress, *66th Annual TUC,* p. 448.

50. *Guardian,* 5 September 1934, p. 9.
51. Oswald Mosley, *Blackshirt Policy,* p. 17.
52. *Daily Worker,* 8 September 1934, p. 1.
53. *Guardian,* 8 September 1934, p. 17.
54. Ibid., p. 10.
55. Oswald Mosley to Trevor Bigham, Scotland Yard, 7 September 1934, MEPOL 2/3074, no. 35EE, PRO.
56. *Guardian,* 8 September 1934, p. 11.
57. British Union of Fascists Deputy Chief of Staff's office, Confidential Memorandum, 8 September 1934, MEPOL 2/3074, no. 36F, PRO.
58. The Committee for Anti-Fascist Activities to All Marshalls and Shock Brigade Unit Leaders, Confidential Memorandum, 9 September 1934, MEPOL 2/3074, no. 17D, PRO.
59. *Daily Worker,* 8 September 1934, p. 1.
60. N. Francis-Hawkins to Abbott of Scotland Yard, 8 September 1934, MEPOL 2/3074, no. 36B, PRO.
61. Great Britain, *Parliamentary Papers* (1934–1935), 10, "Report of the Commissioner of the Police of the Metropolis for the Year 1934," p. 51.
62. *Guardian,* 10 September 1934, p. 9; *Times,* 10 September 1934, p. 9.
63. *Guardian,* 10 September 1934, p. 9.
64. Ibid.; *Times,* 10 September 1934, p. 9.
65. *Guardian,* 10 September 1934, p. 9.
66. Ibid.; *Times,* 10 September 1934, p. 9.
67. *Blackshirt,* 14 September 1934, p. 1.
68. *Guardian,* 10 September 1934, p. 12.
69. Emile Burns, "The Case for Affiliation" (pamphlet), p. 4.
70. Harold Keeble, Police Inspector, Summary—Hyde Park Demonstration, 10 September 1934, MEPOL 2/3074, no. 41A, PRO.
71. Lord Trenchard to Members of the Metropolitan Police Force, Memorandum, 10 September 1934, MEPOL 2/3074, no. 42B, PRO.
72. *Parliamentary Papers* (1934–1935), 10, "Report of the Commissioner of the Police of the Metropolis for the Year 1934," p. 51.
73. *Guardian,* 10 September 1934, p. 10.
74. Trades Union Congress, *66th Annual TUC,* p. 255.
75. Ibid., p. 57.
76. Ibid., p. 59.
77. Ibid., p. 66.
78. Labour Party, *34th Annual Conference,* p. 129.
79. *Guardian,* 27 September 1934, p. 11.
80. National Council for Civil Liberties, *The Record of a Decade of Work for Democracy and Civil Liberty,* p. 15.
81. Colin Cross, *The Fascists in Britain,* p. 125.
82. *Guardian,* 1 October 1934, p. 9.
83. Ibid., p. 11.
84. Cross, *The Fascists in Britain,* p. 125.
85. *Guardian,* 1 October 1934, p. 8.
86. Ibid., 20 October 1934, p. 13.
87. Ibid., 22 October 1934, p. 9.
88. Ibid., 10 October 1934, p. 9; ibid., 12 October 1934, p. 11.
89. Ibid., 19 November 1934, p. 9.
90. National Council for Civil Liberties, *Annual Report and Balance Sheet, 1934,* p. 16.
91. *Guardian,* 26 November 1934, p. 9.
92. Ibid., 6 December 1934, p. 11.
93. *Blackshirt,* 2 October 1937, p. 4.
94. *Guardian,* 19 January 1935, p. 12.

95. Trades Union Congress, *Report of the Proceedings at the 67th Annual Trades Union Congress—Margate, 1935,* p. 480.
96. Benewick, *Political Violence,* p. 194.
97. *Guardian,* 15 April 1935, p. 9.
98. Herbert L. Samuel, *The Political Situation,* p. 2.
99. Trades Union Congress, *67th Annual TUC,* p. 415.
100. *Guardian,* 2 September 1935, p. 11.
101. *Blackshirt,* 25 October 1935, p. 2.
102. Benewick, *Political Violence,* p. 202.
103. *Fascist Quarterly,* 2 (January 1936): 6.
104. Ibid., p. 31. 105. Ibid., p. 4.

Notes to Chapter 8, Renewal of Violence

1. *Fascist Quarterly,* 2 (January 1936): 33.
2. J. L. Douglas, *Spotlight on Fascism,* p. 1.
3. Communist Party of Great Britain, *The March of English History,* p. 5.
4. A. E. Newson, Assistant Secretary of State for the Home Department to Philip Game, 15 October 1935, MEPOL 2/2825, no. 1A, PRO.
5. Great Britain, *Hansard Parliamentary Debates* (Commons), 5th ser., 308:1121–22.
6. Ibid., 309:634. 7. Ibid., 1544.
8. Robert Benewick, *Political Violence and Public Order,* p. 218. Poverty was set as an income of forty shillings per week for a moderate family. Benewick takes his figures from the *New Survey of London Life and Labour,* 3 (1930–1935):345–46.
9. Benewick, *Political Violence,* p. 219.
10. *Hansard* (Commons), 309:1602.
11. Ibid., 1595–1603. 12. Ibid., 1603–5. 13. Ibid., 1608–9.
14. Ibid., 1633.
15. *Daily Worker,* 17 March 1936, p. 1, 18 March 1936, p. 1.
16. *Guardian,* 9 March 1936, p. 13.
17. National Council for Civil Liberties, "Report of a Commission of Inquiry into Certain Disturbances at Thurloe Square, South Kensington, on March 22nd, 1936" (pamphlet), pp. 19–20.
18. *Guardian,* 23 March 1936, p. 11; *Times,* 23 March 1936, p. 14.
19. Philip Game would later write, "Mounted police are extremely useful for this kind of patroling work. They can get about quickly and they have an extraordinary effect with the class of people they will have to deal with." Memorandum from the Commissioner of Metropolitan Police, 16 October 1936, MEPOL 2/3089, no. 16A, PRO.
20. National Council for Civil Liberties, "Report of Commission—Thurloe Square," p. 21.
21. Ibid., p. 24. 22. Ibid., p. 25.
23. *Hansard* (Commons), 310:1227–29.
24. *Guardian,* 23 March 1936, p. 6; *Times,* 23 March 1936, p. 14.
25. *Fascist Quarterly* 2 (April 1936):205–6.
26. *Blackshirt,* 28 March 1936, p. 4.
27. *Daily Worker,* 24 March 1936, p. 1.
28. *Hansard* (Commons), 310:1365–68.
29. Ibid., 1230.
30. National Council for Civil Liberties, "Report of Commission—Thurloe Square," p. 3.

31. *Hansard* (Commons), 310:1361–68.
32. National Council for Civil Liberties, "Sir Oswald Mosley's Albert Hall Meeting, March 22nd: Extracts from Statements of Eyewitnesses" (pamphlet), p. 2.
33. Ibid., pp. 1–11.
34. Ibid., "Report of Commission—Thurloe Square," p. 21.
35. Ibid., p. 4.
36. Philip Game to the Home Secretary, Confidential Report, 17 September 1936, MEPOL 2/3089, no. 17A, PRO.
37. *Hansard* (Commons), 310:1229–30.
38. Norman Kendal to the Metropolitan Police Force, Secret Memorandum, 30 March 1936, MEPOL 2/22, p. 1/1014, no. 3/36, A-2, PRO.
39. *Discussion,* no. 4 (April 1936), pp. 22–23.
40. Ibid., p. 21.
41. *Daily Worker,* 30 March 1936, p. 3.
42. *Discussion,* no. 4 (April 1936), p. 24.
43. Ibid., no. 6 (June 1936), p. 21.
44. Harry Pollitt, *Arms for Spain,* pp. 12–13.
45. Ibid., p. 15.
46. *New Statesman,* 23 May 1936, p. 797.
47. *Guardian,* 18 May 1936, p. 11.
48. *Hansard* (Commons), 312:1633–34.
49. Ibid., 807. 50. Ibid., 2170.
51. *Fascist Quarterly* 2 (July 1936): 335.
52. *Blackshirt,* 13 June 1936, pp. 1–2.
53. Benewick, *Political Violence,* p. 221.
54. *Hansard* (Commons), 331:808.
55. Ibid., 1008. 56. Ibid., 1425–26.
57. *Guardian,* 29 June 1936, p. 9.
58. *New Statesman,* 30 May 1936, p. 850.
59. *Hansard* (Commons), 314:1560–1608. 60. Ibid., 1616–29.
61. *Guardian,* 11 July 1936, p. 12.
62. John Simon to Philip Game, Confidential Memorandum, 16 July 1936, MEPOL 2/3043, no. 1A, PRO.
63. *Guardian,* 13 July 1936, p. 9.
64. Beverley Nichols, *News of England: Or, A Country Without a Hero,* p. 266. Nichols found the attempted assassination strange because political assassination was rare in England, but even stranger because no newspaper except a Fascist organ ever mentioned the incident.
65. *Guardian,* 13 July 1936, p. 9.
66. Ibid., 17 July 1936, p. 15. 67. Ibid.
68. Ibid., 20 July 1936, p. 11; *Times,* 20 July 1936, p. 14.
69. Ibid., 22 July 1936, p. 11.
70. *Hansard* (Commons), 315:1095.
71. Noreen Branson and Margot Heinemann, *Britain in the Nineteen Thirties,* p. 312.
72. Ibid., pp. 310–16.
73. Pollitt, *Arms for Spain,* p. 15.
74. Minutes of Cabinet, 29 July 1936, CAB 85, 55/36/12, pp. 17–18, PRO.
75. *Hansard* (Commons), 315:1706.
76. Philip Game to Members of the Metropolitan Police Force, Confidential Memorandum, 3 August 1936, MEPOL 2, 22/Gen./76, A2, PRO.
77. Philip Game to John Simon, Confidential Report, 9 September 1936, MEPOL 2/3043, no. 10A, PRO.

78. A. E. Newson to Philip Game, Home Office Memorandum, 15 September 1936, MEPOL 2/3043, no. 11A, PRO.

Notes to Chapter 9, Catalyst for Legislative Action

1. Philip Game to John Simon, Confidential Report, 8 October 1936, MEPOL 2/3043, no. 16A, PRO.
2. *Guardian,* 28 September 1936, p. 9; *Times,* 28 September 1936, p. 14.
3. *Guardian,* 30 September 1936, p. 18.
4. *Daily Worker,* 1 October 1936, p. 5.
5. Ibid. 6. Ibid., 2 October 1936, p. 1.
7. Labour Party, *Report of the 36th Annual Conference—Edinburgh,* p. 208.
8. Trades Union Congress, *Report of the Proceedings at the 68th Annual Trades Union Congress—Plymouth, 1936,* p. 424.
9. Communist Party of Great Britain, *The March of English History,* p. 12.
10. *Daily Worker,* 2 October 1936, p. 1.
11. *Times,* 10 October 1936, p. 8; *Guardian,* 13 October 1936, p. 10.
12. *Guardian,* 3 October 1936, p. 12.
13. Robert Benewick, *Political Violence and Public Order,* p. 226.
14. *Daily Worker,* 5 October 1936, p. 1.
15. *Guardian,* 5 October 1936, p. 11.
16. Ibid.
17. *Daily Worker,* 5 October 1936, p. 5; *Guardian,* 5 October 1936, p. 11; *Times,* 5 October 1936, p. 9.
18. *Guardian,* 5 October 1936, p. 11.
19. *Daily Worker,* 5 October 1936, p. 1.
20. Ibid., 5 October 1936, p. 5; *Guardian,* 5 October 1936, p. 5; *Times,* 5 October 1936, p. 9.
21. E. G. Clarke, *The British Union and the Jews,* pp. 6–7.
22. *Blackshirt,* 10 October 1936, pp. 1, 4.
23. *British Union Quarterly* 1 (January 1936): 8.
24. Ibid., p. 9.
25. *Guardian,* 5 October 1936, p. 11; *Times,* 5 October 1936, p. 9.
26. *Times,* 5 October 1936, p. 12.
27. Great Britain, *Parliamentary Papers* (1936–1937), 14, "Report of the Commissioner of Police of the Metropolis for the Year 1936," p. 26.
28. *Guardian,* 5 October 1936, p. 10.
29. Interdivision Memorandum, Metropolitan Police, 5 October 1936, MEPOL 2/3089, no. 4D, PRO.
30. The Special Branch to Philip Game, Confidential Report, 1 November 1936, MEPOL 2/3089, no. 21A, PRO.
31. Ibid.
32. Philip Game to Geoffrey Lloyd, 1 November 1936, MEPOL 2/3089, no. 29A, PRO.
33. *Guardian,* 8 October 1936, p. 11.
34. Ibid., 10 October 1936, p. 14.
35. Ibid., 12 October 1936, p. 9.
36. Ibid., 13 October 1936, p. 14.
37. Ibid., 12 October 1936, p. 10; *Times,* 12 October 1936, p. 11.
38. *Guardian,* 13 October 1936, p. 10.
39. Ibid., 15 October 1936, p. 5.

40. The Special Branch to Philip Game, Confidential Report, 1 November 1936, MEPOL 2/3043, no. 21A, PRO.

41. *Free Speech and Assembly Bulletin,* no. 20 (November 1936), p. 5.

42. Philip Game to John Simon, Confidential Report, 5 November 1936, MEPOL 2/3043, no. 22A, PRO.

43. Philip Game to the Metropolitan Police Force, Memorandum, 5 November 1936, MEPOL 2/3098, minute sheet 4, PRO.

Notes to Chapter 10, The Public Order Act

1. Great Britain, *Parliamentary Debates* (Commons), 5th ser., 317:1375.
2. *Guardian,* 6 October 1936, p. 12.
3. *Fascist Quarterly* 2 (October 1936):476.
4. J. Toole, "Free Speech and Militarized Politics," p. 59.
5. Labour Party, *Report of the 36th Annual Conference—Edinburgh,* p. 164.
6. Ibid., pp. 164–65.
7. *Guardian,* 8 October 1936, p. 4.
8. Ibid., 9 October 1936, p. 12. 9. Ibid., 10 October 1936, p. 13.
10. Ibid., 13 October 1936, p. 14. 11. Ibid., 14 October 1936, p. 9.
12. John Simon, Cabinet Memorandum, 12 October 1936, CAB 85, 24/264/261, copy 46, PRO.
13. Ibid.
14. Minutes of Cabinet, 14 October 1936, CAB 85, 57/62/2, pp. 2–3, PRO.
15. *Guardian,* 15 October 1936, p. 9; *Times,* 15 October 1936, p. 14.
16. *Guardian,* 17 October 1936, p. 17.
17. Ibid., 21 October 1936, p. 9; *Times,* 21 October 1936, p. 14.
18. Minutes of Cabinet, 21 October 1936, CAB 85, 58/36/9, p. 14, PRO.
19. John Simon, Report: Committee on the Preservation of Public Order, 26 October 1936, CAB 85, 24/265/282, copy 43, PRO.
20. Ibid., 3 November 1936, CAB 85, 24/265/290, copy 43, PRO.
21. Ibid.
22. Minutes of Cabinet, 4 November 1936, CAB 86, 62/36/9, pp. 18–19, PRO.
23. *Hansard* (Commons), 316:7.
24. *Hansard* (Lords), 103:4.
25. *Hansard* (Commons), 317:34–35.
26. Ibid., 296. 27. Ibid., 1029–30. 28. Ibid., 235.
29. *Daily Worker,* 3 November 1936, p. 5.
30. *Guardian,* 2 November 1936, p. 12.
31. Ibid., 9 November 1936, p. 11.
32. Ibid., 5 November 1936, p. 10.
33. Great Britain, *Parliamentary Papers* (1936–1937), 5, "Public Order," p. 1.
34. Ibid.
35. *Free Speech and Assembly Bulletin,* no. 21 (November 1936), p. 2.
36. Joseph Baker, *The Law of Political Uniforms, Public Meetings, and Private Armies,* p. viii.
37. *Parliamentary Papers* (1936–1937), 5, "Public Order," p. 2.
38. *Guardian,* 19 October 1936, p. 18.
39. The Haldane Club, "The Law of Public Meetings and the Right of Police Search" (pamphlet), p. 18.
40. *Free Speech and Assembly Bulletin,* no. 21 (November 1936), p. 3.
41. Albert Crew, *The Law Relating to Public Meetings and Processions,* pp. xvi–xvii.
42. Baker, *The Law of Political Uniforms,* p. 13.

43. *Parliamentary Papers* (1936–1937), 5, "Public Order," p. 6.
44. Baker, *The Law of Political Uniforms,* pp. 59–60.
45. *Parliamentary Papers* (1936–1937), 5, "Public Order," p. 4.
46. Ibid.
47. Crew, *The Law Relating to Public Meetings,* p. 17.
48. *Parliamentary Papers* (1936–1937), 5, "Public Order," p. 5.
49. *Free Speech and Assembly Bulletin,* no. 21 (November 1936), p. 8.
50. *Parliamentary Papers* (1936–1937), 5, "Public Order," pp. 3–4.
51. *Free Speech and Assembly Bulletin,* no. 21 (November 1936), pp. 3–4.
52. *Guardian,* 12 November 1936, p. 5.
53. *New Statesman,* 14 November 1936, pp. 761–63.
54. *Daily Worker,* 10 November 1936, p. 3.
55. Ibid., 12 November 1936, p. 4.
56. Ibid.
57. *Blackshirt,* 14 November 1936, p. 1.
58. Ibid. 59. Ibid.
60. *Guardian,* 16 November 1936, p. 10.
61. Ibid., p. 8.
62. *Hansard* (Commons), 117:1350–51.
63. Ibid., 1352. 64. Ibid., 1369–73. 65. Ibid., 189–91.
66. Ibid., 1407. 67. Ibid., 1387.
68. *Guardian,* 21 November 1936, p. 12.
69. *Hansard* (Commons), 318:63–70.
70. Ibid., 102. 71. Ibid., 136. 72. Ibid., 138–45.
73. Ibid., 165–86.
74. Ibid., 1765–66.
75. Ramsey Muir, *The Record of the National Government,* p. 36.
76. *Hansard* (Lords), 103:972; *Parliamentary Papers* (1936–1937), 5, "Public Order."
77. *Daily Worker,* 7 December 1936, p. 5.
78. *Hansard* (Commons), 318:2819.
79. Oliver Cruchley and Ivan Cruchley, "Freedom in Our Time," *Fabian Tract No. 244,* p. 3.
80. *Free Speech and Assembly Bulletin,* no. 23 (January 1937), p. 5.
81. Rajani Palme Dutt, *What Next for the Labour Party?,* p. 1.
82. Philip Game to John Simon, Confidential Report, 1 December 1936, MEPOL 2/3043, 23B, PRO.
83. *British Union Quarterly* 1 (January 1937):11.
84. John Simon, *Retrospect,* pp. 215–16.

Notes to Chapter 11, Public Order and Civil Liberties

1. Philip Game to John Simon, Confidential Report, 3 November 1936, MEPOL 2/3043, 21B, PRO.
2. Ibid., 1 December 1936, MEPOL 2/3043, 23B, PRO.
3. Ibid., 12 March 1937, MEPOL 2/3043, no. 40A, PRO.
4. Lord Jessel to Philip Game, 17 February 1937, MEPOL 2/3089, no. 47J, PRO.
5. Philip Game to John Simon, Confidential Report, 12 March 1937, MEPOL 2/3043, no. 40A, PRO.
6. John Simon to the Commissioner of Police, Home Office Memorandum, 30 March 1937, MEPOL 2/3043, no. 42A, PRO.
7. Robert Benewick, *Political Violence and Public Order,* p. 248.

8. *Times,* 11 June 1937, p. 4.

9. Great Britain, *Hansard Parliamentary Debates* (Commons), 5th ser., 325:846–48.

10. *Times,* 22 June 1937, p. 16.

11. Minutes of Cabinet, 23 June 1937, CAB 88, 26/37/6, p. 9, PRO.

12. *Times,* 29 June 1937, p. 14.

13. *Civil Liberty,* no. 2 (Autumn 1937), p. 2.

14. *Times,* 5 July 1937, p. 8.

15. *Hansard* (Commons), 326:1456.

16. Benewick, *Political Violence,* p. 250.

17. *Times,* 21 September 1937, p. 9.

18. Ibid., 4 October 1937, p. 14. 19. Ibid., p. 16. 20. Ibid., p. 15.

21. Ibid., 6 October 1937, p. 11.

22. *Guardian,* 17 July 1939, p. 12.

23. Oswald Mosley, *Fascism: 100 Questions Asked and Answered,* p. 6.

24. Great Britain, *Parliamentary Papers* (1937–1938), 14, "Report of the Commissioner of Police of the Metropolis for the Year 1937," pp. 12–13.

25. *Parliamentary Papers* (1938–1939), 14, "Report of the Commissioner of Police of the Metropolis for the Year 1938," pp. 8–9.

26. The Special Branch to the Commissioner of the Metropolitan Police, Report, 3 January 1939, MEPOL 2/3043, 133A, PRO.

27. Alfred M. Wall, "Address to the Conference on Fascism and Anti-Semitism," 25 April 1937, pp. 1–2.

28. Oswald Mosley to the Police Superintendent of Hornsey, 18 January 1937, MEPOL 2/3104, no. 2A, PRO.

29. J. Holmes, Inspector's Report of the Hornsey Town Hall Incident, 25 January 1937, MEPOL 2/3104, no. 5A, PRO.

30. Philip Game to the Secretary of State—A Report on the Hornsey Town Hall Disturbance, Memorandum, 2 April 1937, MEPOL 2/3104, no. 3YA, PRO.

31. John Simon to Fred Messer, M.P., 17 May 1937, MEPOL 2/3104, no. 42B, PRO.

32. Ronald Kidd, *British Liberty in Danger,* p. 133.

33. *Civil Liberty,* no. 2 (Autumn 1937), p. 13.

34. *Free Speech and Assembly Bulletin,* no. 27 (July 1937), p. 5.

35. *Civil Liberty,* no. 2 (Autumn 1937), p. 10.

36. Labour Party, *Report of the 37th Annual Conference—Bournemouth,* p. 215.

37. Ibid., p. 216.

Notes to Chapter 12, Conclusion

1. *Guardian,* 31 December 1936, p. 9.

2. "Notes of the Quarter," *British Union Quarterly* 1 (January–April 1937): 8.

3. A rabid anti-Semite, Clarke paraded about in a full-length black leather greatcoat; see Robert Benewick, *Political Violence and Public Order,* p. 280.

4. Ibid., pp. 279–80; Colin Cross, *The Fascists in Great Britain,* p. 166.

5. Benewick, *Political Violence,* p. 281.

6. Ibid., pp. 281–83; Cross, *The Fascists in Great Britain,* pp. 166–67.

7. Benewick, *Political Violence,* p. 282; Cross, *The Fascists in Great Britain,* p. 167.

8. *British Union Quarterly* 1 (May–July 1937):5–6.

9. Benewick, *Political Violence,* p. 272.

10. Philip Game to John Simon, Confidential Report, 7 May 1937, MEPOL 2/3043, no. 50A, PRO.
11. Stafford Cripps, James Maxton, and Harry Pollitt, *The Unity Campaign,* p. 1.
12. Philip Game to John Simon, Confidential Report, 1 March 1937, MEPOL 2/3043, 37A, PRO.
13. London District Congress, Communist Party of Great Britain, *For Social and Industrial Unity to Drive Fascism from London,* p. 3.
14. *Beckenham and Penge Discussion,* no. 1, p. 6.
15. Labour Party, *Report of the 37th Annual Conference—Bournemouth,* p. 158.
16. Harry Pollitt, *Labour's Way Forward,* p. 2.
17. Benewick, *Political Violence,* p. 286.
18. Herbert L. Samuel, *Practical Ethics,* p. 183.
19. Beverley Nichols, *News of England: Or, A Country Without a Hero,* p. 269.
20. Benewick, *Political Violence,* p. 275.
21. John Simon, *Retrospect,* p. 216.
22. Keith Middlemass and John Barnes, *Baldwin: A Biography,* p. 695.
23. John Bullock, *Akin to Treason,* p. 57.
24. Michael Wharton, "A Few Lost Causes," p. 90.

Bibliography

Public Documents

Great Britain. *Hansard Parliamentary Debates*. 5th series. 1919–1939.
Great Britain. London. Public Records Office. Minutes of Cabinet, 1933–1937, CAB 77–89.
Great Britain. London. Public Records Office. Reports, Correspondence, and Memoranda of the Metropolitan Police, 1932–1939, MEPOL 2.
Great Britain. *Parliamentary Papers*. 1914–1939.

Newspapers and Periodicals

Action (London), 1936–1937.
Blackshirt (London), 1933–1939.
British Union News (London), June 1939.
British Union Quarterly (London), 1937–1939.
Civil Liberty (London), 1937–1939.
Daily Mail (London), 1934.
Daily Telegraph (London), 1934–1936.
Daily Worker (London), 1933–1937.
Discussion (London), 1936–1937.
Dod's Parliamentary Companion (London), 1919–1939.
Fascist: The Organ of Racial Fascism (London), 1936–1937.
Fascist Quarterly (London), 1935–1936.
Fascist Week (London), 1933–1934.
Free Speech and Assembly Bulletin (London), 1933–1937.
Labour (London), 1934–1937.
Manchester Guardian (Manchester), 1934–1939.
New Statesman and Nation (London), 1933–1938.
News Sheet (London), 1936.
Punch (London), 1934–1936.
Times (London), 1919–1939.

Primary Sources

Baker, James. *The Law of Political Uniforms, Public Meetings, and Private Armies*. London: H.A. Just, 1937.
"Beckenham and Penge Discussion" (pamphlet). Penge, England: Beckenham and Penge Section, CPGB, 1938.
Bell, Tom. *The British Communist Party: A Short History*. London: Lawrence and Wishart, 1937.

British Union of Fascists. "Blackshirts Back Mosley Because Mosley Backs Britain" (pamphlet). London: BUF Trust, 1937.

———. "The British Union and the Transport Workers" (broadsheet). London: Avenue Printing Works, 1937.

———. Broadsheets and pamphlets, preserved in the Trades Union Congress Library, The British Library, and the London School of Economics Library, London; and Records of the National Council for Civil Liberties, University of Hull Library, Kingston upon Hull, Yorkshire. 1933–1939.

———. "The Empire and the British Union" (pamphlet). London: BUF Publications, 1937.

———. "The Miner's Only Hope" (broadsheet). London: BUF Publications, 1937.

———. "Support Fascism and Save the Fishermen" (broadsheet). London: BUF Publications, 1937.

Brownlie, Ian. *The Law Relating to Public Order*. London: Thornton Butterworth Press, 1968.

Bryant, Arthur. *Stanley Baldwin: A Tribute*. London: Hamish Hamilton, 1937.

Burns, Emile. "The Case for Affiliation" (pamphlet). London: CPGB, n.d.

Campbell, John Ross. "What Is the Use of Parliament?" (pamphlet). London: CPGB, 1924.

Catlin, George E.G. "Fascist Stirrings in Great Britain." *Current History* 39 (1934): 542–47.

Chamberlain, Sir Austen. *Down the Years*. London: Cassell and Co., 1935.

Chesterton, A.K. "The Apotheosis of the Jew" (pamphlet). London: BUF Publications, 1937.

———. *Creed of a Fascist Revolutionary*. London: BUF Publications, 1936.

———. "Fascism and the Press" (pamphlet). London: BUF Publications, 1937.

———. *Oswald Mosley: Portrait of a Leader*. London: BUF Publications, 1936.

———. "What the Jews Did in the War" (pamphlet). London: BUF Trust, 1937.

Chorley, R.S.T. *The Threat to Civil Liberty*. London: Haldane Society, 1938.

Clarke, E.G. *The British Union and the Jews*. London: BUF Trust, 1937.

Clynes, J.R. *Memoirs*. London: Hutchinson and Co., 1937.

Cole, George D.H. and Cole, M.I. *Condition of Britain*. London: Victor Gollancz, 1936.

Cole, M.I., ed. *Beatrice Webb's Diaries, 1924–1932*. London: Longmans, Green and Co., 1956.

Communist Party of Great Britain. "Answer the Fascist Challenge in Hyde Park" (broadsheet). London: Young Communist League of Great Britain, 1934.

———. *Class Against Class*. London: Workers' Bookshop, 1929.

———. "The Class Struggle in Local Affairs." *Our History*, no. 1 (Spring 1956). London: CPGB, 1956.

———. *Communist Political Education: A Manual for Workers' Study Groups*. London: CPGB, 1933.
———. "Fascism Intensifies Crisis" (pamphlet). London: Young Communist League of Great Britain, 1934.
———. "For a Marxist-Leninist School" (pamphlet). Tonbridge, England: CPGB, 1930.
———. "Join the Ranks on September 9" (broadsheet). London: CPGB, 1934.
———. "Let Us Get Together Before It Is Too Late" (broadsheet). London: CPGB, 1934.
———. *The March of English History*. London: CPGB, 1936.
———. "The National Government of Exploiters and Warmongers" (pamphlet). London: Young Communist League of Great Britain, 1934.
———. "The Next Step in Britain, Ireland, and America" (pamphlet). London: CPGB, 1932.
———. *Official Report: Communist Unity Convention*. London: CPGB, 1920.
———. *The Programme of the Communist International*. London: Modern Books, 1932.
———. "The Sedition Bill Exposed" (pamphlet). London: Workers' Bookshop, 1934.
———. *Sidelights on the Cliveden Set: Hitler's Friends in Britain*. London: CPGB, 1938.
———. "To Fascism or Communism?" (pamphlet). London: CPGB, 1931.
———. *The Workers' United Front and the I.L.P.* London: CPGB, 1934.
Crew, Albert. *The Law Relating to Public Meetings and Processions*. London: Sir Isaac Pitman and Sons, 1937.
Cripps, Stafford; Maxton, James; and Pollitt, Harry. *The Unity Campaign*. London: CPGB, 1937.
Cruchley, Oliver and Cruchley, Ivan. "Freedom in Our Time." *Fabian Tract No. 244*. London: Fabian Society, 1937.
Dalton, Hugh. *The Fateful Years*. London: Frederick Muller, 1954.
Dimitrov, Georgi. "What You Can Do Against Fascism and War" (pamphlet). London: CPGB, 1935.
Douglas, J.L. *Spotlight on Fascism*. London: CPGB, 1934.
Drennan, James [William Edward David Allen]. *Oswald Mosley and British Fascism*. London: John Murray Press, 1934.
Driberg, Tom. *Mosley? No!* London: W.H. Allen and Co., 1948.
Dutt, Rajani Palme. *What Next for the Labour Party?* London: CPGB, 1937.
———. *The Workers' Answer to the Crisis*. London: CPGB, 1931.
Eden, Anthony. *Facing the Dictators*. Boston: Houghton-Mifflin, 1962.
Fuller, J.F.C. "What the British Union Has to Offer Britain" (pamphlet). London: Action Press, 1937.
Gallacher, William. "Communism and the Co-ops" (pamphlet). London: CPGB, n.d.
———. "Tariffs and Starvation: An Exposure of the Effect on the Workers of the Empire Fascist Ramp" (pamphlet). London: CPGB, 1932.

Goodhart, A.L. "Thomas v. Sawkins: A Constitutional Innovation." *Cambridge Law Journal* 6 (February 1936): 22–30.

Gordon-Canning, R. *Mind Britain's Business.* London: Greater Britain Publications, 1939.

———. *The Spirit of Fascism.* London: Action Press, 1937.

Gottwald, Klement. *A People's Front.* Moscow: Cooperative Publishing Society of Foreign Workers, 1935.

Great Britain. Kingston upon Hull, Yorkshire. University of Hull Library. Records of the National Council for Civil Liberties. The Albert Hall, Refusal of Lettings. Filing case 7, section 2.

Great Britain. Kingston upon Hull, Yorkshire. University of Hull Library. Records of the National Council for Civil Liberties. Inquiry of Olympia. Filing case 40, section 1.

Great Britain. London. Trades Union Congress Library. Position Papers of the National Council for Civil Liberties [by Ronald Kidd]. File Jc/585, 1936.

Green, John. *Mr. Baldwin.* London: Sampson, Low, Marston, and Co., 1933.

The Haldane Club. "The Law of Public Meetings and the Right of Police Search" (pamphlet). London: Victor Gollancz, 1934.

Hannington, Wal. *The Problem of the Distressed Areas.* London: Victor Gollancz, 1937.

Herbert, A.P. *Independent Member.* London: Methuen and Co., 1950.

Hill, F.D. " 'Gainst Trust and Monopoly" (pamphlet). London: BUF Publications, 1937.

Hyde, Douglas. *I Believed.* New York: G.P. Putnam's Sons, 1950.

Ishmael [pseud.]. "That's Sedition—That Was" (pamphlet). London: Sidney Stanley, 1934.

James, Robert Rhodes, ed. *Memoirs of a Conservative: J.C.C. Davidson's Memoirs and Papers, 1910–1937.* London: Macmillan and Co., 1970.

Joad, C.E.M. *The Case for the New Party.* London: J.C. Bird and Sons, 1931.

Joyce, William. *Dictatorship.* London: BUF Publications, 1933.

———. "Fascism and India" (pamphlet). London: BUF Publications, 1934.

———. "Fascism and Jewry" (pamphlet). London: BUF Trust, 1936.

Kirkwood, David. *My Life of Revolt.* London: George G. Harrap and Co., 1935.

The Labour Party. *Report of the Annual Conference, 1931–1937.* London: Transport House, 1931–1937.

Lansbury, George. *Looking Backwards—and Forwards.* London: Blackie and Son, 1935.

Laski, Harold. *Democracy in Crisis.* Chapel Hill: University of North Carolina Press, 1933.

———. "Freedom in Danger." *Yale Review* 23 (March 1934): 534–51.

Lloyd, George Ambrose (Lord Lloyd of Dolobran). *Leadership in Democracy.* London: Oxford University Press, 1939.

Lloyd George, Gwilym. *Freedom of the Press and the Challenge of the*

Official Secrets Acts. London: National Union of Journalists, 1938.

Loewenstein, Karl. "Legislative Control of Political Extremism in European Democracies." *Columbia Law Review* 38 (April and May 1934): 590–622; 725–74.

———. "Militant Democracy and Fundamental Rights." *American Political Science Review* 31 (June and August 1937): 417–32; 638–59.

Lohia, Rammanohar. *The Struggle for Civil Liberties*. Allahad, India: Foreign Department, All India Congress, 1936.

London District Congress, CPGB. *For Social and Industrial Unity to Drive Fascism Out of London*. London: CPGB, 1937.

MacColl, James E., and Wells, W.T. "The Incitement to Disaffection Bill, 1934." *Political Quarterly* 5 (July 1934): 352–64.

MacDonald, J. Ramsay. *Free Speech in Danger*. London: I.L.P. Publications, 1925.

MacMillan, Harold. *Winds of Change*. New York: Harper and Row, 1966.

Macready, Sir Cecil Frederick Nevil. *Annals of an Active Life*. 2 vols. London: Hutchinson Press, 1924.

Martin, Kingsley. "Fascism and the *Daily Mail*." *Political Quarterly* 5 (April 1934): 273–76.

———. *Fascism, Democracy and the Press*. London: New Statesman and Nation, 1938.

Miles, A.C. *Mosley in Motley*. London: Ex-Servicemen's National Movement, 1937.

Minney, R.J., ed. *The Private Papers of Hore-Belisha*. London: Collins, 1960.

Mirkine-Guetzevitch, B. "The Technique of Liberty." *Political Quarterly* 5 (January 1934): 111–22.

Mosley, Oswald. *Blackshirt Policy*. London: BUF Publications, 1934.

———. *British Union for the British Race*. London: BUF Trust, 1937.

———. *Fascism in Britain*. London: BUF Publications, 1933.

———. "Fascism: 100 Questions Asked and Answered" (pamphlet). London: BUF Publications, 1936.

———. *The Greater Britain*. London: BUF Publications, 1932, 1934.

———. *Mosley: What They Say, What They Said, What He Is*. London: Raven Books, 1947.

———. *Mosley's Mesage to British Union Members and Supporters*. London: BUF Publications, Sept. 1939.

———. *My Answer*. London: Mosley Publications, 1946.

———. *My Life*. London: Thomas Nelson and Sons, 1968.

———. "Taxation and the People" (pamphlet). London: W.J. Hasted and Son, 1939.

———. *Ten Points of Fascist Policy*. London: BUF Publications, 1937.

———. *Tomorrow We Live*. London: Greater Britain Publications, 1936, 1938.

National Council for Civil Liberties. *Annual Report and Balance Sheet, 1934–1937*. London: Stanhope Press, 1934–1937.

———. *Annual Report and Balance Sheet, 1938–1939*. London: Gains-

borough Press, 1938–1939.
———. "A Declaration" (pamphlet). London: NCCL, 1937.
———. "Fascism and the Jews" (pamphlet). London: NCCL, 1936.
———. "Freedom of the Press and the Official Secrets Acts" (pamphlet). London: NCCL, 1937.
———. "Handbook of Citizen's Rights" (pamphlet). London: NCCL, 1954.
———. "Hornsey Town Hall Meeting—Points Upon Which Further Statements Appear Desirable." Mimeographed. London: NCCL, 1937.
———. "The Incitement to Disaffection Bill, 1934: How It Now Stands" (pamphlet). London: NCCL, 1934.
———. "Instructions to Branches, Members, and Affiliated Societies." Mimeographed. London: NCCL, 1934.
———. "A Mock Trial Based on the Sedition Bill" (pamphlet). London: NCCL, 1934.
———. *Notes for the International Conference of the International Judicial Association, 1937*. London: Haldane Society, 1937.
———. Numerous reports and correspondence, 1934–1939. Primarily at the University of Hull and at the Main Office of the National Council for Civil Liberties in London.
———. "Police Methods" (pamphlet). London: NCCL, 1937.
———. "The Public Order Bill" (pamphlet). London: NCCL, 1936.
———. *The Record of a Decade of Work for Democracy and Civil Liberty*. London: Walthamstow Press, 1945.
———. "Report of a Commission of Inquiry into Certain Disturbances at Thurloe Square, South Kensington, on March 22nd, 1936" (pamphlet). London: NCCL, 1936.
———. "Sir Oswald Mosley's Albert Hall Meeting, March 22nd: Extracts from Statements of Eyewitnesses" (pamphlet). London: NCCL, 1936.
———. "Statements of Persons Assaulted by Fascists and of Eyewitness Accounts of Fascist Violence, Fascist Meeting, Hornsey Town Hall, 28th January, 1937." Mimeographed. London: NCCL, 1937.
———. "The Strange Case of Major Vernon" (pamphlet). London: NCCL, 1938.
National Council of Labour. *Fascism: The Enemy of the People*. London: Transport House, 1935.
National Union of Journalists. *The Official Secrets Acts and Individual Freedom*. London: National Union of Journalists, 1938.
Nichols, Beverley. *News of England: Or, A Country Without a Hero*. New York: Doubleday, 1938.
Nicolson, Harold. *Diaries and Letters*. 3 vols. New York: Atheneum Press, 1966.
"Outrageous Violence at Hornsey." *Jewish Chronicle*, 29 January 1937, p. 16.
Paton, J. *Left Turn!* London: Secker and Warburg, 1936.
Payne, W. *A London Busman Reports on Fascism*. London: European Workers' Anti-Fascist Congress, British Delegation Committee, 1936.

Petrie, Charles. *The Life and Letters of the Right Honourable Sir Austen Chamberlain*. London: Cassell and Co., 1940.
Pollitt, Harry. *Arms for Spain*. London: CPGB, 1936.
———. *I Accuse Baldwin*. London: CPGB, 1936.
———. *Labour's Way Forward*. London: CPGB, 1937.
———. *Laski's Mistake*. London: CPGB, n.d.
———. *Serving My Time*. London: Lawrence and Wishart, 1961.
Reisman, David. "Democracy and Defamation." *Columbia Law Review* 42 (May and September 1942): 727–80.
Rosten, Leo G. "The Rise of Oswald Mosley." *Harper's* 169 (September 1934): 492–501.
Samuel, Herbert L. *The Duty of the Liberal Party in Support of a National Government*. London: Liberal Publications Department, 1931.
———. *Memoirs*. London: Cresset Press, 1945.
———. *The Political Situation*. London: Liberal Party Publications, 1935.
Simon, John. *Retrospect*. London: Hutchinson and Co., 1952.
———. *A Word to the Liberals*. London: Victor Gollancz, 1935.
Snowden, Philip. *Snowden: An Autobiography*. London: I. Nicolson and Watson, 1934.
Steed, Henry Wickham. *The Worth of Freedom*. London: Jewish Historical Society of England, 1936.
Strachey, John. *The Menace of Fascism*. London: Victor Gollancz, 1933.
Thomas, James H. *My Story*. London: Hutchinson and Co., 1937.
Thompson, W.H. *Civil Liberties*. London: Victor Gollancz, 1938.
Thomson, Alexander Raven. "Big Fish and Little Fish: Finance, Democracy, and the Shopkeeper" (pamphlet). London: BUF Trust, 1937.
———. "The Coming of the Corporate State" (pamphlet). London: Action Press, 1937.
Trades Union Congress. *Proceedings of the Annual Trades Union Congress, 1932–1939,* ed. by Walter M. Citrine. London: Cooperative Printing Society, 1932–39.
Trades Union Congress, General Council. "United Against Fascism" (pamphlet). London: Cooperative Printing Society, 1934.
Vindicator [pseud.]. "Fascists at Olympia" (pamphlet). London: Victor Gollancz, 1934.
———. "A Strong Hand at the Helm" (pamphlet). London: Victor Gollancz, 1933.
Wade, Emlyn Capel Stuart. "Police Powers and Public Meetings." *Cambridge Law Journal* 6 (1937): 175–81.
Wall, Alfred M. "Address to the Conference on Fascism and Anti-Semitism." 25 April 1937. London: NCCL, 1937.
Wegg-Prosser, Charles F. *Fascism Exposed*. London: Jewish Peoples Against Fascism and Anti-Semitism, 1938.
Weir, Lauchlan MacNeill. *The Tragedy of Ramsay MacDonald*. London: Secker and Warburg, 1938.
Wilson, Francis G. "The Prelude to Authority." *American Political Science Review* 31 (February 1937): 12–27.

Secondary Sources

Allen, Victor L. *Trade Unions and the Government*. London: Longmans, Green and Co., 1960.

Arendt, Hannah. *The Origins of Totalitarianism*. London: George Allen and Unwin, 1958.

Arnot, Robert Page. *Twenty Years*. London: Lawrence and Wishart, 1940.

Arnstein, Walter L. *Britain: Yesterday and Today*. Boston: D. C. Heath and Co., 1966.

Ashworth, W. *An Economic History of England, 1870–1939*. London: Methuen, 1960.

Attlee, Clement R. *The Labour Party in Perspective*. London: Victor Gollancz, 1937.

———, and Williams, Francis. *A Prime Minister Remembers*. London: Heinemann and Co., 1961.

Bagehot, Walter. *The English Constitution*. London: Oxford University Press, 1928.

Baldwin, A. W. *My Father—The True Story*. London: George Allen and Unwin, 1955.

Bassett, R. *Nineteen Thirty-One*. New York: St. Martin's, 1958.

Beer, Samuel H. *British Politics in the Collectivist Age*. New York: Alfred A. Knopf, 1965.

Bell, Daniel, ed. *The Radical Right*. New York: Doubleday and Co., 1964.

Benewick, Robert. *Political Violence and Public Order*. London: Penguin, 1969.

Blaxland, Gregory. *J. H. Thomas: A Life for Unity*. London: Frederick Muller, 1964.

Booth, Arthur Harold. *British Hustings*. London: Frederick Muller, 1956.

Bowes, Stewart. *The Police and Civil Liberties*. London: Lawrence and Wishart, 1966.

Bowle, William. *Viscount Samuel: A Bibliography*. London: Victor Gollancz, 1957.

Boyle, Andrew. *Trenchard*. London: Collins, 1962.

Branson, Noreen, and Heinemann, Margot. *Britain in the Nineteen Thirties*. New York: Praeger, 1971.

Brockway, Archibald Fenner. *Inside the Left*. London: George Allen and Unwin, 1942.

Bullock, Alan. *The Life and Times of Ernest Bevin*. London: William Heinemann, 1960.

Bullock, John. *Akin to Treason*. London: Arthur Barker, 1966.

Carlton, David. *MacDonald versus Henderson*. New York: Humanities Press, 1970.

Chrimes, Stanley B. *English Constitutional History*. London: Oxford University Press, 1967.

Cline, Catherine Ann. *Recruits to Labour*. Syracuse, N.Y.: Syracuse University Press, 1963.

Cole, G. D. H. *A History of the Labour Party from 1914*. London: Rout-

ledge and Kegan Paul, 1948.
Cross, Colin. *The Fascists in Great Britain*. London: Barrie and Rockliff, 1961.
Dalton, Hugh. *Call Back Yesterday*. London: Frederick Muller, 1953.
Dicey, A. V. *Introduction to the Study of the Law of the Constitution*. 9th ed. London: Macmillan and Co., 1939.
Divine, David. *Mutiny at Invirgordon*. London: MacDonald and Co., 1970.
Douglas, Roy. *The History of the Liberal Party: 1895–1970*. Rutherford, N.J.: Fairleigh Dickinson University Press, 1971.
Foot, Michael. *Aneurin Bevan*. 2 vols. London: MacGibbon and Kee, 1962.
Granzow, Brigitte. *A Mirror of Nazism: British Opinion and the Emergence of Hitler, 1929–1933*. London: Victor Gollancz, 1964.
Graves, Robert, and Hodge, Allan. *The Long Weekend*. New York: W. W. Norton, 1963.
Guttsman, W. L. *The British Political Elite*. London: MacGibbon and Kee, 1964.
Hamilton, Alistair. *The Appeal of Fascism*. London: Anthony Blond, 1971.
Hamilton, Mary A. *Arthur Henderson: A Biography*. London: W. Heinemann, 1938.
Hardie, Frank. *The Political Influence of the British Monarchy, 1866–1952*. London: B. T. Batsford, 1970.
Harvey, James, and Hood, Katherine. *The British State*. London: Lawrence and Wishart, 1958.
Heuston, R. F. V. *Essays in Constitutional Law*. London: Stevens and Sons, 1964.
Hyde, H. Montgomery. *United In Crime*. London: William Heinemann, 1955.
Jackson, Robert. *The Chief*. London: George G. Harrap and Co., 1959.
Jones, J. R. "England." In *The European Right*, ed. by Hans Rogger and Eugen Weber. Berkeley: University of California Press, 1965.
Kaufman, Gerald. *The Left*. London: Anthony Blond, 1966.
Keir, David Lindsay. *The Constitutional History of Modern Britain, 1485–1951*. London: Adam and Charles Black, 1953.
Kidd, Ronald. *British Liberty in Danger: An Introduction to the Study of Civil Rights*. London: Lawrence and Wishart, 1940.
Klugmann, James. *History of the Communist Party of Great Britain*. 2 vols. London: Lawrence and Wishart, 1968–1969.
MacElwee, William. *Britain's Locust Years, 1918–1940*. London: Faber and Faber, 1962.
MacFarlane, L. J. *The British Communist Party*. London: MacGibbon and Kee, 1966.
McHenry, Dean Eugene. *His Majesty's Opposition: Structure and Problems of the British Labour Party, 1931–1938*. Berkeley: University of California Press, 1940.
Macleod, Iain. *Neville Chamberlain*. London: Frederick Muller, 1961.
Mandle, W. F. *Anti-Semitism and the British Union of Fascists*. London: Longmans, Green and Co., 1960.

Marcham, Frederick George. *A Constitutional History of Modern England, 1485 to the Present*. New York: Harper and Bros., 1960.
Marwick, Arthur. *The Deluge*. Boston: Little, Brown & Co., 1965.
Middlemass, Keith, and Barnes, John. *Baldwin: A Biography*. London: Weidenfeld and Nicolson, 1969.
Mowat, Charles L. *Britain Between the Wars, 1918–1940*. Chicago: University of Chicago Press, 1955.
Muggeridge, Malcolm. *The Thirties, 1930–1940, in Great Britain*. London: Collins, 1967.
Muir, Ramsey. *The Record of the National Government*. London: George Allen and Unwin, 1963.
Newton, Kenneth. *The Sociology of British Communism*. London: Allen Lane, 1969.
Nolte, Ernst. *Three Faces of Fascism*. London: Weidenfeld and Nicolson, 1965.
———. *King George V*. London: Constable and Co., 1952.
Pelling, Henry. *The British Communist Party: A Historical Profile*. New York: Macmillan Co., 1958.
———. *A Short History of the Labour Party*. New York: St. Martin's, 1968.
Priestly, Harold Edford. *Voice of Protest: A History of Civil Unrest in Great Britain*. London: Leslie Frewin, 1968.
Pritt, Denis Nowell. *From Right to Left*. London: Lawrence and Wishart, 1965.
———.*The Mosley Case*. London: Evans, Spencer, and Co., 1944.
Pye, Lucian, and Verba, Sidney, eds. *Political Culture and Political Development*. Princeton: Princeton University Press, 1965.
Raymond, John, ed. *The Baldwin Age*. London: Eyre and Spottiswoode, 1960.
Richardson, Harry W. *Economic Recovery in Britain, 1932–1939*. London: Weidenfeld and Nicolson, 1967.
Roberts, Bechofer. *Stanley Baldwin: Man or Miracle*. London: Robert Hale and Co., 1936.
Rogger, Hans, and Weber, Eugene, eds. *The European Right*. Berkeley: University of California Press, 1965.
Rudlin, Walter A. *The Growth of Fascism in Great Britain*. London: George Allen and Unwin, 1935.
Sacks, Benjamin. *J. Ramsay MacDonald in Thought and Action*. Albuquerque: University of New Mexico Press, 1952.
Salmon, William. *The Law and Individual Liberty*. London: Haldane Society, 1970.
Samuel, Herbert L. *Belief and Action*. London: Pan Books, 1953.
———. *Practical Ethics*. London: Thornton Butterworth, 1935.
Skidelsky, R. J. A. "Great Britain." In *European Fascism*, ed. by S. J. Woolf. London: Weidenfeld and Nicolson, 1968.
Stewart, Michael. *The British Approach to Politics*. London: George Allen and Unwin, 1955.
Strauss, Patricia. *Bevin and Co*. New York: G. P. Putnam's Sons, 1941.

Street, Harry. *Freedom, the Individual, and the Law*. Hammondsworth, Eng.: Penguin Books, 1963.
Symons, Julian. *The Thirties*. London: Cresset, 1960.
Taylor, A. J. P. "Confusion of the Left." In *The Baldwin Age*, ed. by John Raymond. London: Eyre and Spottiswoode, 1960.
———. *English History, 1914–1945*. New York: Oxford University Press, 1965.
Thayer, George. *The British Political Fringe: A Profile*. London: Anthony Blond, 1965.
Thompson, Anthony. *Big Brother in Britain Today*. London: Michael Joseph, 1970.
Thompson, Edward P. *Fascist Threat to Britain*. London: CPGB, 1948.
Wade, Emlyn Capel Stuart, and Phillips, G. Godfrey. *Constitutional Law*. London: Longmans, Green and Co., 1960.
Webb, R. K. *Modern England*. New York: Dodd, Mead, and Co., 1970.
Weiss, J. *The Fascist Tradition*. London: Harper and Row, 1967.
West, Rebecca. *The New Meaning of Treason*. New York: Viking, 1964.
Wharton, Michael. "A Few Lost Causes." In *The Baldwin Age*, ed. by John Raymond. London: Eyre and Spottiswoode, 1960.
Williams, David. *Keeping the Peace*. London: Hutchinson and Co., 1967.
———. *Not in the Public Interest*. London: Hutchinson and Co., 1965.
Williams, Francis. *Ernest Bevin: Portrait of a Great Englishman*. London: Hutchinson and Co., 1952.
Wood, Neal. *Communism and the British Intellectuals*. New York: Columbia University Press, 1959.
Woolf, S. J., ed. *European Fascism*. London: Weidenfeld and Nicolson, 1968.
Young, G. M. *Stanley Baldwin*. London: Rupert Hart-Davis, 1952.

Index